RECTO VERSO: REDEFINING THE SKETCHBOOK

Ashgate Studies in Architecture Series

SERIES EDITOR: EAMONN CANNIFFE, MANCHESTER SCHOOL OF ARCHITECTURE,
MANCHESTER METROPOLITAN UNIVERSITY, UK

The discipline of Architecture is undergoing subtle transformation as design awareness permeates our visually dominated culture. Technological change, the search for sustainability and debates around the value of place and meaning of the architectural gesture are aspects which will affect the cities we inhabit. This series seeks to address such topics, both theoretically and in practice, through the publication of high quality original research, written and visual.

Other titles in this series

The Architectural Capriccio
Memory, Fantasy and Invention
Lucien Steil
ISBN 978 1 4094 3191 6

The Architecture of Pleasure
British Amusement Parks 1900–1939
Josephine Kane
ISBN 978 1 4094 1074 4

No Matter: Theories and Practices of the Ephemeral in Architecture
Anastasia Karandinou
ISBN 978 1 4094 6628 4

The Challenge of Emulation in Art and Architecture
Between Imitation and Invention
David Mayernik
ISBN 978 1 4094 5767 1

Building Transatlantic Italy
Architectural Dialogues with Postwar America
Paolo Scrivano
ISBN 978 1 4724 1483 0

Forthcoming titles in this series

The Architecture of Edwin Maxwell Fry and Jane Drew
Twentieth Century Architecture, Pioneer Modernism and the Tropics
Iain Jackson and Jessica Holland
ISBN 978 1 4094 5198 3

Recto Verso: Redefining the Sketchbook

Edited by

Angela Bartram
University of Lincoln, UK

Nader El-Bizri
The American University of Beirut, Lebanon

Douglas Gittens
University of Lincoln, UK

ASHGATE H JS

Published by
Ashgate Publishing Limited
Wey Court East
Union Road
Farnham
Surrey, GU9 7PT
England

Ashgate Publishing Company
110 Cherry Street
Suite 3-1
Burlington, VT 05401-3818
USA

www.ashgate.com

British Library Cataloguing in Publication Data
A catalogue record for this book is available from the British Library.

Library of Congress Cataloging-in-Publication Data
Recto verso : redefining the sketchbook / by Angela Bartram, Nader El-Bizri and Douglas Gittens.
    pages cm. -- (Ashgate studies in architecture)
    Includes bibliographical references and index.
    ISBN 978-1-4094-6866-0 (hardback) -- ISBN 978-1-4094-6867-7 (ebook) -- ISBN 978-1-4094-6868-4 (epub) 1. Artists' preparatory studies. 2. Notebooks. 3. Architecture--Sketch-books. I. Bartram, Angela, editor of compilation. II. El-Bizri, Nader, editor of compilation. III. Gittens, Douglas, editor of compilation. IV. El-Bizri, Nader, author. By way of an overture.
    N7433.5.R43 2014
    741--dc23

                                                                            2013045805

ISBN: 9781409468660 (hbk)
ISBN: 9781409468677 (ebk – PDF)
ISBN: 9781409468684 (ebk – ePUB)

MIX
Paper from
responsible sources
FSC
www.fsc.org   FSC® C013985

Printed in the United Kingdom by Henry Ling Limited, at the Dorset Press, Dorchester, DT1 1HD

Contents

List of Illustrations

1 By Way of an Overture: Classical Optics and Renaissance Pictorial Arts

2 Parerga – Carnet de Croquis: 'ni oeuvre, ni hors d'oeuvre'

3 Palimpsest

4 The Ontological Sketchbook

5 Plotting the Centre: Bramante's Drawings for the New St. Peter's Basilica

13   My Arguments with the World

13.1   Police and the rest of us speaking about drawn lines, through lines drawn as Bush drives by. Published in *The Sydney Morning Herald*, 6 × 12 inches, 2007. Source: Drawing: Mario Minichiello, 2007

13.2   *'The Pigs Will Fly'.* APEC: in response to the leader of world's richest nations arriving. Published in *The Sydney Morning Herald* 2007, 2nd–9th September 2007, weekend edition, removed from news web by government request, 17 × 12.5 inches. Source: Drawing: Mario Minichiello, 2007

13.3   *'Police protect the rich and property'.* Outside the Conference building, in response to the leaders staged 'photo-shoots'. Policing APEC: here the police line facing out with the city's richest business community who are protected behind the lines. Published 2nd–9th September 2007, weekend edition, 12.5 × 17 inches. Source: Drawing: Mario Minichiello, 2007

14   The Sketchbook as Collection: A Phenomenology of Sketching

14.1   British Museum Sketchbook Pages. Selection of images from the author's sketchbook, these were drawn *in situ* at the British Museum. The multiple projections used in the sketches are particularly important in showing ways of describing and understanding objects more fully than a solely perspectival representation. Source: Image: Raymond Lucas 2011

14.2   British Museum Sketchbook Pages. Selection of images from the author's sketchbook, these were drawn *in situ* at the British Museum. The multiple projections used in the sketches are particularly important in showing ways of describing and understanding objects more fully than a solely perspectival representation. Source: Image: Raymond Lucas 2011

14.3   British Museum Sketchbook Pages. Selection of images from the author's sketchbook, these were drawn *in situ* at the British Museum. The multiple projections used in the sketches are particularly important in showing ways of describing and understanding objects more fully than a solely perspectival representation. Source: Image: Raymond Lucas 2011

15   Notebooks and Narratives: The Secret Laboratory of The Architect's Sketchbook

15.1   The secret laboratory exhibition. Source: Image: Paul Clarke

15.2   The interchanging sketchbooks of Jane Larmour and Patrick Wheeler. Source: Image: Paul Clarke

15.3   The sketchbook as device. Source: Image: Paul Clarke

16   Sketchbook or Reflective Journal? Documenting the Practical PhD

16.1   Venus Drawings. Source: Image: Christine Turner 2009

Notes on Contributors

ROOHI S. AHMED

Roohi S. Ahmed lives and works in Karachi, Pakistan. She teaches at the Indus Valley School of Art and Architecture (IVS) in Karachi. As a multi-disciplinary artist, her work often draws upon cartographical references in order to investigate the ontological realities of human existence in a degenerating political, social and religious environment. Ahmed has exhibited widely throughout Pakistan and her work has featured in the 11th Asian Art Biennial in Bangladesh and numerous other international exhibitions. She is currently on a sabbatical to pursue an MFA at COFA. She has coordinated the Foundation Programme at the IVS and lectured for the University of Karachi's Visual Studies Department. Ahmed was artist in residence at Vasl (Pakistan), Coast (UK) and Cicada Press (Australia). She curated the exhibition *Simply Paper!* Co-curating credits include: *Michael Esson: A Survey of Drawing; Michael Kempson: A Survey of Prints, Aboriginal Dreams* and *Let's Draw the Line and 6X6: The Labyrinth in Karachi.*

ANGELA BARTRAM

Angela Bartram works in live art, video, sculpture and published text. Bartram's artwork has been included in a variety of exhibitions, including more recent exposure at: *Miami International Festival of Performance* (2013); at the gallery Grace Exhibition Space' (New York 2012); *Bristol Live Open Platform* (Arnolfini 2012); *Action Art Now* for O U I International Performance (York 2011); *The Future Can Wait* (London, 2008 and 2009); *EAST International* (Norwich 2009); *The Animal Gaze* (London 2008, Plymouth 2009, Sheffield 2011); *EAST goes East* (Krakow 2010) and *Animalism* (Bradford 2009). Recent published texts include: 'Between Bodies: an Artist's Account of the Oral Connection Between Human and Dog,' in *Intimacy Across Visceral and Digital Performance* (M. Chatzichristodoulou and R. Zerihan 2012); 'Response Oral / Response' in *Total Art Journal*, Volume 1: 2 (N. Loveless, 2012; *Performing Lost Space: Recording Architectural Detail With the Body* (2012); 'Oral / Response' in *Emergency Index* (Y. Guzman and M. Yankelevich 2012); 'One Woman and Her Dogs' in *Mutual Dependencies* (K. Meynell 2011) and 'The Sacrifices

Made by Audiences: The Complicit Discomfort of Viewing Performance Art' in *Cultural and Ethical Turns: Interdisciplinary Reflections on Culture, Politics and Ethics* (B. Garne, S. Pavlenko, S. Shaheen and A. Wolanski 2011). Bartram completed a PhD at the University of Middlesex and is a senior lecturer in fine art at the University of Lincoln. She is also co-collaborator in the research partnership Bartram O'Neill with Mary O'Neill.

PAUL CLARKE

Paul Clarke is an architect, writer and senior lecturer in architecture. He is the Course Director and 6th year studio coordinator for the Master of Architecture programme at the School of Architecture and Design at the University of Ulster in Belfast, where he is a member of the Research Institute of Art and Design. His design work has been published in a number of key architectural journals, including *Frame* and *Architecture Today*. Clarke has written extensively on themes of the 'Contemporary City', 'Modernism', 'Le Corbusier', and 'Urbanism' and has collaborated on books on the work of the Scottish architect Charles Rennie Mackintosh. His interests include the relationship between architecture, film and sound as well as architectural drawing and representation. He is the curator and co-designer of a touring exhibition and research project called 'The Secret Laboratory' which explores the hidden world of architects' sketchbooks.

ROBERT CLARKE

Robert Clarke trained as a painter at the Royal College of Art (1980–1983) and completed his doctorate (*A Phenomenology of Ships: Time, Memory and Appearance*) at Birmingham Institute of Art and Design in 2003. He has taught in a range of contexts including both practice and theory. Clarke's notebooks and drawings have been widely exhibited, he was a Jerwood Drawing Prize winner in 2006 and artist in residence at the Dock Museum Barrow in 2007. Clarke teaches drawing on the NSEAD artist-teachers' postgraduate scheme. Since 1997, he has published academic papers on tradition, art education, aesthetics and phenomenology.

NADER EL-BIZRI

Nader El-Bizri is an Associate Professor in the Civilization Sequence Program, and the Director of the Anis Makdisi Program in Literature at the American University of Beirut. He is also an associated researcher in history of philosophy and science at the Centre National de la Recherche Scientifique in Paris. Prior to this, he was a Principal Lecturer (Reader) in architecture at the University of Lincoln. Previously, he has lectured at the University of Cambridge (1999–2010), and held a visiting professorship at the University of Lincoln (2007–2010), a senior research fellowship at The Institute of Ismaili Studies, London (2002–2010), and a lectureship post in architecture at the University of Nottingham (2000–2002). He also taught at Harvard University (1994–1995). He holds a PhD in philosophy from the New School for Social Research in New York (1999), an MArch-II from the Harvard Graduate School of Design (1994) and a BArch from the American University of Beirut (1989). His areas of expertise are in architectural humanities, history of philosophy and science and phenomenology. He maintains active memberships in international societies such as the American Philosophical Association and the Architectural Humanities Research Association and he is an elected council member of the Société Internationale d'Histoire des Sciences et des Philosophies Arabes et Islamiques (CNRS, Paris). El-Bizri has published widely, and contributed to various BBC radio and TV programs. He also serves on the editorial boards of various book series and journals published by Oxford University Press, Cambridge University Press, E. J. Brill, and Springer. Moreover, he has acted as a consultant to the Science Museum in London, the Aga Khan Trust for Culture in Geneva, and the Solomon Guggenheim Museum in New York and Berlin. Besides his academic profile, he practiced as an architect and designer in London, Cambridge, New York, and Beirut.

DOUGLAS GITTENS

Douglas Gittens is an experienced architectural designer and academic involved in the creative industries. He is a researcher and senior lecturer at the Lincoln School of Architecture, where he is Programme Leader for the BA (Hons) in Interior Architecture and Design. He is also an active member of the Architectural Contexts Research Group and the Drawing Research Group at the University of Lincoln, and a member of the Architectural Humanities Research Association (AHRA). His research interests include spatial theory, the phenomenology of architecture, architectural representation and the documentation of architectural memory and lost space. He is also engaged in drawing-based research activities that are concerned with the action of drawing and the creative process, and with the investigation of drawing as a problem-solving tool and drawing as a method in research.

JOHN HENDRIX

John Hendrix is Professor of Architectural History at the University of Lincoln and an adjunct professor at Roger Williams University in Rhode Island, USA. Hendrix has written and edited several books on art, architecture, and philosophy, such as: *The Cultural Role of Architecture; Renaissance Theories of Vision, Architecture as Cosmology; Lincoln Cathedral and English Gothic Architecture; Robert Grosseteste; Philosophy of Intellect and Vision; Architecture and Psychoanalysis: Peter Eisenman and Jacques Lacan; Aesthetics and the Philosophy of Spirit; Architectural Forms and Philosophical Structures; Platonic Architectonics: Platonic Philosophies and the Visual Arts; Neoplatonic Aesthetics; Neoplatonism and the Arts* and *The Relation Between*

Architectural Forms and Philosophical Structures in the Work of Francesco Borromini in Seventeenth-Century Rome.

RACHEL HURST

Rachel Hurst is a Senior Lecturer at the University of South Australia and a PhD Candidate at RMIT. Hurst's research explores theories of domesticity and the everyday and her PhD addresses themes of architectural drawing and representation, analogue crafts and curatorial practices in architecture. She has published over thirty articles, papers and creative works on the relationship between architecture and food, including publications in *Eating Architecture* (MIT Press 2004) and *Food + the City* (Architectural Design 2005). Hurst also writes regularly for the Australian design media. In 2004 she curated the inaugural Architecture Symposium *Food & Architecture* for the Adelaide Festival of Arts, with eight international and national speakers (including Marco Frascari) and *The Grimoire of Architecture: A Symposium on the Drawings and Work of Marco Frascari*. Hurst was awarded a Commendation by the Australian Institute of Architects (AIA) in 2008, the Neville Quarry Architectural Education prize and in 2009 she was a juror for the National AIA Architecture Awards. Hurst also serves on both the South Australian and Tasmanian chapter juries. She has contributed to thirteen exhibitions as co-curator and/or exhibitor and in 2013 is co-curating *Manual* at the SASA Gallery, Adelaide.

RAYMOND LUCAS

Raymond Lucas is Senior Lecturer in Architecture at Manchester School of Architecture (MMU). Lucas holds a PhD in social anthropology with the thesis 'Towards a Theory of Notation as a Thinking Tool,' which sought to understand drawing and other inscriptive practices as equivalent forms of knowledge-production to the text, positing that a series of drawings can constitute theory. This interest in drawing continued through several research projects, most notably 'Multimodal Representations of Urban Space' for the UK's AHRC & EPSRC scheme *Designing for the 21st Century*. The project resulted in a method for sensory notation, and a graphic representation of a complete sensory experience of space. Lucas co-ordinates the Humanities for the BA in Architecture at MMU, and runs a course on 'Architecture & Observation,' which places emphasis on descriptive practices from sketching and cartography to ethnographic participant-observation.

MARIO A. MINICHIELLO

Mario A. Minichiello is Head of School and Professor of Visual Communication at Birmingham City University [BIAD]. He previously held posts at Loughborough University, and acted as Head of the Visual Communication Department (LCAD) and as a QAA reviewer. Minichiello has taught at De Montfort University and served as a consultant to the BBC, the *Guardian* and the *Financial Times*. Moreover, he is a freelance artist who has lectured widely in places such as the RCA, and was visiting professor and research fellow at the Sydney College of the Arts. His work aims to develop a better understanding of the role of drawing as both a language for art and design practice, and as a means of thinking and researching social and personal issues. Examples of this research are evident in a project with the Birmingham Children's Hospital, as conducted with Professor D. Kelly and her team, and in the recent Ikon Lunar debates. Besides Minichiello academic and professional experience he also serves as a member of several boards and advisory committees.

CATALINA MEJIA MORENO

Catalina Mejia Moreno is a PhD candidate in Architectural Theory and Criticism at the School of Architecture, Planning and Landscape at Newcastle University. She is an architect having graduated from the Universidad de los Andes (Bogotá, Colombia) and holds an MA in Architectural History from the Bartlett School of Architecture (London, UK). Her research interests address questions around the various modes of architectural representation with an emphasis on the relationship between writing and architecture. Her investigations aim at understanding representation and creative possibilities in the field of architectural studies.

MIRIAM STEWART

Miriam Stewart is Curator of the 'Collection' in the Division of European and American Art at the Harvard Art Museums/Fogg Museum. She specialises in drawings, and has a particular interest in artists' materials and sketchbooks. She has contributed to many publications including: *David to Corot: French Drawings at the Fogg Art Museum*, 1996; *Sargent at Harvard*, 1999; *A Private Passion: 19th-century Paintings and Drawings from the Grenville L. Winthrop Collection, Harvard University*, 2003; and *John Singer Sargent's 'Triumph of Religion' at the Boston Public Library: Creation and Restoration*, 2009. She has organised many exhibitions devoted to drawings, including *Aubrey Beardsley, Sargent in the Studio* and *Under Cover: Artists' Sketchbooks*.

ABDULLAH M. I. SYED

Abdullah M. I. Syed was born in Karachi, Pakistan. He works and lives in both Karachi and Sydney, where he is completing his PhD in fine arts practice at the College of Fine Arts (COFA), UNSW. Syed has a BA in Design (1999), a MEd (2001) from the University of Central Oklahoma (UCO) and a MFA (2009) from COFA. Syed is an artist, freelance designer and curator. He has coordinated the Design

Department at the University of Karachi, Pakistan and lectured at UCO, USA. His artwork has been featured in exhibitions in Bangladesh, Sharjah, USA, Australia, Hong Kong, India, the UK and Pakistan. Syed was artist in residence at Cicada Press, Sydney (2009) and Blacktown Art Centre (2011). His co-curating credits include: *Michael Esson's: A Survey of Drawing, Michael Kempson's; A Survey of Prints, Aboriginal Dreams, Let's Draw the Line, and 6/6* and *Labyrinth in Karachi.* Syed has received awards including the 'Individual Artist of Oklahoma Award for Installation' (2003), the 'COFA Senior Artist from Asia Scholarship' (2006), the 'UNSW's Postgraduate Research Scholarship' (2009) and the 'Blacktown Art Prize' (2010), Sydney.

NICHOLAS TEMPLE

Nicholas Temple is an architect and professor of architecture at the University of Huddersfield, with research interests in the historical and cultural contexts of architecture and the city, with specific focus on the European traditions. He has previously taught at University of Lincoln, Liverpool University, University of Nottingham, University of Pennsylvania and Leeds Metropolitan University, and was a visiting lecturer at the Moscow Architectural Institute and the Ion Mincu Institute in Bucharest. A graduate of Cambridge University, and a Rome Scholar in Architecture at the British School at Rome (1986-88), Temple was recently awarded the *Paul Mellon Rome Fellowship* (2012). His published works include *Disclosing Horizons: Architecture, Perspective and Redemptive Space* (Routledge, 2007) and *renovatio urbis: Architecture, Urbanism and Ceremony in the Rome of Julius II* (Routledge, 2011).

CHRISTINE TURNER

Christine Turner is a PhD candidate in fine art at Liverpool John Moores University in the School of Art and Design. Her research concerns the practice of drawing and painting and her PhD is entitled 'An Enquiry into the Significance of Drawing and Painting the Human Form in Contemporary Fine Art Practice.' The practice integrates a personal and idiosyncratic presentation of how the human form is visually represented. Turner is an artist who has exhibited nationally and has works in public and private collections. Her research interests remain in the role of the practice-based art and design PhD and the potential for the development of knowledge through drawing.

LI WENMIN

Born in China and currently living and working in Sydney, Li Wenmin has studied at the College of Fine Arts, The University of New South Wales since 2001 and obtained her PhD in drawing in 2009. Li has presented her research on themes that investigate the relationships between Chinese traditional painting and contemporary drawing at different conferences in Sydney, the UK and China. Li's work as a practising artist has been exhibited internationally in Australia, the UK, Japan, China and Hong Kong. She currently lectures at the College of Fine Arts, The University of New South Wales.

Acknowledgements

Angela Bartram, Nader El-Bizri, Douglas Gittens

We would like to thank John Plowman and the Drawing Research Group of the University of Lincoln for initiating and staging the conference, *Recto-Verso: Redefining the Sketchbook,* in February 2011 at the Collection in Lincoln that inspired this volume. We would also like to acknowledge the contribution of the conference's accompanying exhibition *The Moment of Privacy has Passed*, as curated by John Plowman and shown at the Usher Gallery, Lincoln in 2010–11, and the support given during the installation of the exhibition by Maggie Warren, Richard Wright and Barbara Griffin. We would like to give indebted thanks to our colleagues Lisa Mooney and Nick Temple who supported and encouraged this publication, and to the University of Lincoln.

We also give thanks to the authors who have developed papers from the conference for this edited volume of studies. Thank you also to the editorial team at Ashgate for their friendly manner, their professionalism and for their patience, with special gratitude to the commissioning editor, Valerie Rose.

We dedicate this edited volume to the memory of the late Marco Frascari.

Introduction

Angela Bartram, Nader El-Bizri, Douglas Gittens

OVERVIEW

Some of the chapters that are gathered within our edited volume of studies were based in part on adapted and expanded versions of contributed papers that were originally presented at an international colloquium and exhibition in February 2011, held at The Collection (the art and archaeology gallery in Lincoln, UK) in association with the Faculty of Art, Architecture and Design at the University of Lincoln. Additional texts were specifically composed for this volume, and the original colloquium papers were rewritten to meet our editorial directives and publication rationale.

The thematic orientations of the chapters of this edited volume are interdisciplinary in character, and they cover diverse topics across a variety of methodological approaches in research, which include art theory, architectural humanities, philosophical discourse, along with reflections on curatorial practices and pedagogical analyses.

This volume explores variegated aspects that figure in terms of placing the sketchbook within contemporary practices and modes of thinking in the artistic, design–orientated and architectural domains. Part of this line of investigation is undertaken against the background of the most recent developments in information processing and communication technologies, whilst also accounting for the impact that these have on the theoretical and practical conceptions of traditional forms of drawing, and of the graphical modes of representing artistic, architectural and design-based ideas. The enquiry also considers the contexts in which drawing and sketching become intimately interwoven with textual commentary, or the registering of thought through the co-entanglement of images with texts, of icons with words. It also includes reflections on the traditional role of the sketchbook as creative archival system for ideas development, reflection and progression within the practice of art, design and architecture, where it acts as a necessary accompaniment to the methods and processes in which more formal works are realized.

The themes that guided the composition of the individual chapters, and underpinned the editorial directives behind the unity of this volume, evoked notions such as the 'trace', in understanding the essence of the sketchbook, or in terms of accounting for its 'curated' character, the 'itinerant' and 'pedagogic' traits of its production and interpretation, and the 'physical handiness' of its presence as art-object versus its 'digitised' novel manifestations. These orientations deal with philosophical and psychological concepts that investigate relatable phenomena of perception, embodiment, spatiality and temporality. In addition, they probe the impact of novel developments in digital technologies and the techniques of production in terms of new forms of drawing, sketching and visual representation. Such studies cast the sketchbook in a new light in order to illuminate its metaphysical presuppositions, and its emplacement against the background of representational thinking and imaging. Moreover, this elucidates the spheres of the theoretical and practical assimilations of the sketchbook within artistic and architectural modes of thought and production, along with the meditation on the criteria of redefining the sketchbook and its role within pedagogic domains and curatorial contexts. The curation of sketchbooks, as a method to demonstrate and make visible formative ideas and their development, has become of increasing interest for galleries in recent years, and this edited volume aims to offer a suggestion of why their importance has gained significance in this way.

Diverse issues are examined herein, including the ontological aspects of the sketchbook in the way it is immersed within lived experiences, or what classical phenomenology in the Husserlian tradition refers to as the 'life-world' (*Lebenswelt*). These enquiries are also guided by philosophical insights, such as the Heideggerian leitmotifs in the existential analytic of '*Dasein*', or the critique of the metaphysical underpinnings of 'truth in drawing and painting' as embodied in Derrida's reflections on the classical Greek notion of the '*parergon*' or on its character as 'supplement' and 'accessory'. The investigations are also supported by meditations on the liminal and interfacial character of the sketchbook in particular, or, more generally, in connection with the essence of the graphical icon and imagery, by way of contrasting the objective presence of an actual drawing versus its representational positing at a conceptual level or through imagination. Such lines of investigation evoke the workings of memory and of weaving biographical recordings with topological and cosmological attributes. They also draw out spatial-temporal modulations that demarcate the anatomies of sketches and of graphical traces, or of the physical embodiment of the sketchbook as material object, or as a given *thing* in the world – an object given exhibitable status in its own right, and offered as a portal into the imagination of the creative process. Furthermore, these enquiries are not restricted to the domains of exploring European intellectual and artistic traditions; rather they also deal with intercultural and cross-cultural determinants. Included in this discourse are reviews of practices in Chinese artworks or Islamic calligraphy, and situational contexts that deal with historical exemplars, such as Roman and Renaissance art, or modern practices in geographical-cultural regions like Pakistan. The spheres of investigation articulate bodily experiential fields of perceptual encounters that are 'lived' in everydayness amidst the vast urban milieu and its societal orders. The sketchbook is therefore taken as a theme for exploring the city and the geographies of travel. This covers situational settings for probing the intimacies of private spaces and the conditions of their broad cultural exposures in the public domain of curatorial praxis, the collection and trading of artworks, and the pedagogic exchanges within studio-based experimentations. These lines of investigation are also intertwined with reflections on the unfolding of technology in the hybrid spheres of reinventing the sketchbook in digitised settings or design-laboratories. With the emergence of new specific forms of demarcating the range of expected skills in the use of computerized tools, the advance of digitisation presents novel problem-solving techniques that are imposed on the traditional use of the sketchbook or that get intertwined with it, or even evoking scepticism regarding the relevance of manual sketching altogether.

Given its wide-ranging scope, this edited volume covers the spectrum of the visual arts in their thematic orientations within universal rituals and practices associated with the sketchbook. This is reflected in the diverse disciplinary and praxis spheres that shaped the chapters of this volume and included the authorial contributions of art and architecture historians and theorists, practicing architects, artists and designers, in addition to philosophers. As a consequence, the volume assembles an international company of writers, all of whom draw upon manifold theories, practices and reflections that are common to the contemporary conceptualizations of the sketchbook and of its associated environments (be it in studios, workshops, ateliers, schools, museums and exhibition spaces, public-art sites, etc.). The contributions of the authors of the chapters offer multiple intertwined and complementary dialogues in which the sketchbook can be understood as a pivotal working tool that contributes to the creative process and the formulation and manufacturing of visual ideas, and their dissemination within academic, professional, pedagogic and curatorial settings. These enquiries address in variegated forms the doubts that may be levelled at the validity of the sketchbook in the age of modern technology, as an instrument of practice and creativity, and as an educational device. The probing reflections on the value of the traditional 'paper and bound' sketchbook, with its associated modes of making and sketching, and as also set within their historical horizons, do not eclipse the penchant to explore the advantages afforded by digital technologies, or in appreciating certain hybrid experimental ways of combining the conventional with the novel. A plethora of 'how to do books' exist that specifically deal with the vocational aspects of the sketchbook and many of these publications are aimed at educational markets. By contrast, this volume specifically addresses the philosophical, theoretical, historical and psychological significance of sketchbooks and their socio-cultural relevance to praxis in art, architecture and design; especially as a cognitive 'sounding boards' and 'ideas stores'.

SYNOPTIC ACCOUNTS OF THE CHAPTERS

To give a more concrete account of the themes and topics that are addressed within this volume, and the variation in method, disciplinary approach, and conceptual framing, we shall offer hereinafter a synoptic survey of the contents of each of the chapters.

By way of an 'overture' that complements this 'Introduction', the first chapter, which is composed by Nader El-Bizri as an *Exordium historicum*, offers an overview that places in relief the recent technical and conceptual developments modulating the reception and definition of the sketchbook, and of sketching, in the age of modern techno-science. This state of affairs is situated against the background of historical precedents, particularly in Renaissance art and architecture, which emerged in response to the adaptive assimilation of science and technology within artistic and architectural modes of thinking and making. A special emphasis is placed in this context on exploring the Renaissance *perspectiva* traditions in the pictorial arts, and their mathematical underpinning by the classical Greco-Arabic-Latin sources in the science of optics.

The second chapter, also authored by Nader El-Bizri, deals with ontological and phenomenological directives; particularly as set within Derrida's account of the '*parergon*'. This line of enquiry addresses the sketchbook from the standpoint of thinking about the relativity of the 'supplement' in signification and in its presupposition of 'what lacks' and resides as 'accessory' outside the *ergon* (qua work) whilst also en-framing it (*l'encadrer*; *Ge-Stell*). The 'sketchbook' is conceived herein as '*ergon*' that has the potentiality to be instead of being that which exists in actuality *per se*. This is argued by El-Bizri to be the case in spite of the 'object-character' of the physical *graphèmes* (graphical entities) that the 'sketchbook' receives by way of materially and physically registering the motions of the forms of presentation as a movement of the *Darstellung* (the portraying depiction of a shifting representation). This chapter offers a critical interpretation of Derrida's analyses of the pictorial arts in *La vérité en peinture* (*Truth in Painting*), as these were set against the backdrop of a metaphysical critique of a fundamental ontology that is set at work within Heidegger's *Der Ursprung des Kunstwerkes* (*The Origin of the Work of Art*).

In Chapter 3, John Hendrix deals with the sketchbook as a palimpsest that continues to be important for the *parti* in the architectural design process. Hendrix blends the historical with the theoretical. He argues that, while information technology and cybernetics are vital in the development and execution of modern designs and their *parti*, it remains to be the case that computer-aided tools cannot readily replace certain functions of the traditional sketchbook, wherein sketches can more completely represent the relation between the human mind, thought and psyche, and compositions in art or architecture. The best example of this is the quality of palimpsest in the sketchbook, where layers of forms and ideas overlay each other, and traces of partially erased markings can rise to the surface and become part of the form. Hendrix analyses such palimpsest-qualities in drawings by Francesco Borromini, in the seventeenth century, and in those of Peter Eisenman in the twentieth century. He also identifies the quality of palimpsest with some urban landscapes, and Rome being the best example, where buildings or streets are composed of traces of past built-forms and pathways. However, most importantly, Hendrix holds that the essence of the palimpsest can be found in the human mind, where layers of consciousness are composed of traces, memory-fragments of visual and aural forms, of recollections and dream-like images. Through an analogical connection with the palimpsest, the sketch emulates the human mind, and serves as a tool in drawing and painting, in architectural composition and urban design, which connects the built environment to the human mental faculties. The sketch would thus continue to be a mechanism that assists in producing increasingly creative, insightful, and meaningful modes of design.

The philosophical and theoretical orientations continue to figure prominently in chapter four, as authored by Robert Clarke, who explores the ontological nature of the sketchbook in which the intimate experience of drawing opens up a special indeterminate sense of being immersed in the world. He argues that such absorbed immersion is neither passive nor predictable, but aptly demonstrates the Heideggerian notions of *Zuhandenheit* (ready-to-hand) and *Vorhandenheit* (present-to-hand) in relation to the indivisible nature of consciousness and the world. Clarke aims at establishing the foundation for examining the unique possibilities of the sketchbook as an intimate referent of presence in the self and its expressiveness of its being-in-the-world, as focused within fleeting moments of recognition (*Augenblick*) in which both viewer and viewed get mutually transformed. The chapter refers to its author's own practice of drawing, which, for twenty years, exclusively used the sketchbook in its unfolding.

In the fifth chapter, Nick Temple grounds his theoretical orientations in historiography by way of closely examining Bramante's drawings for St. Peter's Basilica, whilst mediating his analyses by appealing to Renaissance humanists and theologians besides the architects. Temple aims at showing how the idea of divine infinitude can be transcribed unto the situational context of an architectural problem at the symbolic and practical levels. He argues that the search for geometrical precision in the articulation and connectivity of spaces was counterbalanced by an equal concern for their 'reception' and accommodation within a pre-existing urban context and cultural milieu. The sketch served as a contemplative datum to reconcile these relationships, whereby the marks on paper – with their approximations to certain exemplary models – provided indicators, or gestures, for more concrete relationships, as yet undefined, but nevertheless open to new possibilities and potential realizations. Temple considers how Bramante sought to reconcile through drawing the philosophical/theological notions of the 'centre' with the requirements to accommodate existing spatial and topographical conditions, as they relate to the location of the tomb of St. Peter.

In the sixth chapter, Li Wenmin focuses on the notion of the 'trace' and the way a sketch acts as a preparatory intervention in laying down the possibilities for the emergence of the markings of visual activities. She seeks to show how sketching partakes in analysis through several kinds of visual imagery by examining Chinese traditional painting. Certain patterns of pictorial enquiry and depiction rise through these modes of sketching, which display a common method carried out in praxis by the artists. The Chinese approach aims at capturing the likeness and the essence of the depicted object, which distinguishes the significance of sketching in its preparatory function from how the sketch figures within European-based legacies; namely as these evolved in the Renaissance and in modern avant-garde art. Chinese sketches rest on evoking the emotions, which arise during the experiences of observation in order to draw from imagined images the actual markers of the artistic making activity, and the guiding of its creative impulses.

In Chapter 7 Douglas Gittens situates the sketchbook between the virtual and the actual. He grasps the sketchbook in this context as a field of potentialities, and as an interactive network that allows free-flowing theoretical and imaginative applications to unfold within a process of incubation, whilst also facilitating the emergence of ideas. In this respect, the sketchbook acts as a virtual domain that assists in actualising latent potentialities through which the realm of ideas embodies a world of objects. The sketchbook offers the designer an alternative mode of engagement with the artwork that circumvents the restrictions of everyday design-practice. In this chapter, Gittens argues that the sketchbook is an inherently fluid and transient space for the designer, and that, by merit of its nature, it is a liminal and unstable interface through which creative potentialities and practical endeavours become intertwined. Such analyses are furthermore orientated by a reading of Deleuze in which the sketchbook is seen as an immanent field of potentiality through which the virtual can find expression in the actual.

Chapter 8 weaves the autobiographical with the artistic and architectural activity, and takes the sketchbook as an intimate diary upon which Rachel Hurst reveals how a love affair evolved through the medium of sketches. Hurst endeavours to show how certain genres of diaries and journals record the emergence of love affairs, or how they document the first awakenings of amorous interests and passions. Hurst's chapter considers the significance of *eros* in sketching, and then extrapolates on this in terms of including an account of *a love of the other* as it gets also entangled with loving drawing. She uses the drawing-journals of two architects in order to examine the sketch as a revelatory trace, whilst chronicling their liaison between the copious lines of architectural depictions. The drawings do not only map spatial objects and observations, perceived simultaneously but differently by both authors, but they also constitute a poetized form of architectural discourse and conversation between them.

Chapter 9 follows through with the autobiographical thematic penchant, and the evocation of lived experience as it manifests itself by way of a performativity-based analysis of drawing and sketching. In this chapter, Catalina Mejia Moreno entangles reflections on the sketchbook with her own embodiment, specifically by way of grasping her own body and its wounds as 'a site' for writing and drawing. The sketchbook is posited here as a written/drawn artefact that performs unvaryingly with a site-writing project, and as a means for exploring textual and material possibilities (the patterning of words on a page, the design of the page itself – its edges, boundaries, thresholds, surfaces, the relation of one page to another). The sketchbook becomes a place where possible new meanings emerge from processes of drawing, writing, cutting, and pasting; and through it, the material evidence of new critical explorations and possibilities become manifest.

Chapter 10, which is authored jointly by Roohi Shafiq Ahmed and Abdullah Muhammad Iyhab Syed, deals with curatorial issues that surround a show in Karachi that surveyed the drawing practices of twenty-two Pakistani artists. The exhibited preliminary sketches and subsequent finished drawings reveal a unique phase of the artists' visual practices, and show responses to collective or personal tragedies and triumphs. The chapter aims at identifying the role of drawing in exercising self-imposed censorship within the spheres of art practice in the Pakistani societal milieu. Studying the sketchbooks reveals the social, religious, political and personal underpinnings of sketching in this contemporary Pakistani art scene, whilst oscillating between the notions of hiddenness in meaning versus the revealing of what has been imagined and is eventually presented publicly.

In Chapter 11, Angela Bartram analyses the sketchbook from the standpoint of its use and purpose, which is to collect the initial ideas of the artist, designer or maker in the manner that suits their practice. The sketchbook is grasped herein, as a receptacle in which initial intimate creative outpourings are invested safely and privately. An object made by the author for the author, and theirs to do with as they wish. To this end, a discussion ensues on the creative permanence and object validity of the sketchbook used fully and to capacity in relation to its historic sacrificing and destruction. Nonetheless, whilst this chapter examines the sketchbook as a throwaway commodity, it still addresses the nature of its inherent worth as an active participant in creativity and challenges the notion of taking the redundant sketchbook as being precious through a focus on its agency. Bartram ultimately argues that the sketchbook be disregarded as an ultimate act of keeping creativity a private occupation, despite reactionary protest for it to be saved as a demonstrative object of the process.

In Chapter 12, Miriam Stewart delves into curatorial issues by accounting for the interpretation, preservation, and displaying of sketchbooks against the background of analysing their meaning, their survival and physical characteristics. She holds that the sketchbook provides a glimpse of the artist at work; assembling ideas for future projects, documenting travels, making lists, etc. The sketchbook may provide a collated view of the artist's process – a way to see ideas in proximity, one leading to the next, or it may be a disparate record of passing sketches or notations, taken days, weeks, or years apart. Examining a sketchbook can seem somehow animated by transgression, as if we were looking over the artist's shoulder, invading her/his space, and prying into her/his private diary. Kept close to the body, the sketchbook can seem to be a bodily extension of the artist, and is as such 'ready-to-hand'. Failure to recognize drawings as sketchbook-pages can limit our understanding and interpretation of their meaning, allowing only an incomplete picture of the artist's process.

In Chapter 13, Mario Minichiello considers the sketchbook to be 'a site' for the artist's 'arguments with the world'. Minichiello explores how sketchbooks can be used to develop a personalized approach to drawing and to visual thinking. For the artist and designer the sketchbook remains a private and convenient place to engage with drawing as a means of contemplating the world. As a process, it underpins the development of visual memory, of researching ideas and securing a personal point of view. In this way drawing contributes to the generation of knowledge and helps in focusing the development of an individual's critical thinking. For Minichiello, the sketchbook probes the world in alternative ways to that of electronic and photographic media. He also explores how the sketch can often circumvent the censorship imposed on mass media, thereby providing a unique visual analysis of the socio-political realm. This chapter ultimately shows how the use of drawing can become a poignant form of *reportage* or as a registering record of enquiry and socio-political analysis.

Chapter 14 by Raymond Lucas approaches the sketchbook (as opposed to the loose-leaf or individual sketch) with a particular reference to the phenomenon of *collecting*. The collector as an individual has several traits in common with the sketcher, as well as some notable differences. The collector has been a figure in critical theory and anthropology that is celebrated and critiqued in equal measure. Collecting has associations not only with colonialism, objectification, and materialism, but it also engages curiosity, aesthetics, and preservation. Each of these aspects is present in the serial form of the sketchbook. Lucas evokes the views of Baudrillard and Elsner around the phenomenon of *collecting* in relation to context, time, and objectification. Lucas argues that the sketchbook bears witness and mediates processes by which artists, architects, and designers seek to understand the world.

In Chapter 15, Paul Clarke focuses on the narrative that emerges from sketching, whereby the sketchbook becomes an experimental setting, and a laboratory of visual ideas that are intermingled with textual fragments and registered thoughts. His chapter frames the sketchbook as an historical 'device' that served the education of architects. He therefore wonders whether it can still be an indispensable aid amidst the complex representational fields of computer-modelling. He examines the manner a sketchbook becomes a 'portable workspace' that extends the studio beyond a fixed location, or that offers a unique medium for critical thinking and design. Using contemporary case-studies, he examines the contrasting approaches used in the sketchbooks of a range of architectural settings; including studio teaching pedagogies as they are unfolding in the digital age. Clarke argues that by aiming to catalogue, research, and codify different approaches and working-methods, rich and diversified sources of creativity and critical methodology get opened up, which in their turn inform the studio practices. His study reveals continuities with how sketchbooks have been used in the past as storehouses of reflective thought and memory, and the way they may still open up the horizons of research in architecture against the backdrop of modern information technology.

In Chapter 16, Christine Turner considers the sketchbook as a reflective journal that can serve research within higher education settings. However, she also recognizes the challenges that face conventional modes of manual sketching in the age of the advent of digital technologies. The sketchbook may nowadays be seen as a compromised device, particularly in the fine arts that are also privileging conceptual approaches over sketching and drawing, let alone the dominance of computer-aided methods of tracing and rendering. She argues that the shift to conceptual-art-praxis has been exacerbated by art and design educational progressions towards serving academic-research cultures. Her chapter demonstrates how the divide and dichotomy between theory and practice, which is acutely manifested in debates surrounding art-research, may be also witnessed in the methods of developing a doctoral enquiry *cum* project. She holds that contrariety between the pragmatic and speculative creative development is intimately present in the sketchbook. Through her own doctoral research artwork, she aims at demonstrating the problematic dynamics of constructing a practical research thesis that is creatively fluid on one hand, but academically rigorous on the other. She also takes this state of affairs to be reflective of the dual quality in the sketchbook, which offers a peculiarly potent arena for critical and contemplative practice, and therefore remains crucial to contemporary art and design in academe and higher education.

CONCLUDING REMARKS

Looking at the breadth and diversity of the themes of the chapters that are gathered in this edited volume, and the conceptual threads that link them together, a comprehensive account of the various aspects that surround the redefinition of the *sketchbook* in the age of digital technologies is secured with architectonic unity and depth in enquiry. It is in this respect that we hope this gathering of studies would constitute a welcome addition to the constellation of books that deal with art, architecture and design, especially in connection with the investigation of the theoretical and practical dimensions of drawing and sketching, with the *sketchbook* being situated herein at the heart of such meditations.

It is our delightful duty in this context to thank all the authors who made contributed chapters to this edited volume of studies. This publication would not have been realizable without their commitment, patience and dedication in meeting the editorial directives and production timeframes. We are also thankful to the editors at Ashgate, who accompanied us through the journey of bringing this volume to publication, and our special thanks go here to Valerie Rose. We are grateful to our colleagues and friends who encouraged us to pursue this publication, and we especially express our gratitude to Lisa Mooney, Nick Temple, and John Plowman, who, at the time of launching this initiative, were supportive of our research at the University of Lincoln. At the theoretical level, we benefitted from the anonymous reports of the specialist referees that were commissioned by Ashgate to review our volume at the earlier stages of its composition, and this blind-refereeing process assisted us in refining the contents of the chapters and brought their themes to a greater focus and coherence. We are also indebted to the authority of Martin Kemp, who was a keynote speaker at the Lincoln international colloquium, and for his insightful remarks at the initial stages of shaping this publication project. We also dedicate this edited volume to the memory of the late Marco Frascari, who from the onset supported our endeavour to publish this volume.

1

By Way of an Overture:
Classical Optics and Renaissance Pictorial Arts

Nader El-Bizri

PREAMBLE

The various chapters of this edited volume offer perspectives that affirm the intertwining of the acts of sketching/drawing with the processes of making (or unmaking) the sketchbook. These experiential and conceptual aspects emphasize the practical and philosophical reflection on the status of the sketchbook in art, design and architecture, and its interconnectivity with the acts of sketching/ drawing across these disciplines. Such processes have been metamorphosed through the passage of time and in being historically determined, since sketching and the sketchbook constitute respectively an act and an artefact whose uses and values are commonly shared by these creative disciplines. Even though the principal focus in this edited volume is on the theoretical attributes of the acts of sketching/drawing, and of the associated activities that surround them, along with their co-entanglement with the physicality of the phenomenal presence of the sketchbook as a given sensible 'thing' or an 'object' of sense-perception, this conceptual orientation is not meant to be ahistorical in character and it remains guided by cultural determinants. Whilst it is the case that the standing of sketching/drawing in their traditional sense (namely as what is not directly mediated via cybernetic and digital information processing and communication technologies) is confronting variegated pressures and challenges in our more recent times, it remains to be the case that the activities of sketching/drawing have always been historically and culturally bound, and through them, the production of the sketchbook being itself accordingly tailored and apportioned. Although the theories of phenomenology are dominant in the constellation of studies that are gathered in this edited volume, the historical nuances are not left out, but rather they are assumed within orientations that focus on contemporary predicaments and expectations surrounding the phenomenon of the sketchbook, which solicit the rethinking of its definition and significance. It is in this context that the emphasis is set on recent history in its theoretic and practical angles. Nonetheless, to offer a more rooted historical apercu, this overture acts as an *exordium historicum*, in view of picturing a framework that better assists in situating the studies that are collected under the covers of this volume. This will be undertaken by way of synoptically picturing one of the most profound ruptures in European sketching/drawing practices, which took place prior to our modern transitional epoch, as exemplified by Renaissance pictorial arts and their adaptive assimilation of the exact sciences of their age. This exordium aims at providing a historical prologue that complements the philosophical reflections on the shifting landscapes of the modern paradigms of sketching/drawing, which may be indicative of the emergence of a new and unprecedented fissure in the pictorial arts. This undertaking is not fused with the organizational and curatorial aspects of the editors'Introduction', and its concerns of arranging a singular text out of manifold chapters constituting organic sets of scholarship. Whilst the editors' 'Introduction' explains the themes of this text and their philosophical underpinnings, the present 'Overture' serves as an historical prelude that suggests additional directions in research, which are attuned to the works of art historians and theorists such as Hubert Damisch, Martin Kemp, Mario Carpo and Patrick Maynard.[1] This line in thinking does not thusly assume that sketching/drawing constituted activities that were historically fixed or that can be contemplated as being metaphysically stable.

The historical and cultural longstanding Renaissance episodes of the convergences between the arts and the sciences offer us instructive scenes. These hint in particular at the way we can also account for the ameliorations in the artistic and scientific spheres, which witnessed novel expressions and adaptive adjustments at the beginnings of the twentieth century through modern fascinations with technique and machines. A similar state of affairs has been already unfolding and underway, albeit in more sharpened modes of the unlocking of the powers of techno-science, at the turn of our new millennium. The impress of techno-science is thought-provoking in the sense that is calls for thinking about what withdraws from our world and experiential realms, which leads us back unto rethinking our worldly reality and its fields of experience. The theme of this present *exordium historicum* overture would therefore examine some key aspects of the connections and distinctions between the pictorial arts and the exact sciences, as these were manifested in the context of the theories and practices of *perspectiva* in the Italian Renaissance, while also taking into account the way they would potentially inform our assessment of modern expressions of the interconnections between art and techno-science.

ARS SINE SCIENTIA NIHIL EST – SCIENTIA SINE ARTE NIHIL EST

The *dicta*: *'ars sine scientia nihil est'* ('art without knowledge [science] is nothing') and 'knowledge [science] without art is nothing' (*'scientia sine arte nihil est'*) are best expressive of the co-entanglement of the arts with the sciences, as these found one of their intense expressions through the humanistic theoretical treatises of Renaissance scholarship, and via their diverse architectonic applications in the expansion of material culture. The boundaries that may have separated art from

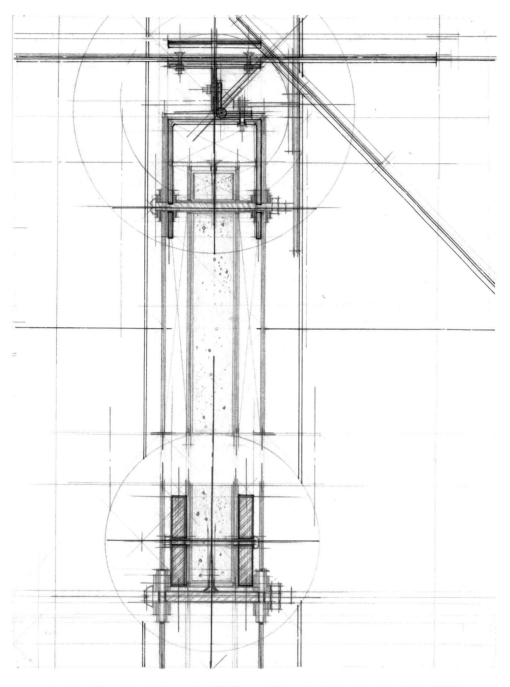

1.1   Study for an installation at the GSD, Harvard University. Original drawing: Nader El-Bizri

science became at times blurred in the Italian Renaissance, especially as this was set against the epistemic backdrop of a gradual and systemic deconstruction of the antique and millennial Aristotelian physics. One of the main aspects of establishing scientific grounds for the praxis of visual and plastic art, and the associated artistic underpinning of reflections on the applications of the exact *cum* natural sciences, was modulated through contemplations of the connection and distinction between the *perspectiva naturalis* of natural visual-perception (as studied in the classical Greco-Arabic science of optics) and the *perspectiva artificialis* of pictorial representation of the perceptual field of vision (as enacted in Renaissance architectural drawing, painting and selected relief sculpting). The leitmotifs of *perspectiva* offered an optimal context for investigating the relationships between science and art, in terms of probing the optical and geometric foundations of the pictorial representation of natural phenomena in a painted spatial-depth, while experimenting with the manner projective drawing in geometric perspective contributed to the constitution of knowledge about the visible reality. These endeavours were intermediated via the agency of perfecting the so-called '*costruzione legittima*' (legitimate construction) in establishing linear and central single-point perspectives within the Italian Renaissance pictorial arts of the *Trecento*, *Quattrocento* and *Cinquecento*.

VIRTUAL REPRESENTATIONAL SPACE

The co-entanglement of the elements of the pictorial arts with the scientific taxonomies in the Renaissance may have been animated at its core by ontological-theological motives in establishing metaphorical and symbolic connections between a scriptural-textual exegesis and a presupposition of visual atonement in measuring reality via a *visio intellectualis* (intellective vision). This was the case despite the fact that the visual illusory depiction of spatial depth, in the geometric constructions and projections of perspective, alluded theologically to higher orders of 'reality' that transcended the way the 'real' manifested itself empirically and experientially in visual perception. The visualization of reality and the picturing of the world were mediated via the agency of perspective in terms of transforming the *natural visual theory* into a *pictorial theory*.[2]

The epistemic, veridical, and apodictic criteria of *scientia*, as a source of reliable and sound rational knowledge, when conducted within the parameters of precision in logical reasoning and controlled experimenting, is not dependent on personal choices as it is for instance the case with the spheres of theory and praxis in art, which do not necessitate strict rules of proof and demonstration. This aspect in the explorative horizons of the visual and plastic arts opened up new spheres of inquiry that were imaginatively inventive, and relatively at liberty in not following with stricture the principles of scientific logic. This also assisted in the constitution of imaginary models of empirical reality through pictorial representational spaces and visual narratives, which themselves offered contexts for informing the spatial and architectonic qualities of actualized physical architectural realities, specifically through the agency of design and its approximation of the realization of its formal-material hypotheses.

The rigorous rationality that underpinned the coherence of representational space in modelling an imaginative reality within the spectacle of linear central perspective was based on an inner geometric system of points, angles, axes, converging lines and triangles. The representational space of pictorial perspective is imagined, and depicted afterwards, or in succession, through the structuring order of geometric construction and projection, to be furthermore refined by way of colour and the anatomy of figurative forms of human and living beings, with their gestures and choreographies, which all manifest a virtual new reality that is saturated with communicative visual metaphors, symbolic meanings, and narratives. These became vital in their turn in terms of highlighting the role of imagination in pictorial and figurative representation, and in the un-concealment of the hidden physical and mathematical principles of reality. The science that grounded the pictorial arts became itself served by the unfolding of such applications in founding the role of imagery in the scientific modelling of realities that would remain otherwise imperceptible in the course of lived experiential and empirical ambient settings of our human sensibility and its sensorial conditions.

The designer, the painter-architect, contemplates and imagines certain spatial and architectonic possibilities, which belong to reflections on a given pictorial or architectural context, and are mediated via concepts that set down the theoretical hypotheses of design. Such processes unfold through conjectures and the exploration of the most probable possibilities by testing them through drawing, drafting, tracing, and in terms of scaled models, as physical 'maquettes'. This also applies to most site-specific expressions of art, such as installations, wherein sketching through drawing and making is integral, or even in practices of depicting spaces irrespective of given disciplines, like painting architectural interiors. These procedures enact calculative, intuitive, and imaginative strategies that attempt to approximate in actualization what can possibly be done in tangible terms within physical reality. The logic of geometry, physics (statics), architectonics, material mechanics, formal and spatial qualities, atmosphere in imagined sensorial experiences, all bring science and art together in design, while also being oriented by the agency of language in articulating thinking and the manner it depicts the gradual emergence of a composite of form and matter in making. Artistic visions are therefore all along entangled with scientific abstractions.

The pictorial representational space that is depicted through artificial linear central perspective makes the seeming sense of infinity manifest in virtual visual terms. The material painting on the surface of the canvas appears as a window that is carefully opened up into a given region of an imagined reality, which is chosen through the agency of the painter, their inherence in history, culture and language, and is offered as a complex web of narratives to the observers, be it contemporaneous patrons, or eventually the anonymous spectators who stretch as the on-looking ghosts of posterity. A human viewpoint on the world is established by seeing reality in perspective. A relationship is set between the finite distance of the painter-observer from the surface of the painted canvas, and the implied sense of infinity within the representational virtual space of the depicted portion of imagined reality in the painting. Similar relationships have, to some extent, been theorized in the form of 'a contract between artist-artwork-performer-spectator'.

PERSPECTIVA

Two pyramids-cones of visibility intersect in seeing by way of perspective: the finite pyramid-cone of vision of the *perspectiva naturalis*, as studied in optics in connection with direct visual perception, and the pyramid-cone of the *perspectiva artificialis* in the pictorial order, which tends towards infinity. The pyramid-cone of vision in the *perspectiva naturalis*, as entailed by direct visual perception, is finite and determined by the nearness of its vertex (which is at the centre eye of the painter-observer) to its base (as the surface of the contemplated canvas). As for the pyramid-cone in the *perspectiva artificialis* pictorial order, it gives the semblance of tending towards infinity through the converging geometric lines that meet in the centring-vanishing point, or in the various triangles that form the two-dimensional depiction of a pyramid when meeting in one point. This geometry is embedded in the single-point linear and central construct of pictorial perspective, which is established from the viewpoint of a fixed angle of vision. The *perspectiva artificialis* is static and marked by fixity, in contrast with the manner the eyes continually move and vibrate in scanning the visual field in the *perspectiva naturalis*. The representational space that is depicted via the *perspectiva artificialis* is itself static and fixed, while opening up to a sense of seeming infinitude. The single-point linear and central construct of pictorial perspective, with the fixity and static quality of its representational order, offers an idealized context for abstractness in geometric space, which is unlike what is brought into appearance within the horizons of natural visual perception. Artificial perspective reveals a symbolic order that is modulated by the exact rules of geometry, and it grants an abstractive viewpoint on what remains hidden from natural sight in the concrete fields of empirical and sensible experience. Artificial perspective lets something *omnipresent* appear, through its geometric order; and yet, there is also the virtual sense by which the painter-observer is also looked at from within the painting when gazing at it. The contemplation of the painting reveals a virtual viewpoint from a seeming infinity, that looks back at the painter-observer and beyond, and is situated at the vertex of the pyramid-cone of the *perspectiva artificialis* within the pictorial space; namely, as the centring-vanishing point where parallels in pictorial-depth tend towards it as the *infinite*, while meeting in it when they are simply seen as geometric lines traced on a two-dimensional surface. As if the painter-observer is also supposedly seen from infinity, in a gaze coming from within the painting that remains *omnivoyant*, given the fixity of the angle of vision in the geometric representational structure of the single-point linear and central pictorial perspective. This phenomenon is attested with portraiture whereby the subject appears to be looking at the painter in destabilizing visual exchanges between viewer-and-viewed, or in the context of sculpture as well, wherein the subject's gaze is direct. This outlook is densely expressed in Nicolaus Cusanus's '*Figura paradigmatica*', in his *De coniecturis* (*On conjecture*; ca. 1440 CE), which shows two intersecting pyramids, one of light (*lux*), as the *pyramidis lucis*, and the other of shadow (*tenebrae*), as the *pyramidis tenebrarum*, which respectively evoke the ideas of unity and manifoldness. Perspective is posited in this context as a channel of communication between divinities and mortals.[3] As if the idealized representational space of pictorial perspective carries also a deeper sense of reality in unveiling the geometric order that grounds and structures the visible universe. In opening up to the infinite, the virtual reality of the painting, as an object of sensible experience, and in its materiality as some *paint* brushed on a canvas surface, becomes itself a portion of a much wider world that is enacted by the visual art with its communicative meaningful and symbolic internal complexities.

THE SCIENCE OF OPTICS

Sketches, drawings, paintings, relief sculpting, were all modulated via the multiple theoretical and applied refinements of Renaissance 'perspectivism'. These visual arts articulated novel modes of accounting for theories of vision and light. Besides the reliance on elements from Ptolemy's book of optics, another principal reference-source in the classical Greco-Arabic science of optics was made available through the Latin renditions of the *Kitab al-Manazir* (*Book of Optics*; translated in Latin as *Perspectiva* or *De Aspectibus*)[4] of the eleventh-century Arab polymath, al-Hasan Ibn al-Haytham (known in Latinate renderings of his name as 'Alhazen' or at times as 'Alhacen'). Ibn al-Haytham's treatises in geometry and conics (following the tradition of Archimedes and Apollonius of Perga) also impacted Renaissance scholars of the calibre of Biagio Pelacani da Parma,[5] Francesco Maurolico, Ettore Ausonio, Egnazio Danti, and Francesco Barozzi.[6] Ibn al-Haytham's *Optics* was assimilated in Renaissance scholarly circles, partly through the mediation of thirteenth-century Franciscan opticians, most notably of figures like Roger Bacon and more so with the Polish mathematician and natural philosopher Witelo (Vitello). The Latin versions of Ibn al-Haytham's *Optics* partly impacted the perspective theories of Leon Battista Alberti in the *De pictura* (*On Painting*), and they were more directly influential, along with Witelo's legacy, on Lorenzo Ghiberti in his *Commentario terzo* (*Third Commentary*).[7] A printed edition of Ibn al-Haytham's Latin version of the *Optics* was established by Friedrich Risner in 1572 in Basle, under the title: *Opticae Thesaurus*, which was eventually consulted by seventeenth-century scientists and philosophers of the calibre of Kepler, Descartes, Huygens, and possibly also by Newton. The recognition of Ibn al-Haytham's *oeuvre* is also evident in the high station he was accorded by the seventeenth-century German scientist Johannis Hevelius, whereby the frontispiece of the latter's *Selenographia sive Lunae Descriptio* (a treatise on surveying the moon, dated 1647 CE) depicts Ibn al-Haytham standing on the pedestal of *ratione* (reason), with a compass in his hand and a folio of geometry, while Galileo stands on the pedestal of *sensu* (observation), holding a telescope.

Even though Ibn al-Haytham's mathematical and optical research was foundational in the domains of the exact sciences and their scientific applications, it was not in itself metamorphosed into artistic theoretical or practical spheres. Ibn al-Haytham's preoccupations were centred on experimental methods of inquiry and controlled testing, which combined geometry with physics (natural philosophy; *philosophia naturalis*) and rested on studies in optics that aimed at investigating the optimal veridical conditions of visual perception, which would ground the reliable empirical recording and analysis of accurate observational data. Moreover, the classical (mediaeval) *milieu* of the intellectual history of ideas in Islamic civilization had its own distinctive outlooks on the visual arts, which in general focused on abstractive stylizations, geometric patterning and configuration, and on a mediated epigraphic and calligraphic take on visual representation, on miniatures and manuscript illuminations, with their associated scriptural, literary, and epistemic narrations.

The Islamic conceptions of representational space and their theological *cum* religious presuppositions were historically and culturally different from the ones that have been practiced at the time in the European mediaeval context, which in their turn found their own separate ameliorations by way of gradual and novel modes of pictorial depiction via the agency of the experimental-geometrical development of perspective constructions and projections. Ibn al-Haytham's transmitted and adapted legacy in geometry and optics (from Arabic to Latin, and then in parts into Italian too) proved to be pivotal in the European art *milieu*, which had become readied and conditioned to experiment with the approximations of realist modes in rendering the pictorial form of spatial depth and of its architectonic heuristics. This state of affairs also went along with particular penchants in theological thinking that emerged from within the Renaissance expressions of Christian faith and of the material cultures of Christendom.

A THEORY OF VISION

In the *Due Regole della prospettiva pratica* (rules on practical perspective; first published in 1583 CE),[8] Jacopo Barozzi da Vignola dedicated a chapter to refute the idea of constructing linear perspective through two vanishing points that correspond with binocular vision. In this, he deployed arguments that accorded with Ibn al-Haytham's findings in optical research on the psychological-neurological-physiological aspects of vision, by way of accounting for binary visual perception, and the fusion-unification of the visible form of the object of vision, when the light rays emitted from the visible lit surfaces of that object make their final impress, via the eyes and the optical nerves, on the last sentient located in the anterior part of the brain (principally in Ibn al-Haytham's *Optics*, Book I, Chapter 6).[9] Ibn al-Haytham focuses in this on the cones in central vision that receive light and colours, and he does not evoke in this context what can be grasped as retinal receptors of light and colour in peripheral vision. This aspect of binocular vision, and its implications in terms of thinking about the method of constructing linear perspective in pictorial representational art, attracted also the comments of the Renaissance mathematician Egnatio Danti who sustained similar views as those of da Vignola, as he commented on the latter's opus.[10] Danti also displayed signs of his awareness with regard to the science of optics, in lines that accorded with Ibn al-Haytham's theories. Ultimately, linear perspective is said to have a single centring-vanishing point instead of two, hence, being mono-focal and central, without contradicting the nature of binocular vision. However, the traditions practiced in the *Trecento* pictorial renderings, based on asserting binocular vision, tended to posit two vanishing points that are correlative with the two eyes of the observer, without being in this bifocal, in the sense of having a two-point perspective that is associated with relatively more modern constructs (like the ones that are also trifocal, or curvilinear, etc.). Notwithstanding, the science of optics, as exemplified by Ibn al-Haytham's theory of visual perception, and his analysis of binocular vision, allowed for two pictorial interpretations: the *first* consists of positing a single centering-vanishing point in mono-focal central linear perspective, which correlates with the presupposition of a single cone of vision receiving the seen spectacle by the observer, while the *second* allows the positing of two vanishing points in asserting binocular vision. The latter was exemplified in what we may call: 'the heterodox [*Trecento*] perspective', which posits two vanishing-points; like, for instance it was the case with Lorenzo Ghiberti's *Christ Amongst the Doctors* (fourth panel of the North door at the Baptistery of San Giovanni).

COSTRUZIONE LEGITTIMA

The *problématique* of the '*costruzione legittima*' (legitimate construction of perspective) centred on the consequences of doubling the unique centring-vanishing point of perspective, and on debating the risks of distortions, or of compromising the spatial unity of the representational pictorial field. The manipulation of heterodox two-point perspectives, in terms of depicting central foreground figures against architectural background settings, to neutralize the effects of diplopia (double vision), did not always succeed in avoiding visual distortions, or in securing the unity of the painted representational space.[11]

The pictorial interpretation based on the heterodox positing of two-vanishing points (like it was the case with Gentile de Fabriano's *The Tomb of Saint Nicholas*), reflects an optical awareness of the need to accommodate binocular vision instead of monocular sight. However, this consciousness does not account for the fusional convergence of the two images formed on the crystalline of the eyes, and their unification in terms of the physiological-neurological-psychological determinants of vision, as analyzed by Ibn al-Haytham. Rather, this practice rests on an analysis of binocular vision that attempts to overcome the effects of diplopia and parallax (displacement of apparent position of the visible object) phenomena, under normal physiological conditions of eyesight. Such dimensions were also carefully studied in Ibn al-Haytham's optical experiments, in terms of investigating the implications of distance in vision (nearness to the eyes in particular), and of ocular convergence or its insufficiency, of visual alignments and misalignments, of parallax phenomena and stereopsis (perceived spatial depth), with their various effects on the positioning of the eyes and the physiological-ocular effort in focusing sight on certain objects within a given spectacle, with the potential also of generating errors in visual perception (principally as studied in Book III, chapter 2 of the *Optics*).

Binocular diplopia, commonly known as 'double vision', entails the simultaneous perception of two quasi-displaced-images of a single object, which results from the misalignment of the two eyes relative to one another, and due to *convergence insufficiency*. This is not a disorder when the object of vision is brought at a near distance to the eyes, and results from normal physiological conditions of convergence, which require additional effort in focusing the two eyes on an object that is very close to them, and seeing it against the background of other more distant objects. Binocular vision is normally accompanied by *singleness of vision* or *binocular fusion*, in which a single image is seen despite each eye having its own image of the object of vision. Moreover, stereopsis exploits the parallax, in terms of the displacement of a single object viewed via two different lines of sight of the eyes, along with the binocular fusion of these two resultant images, leading ultimately to seeing spatial depth.

The theoretical presuppositions guiding the construction of mono-focal linear perspective were grounded on a sound optical analysis of binocular vision and the singleness of vision in terms of binocular fusion, as for instance these were investigated by Ibn al-Haytham. This relied on the psychological, physiological, and neurological determinants of visual perception, which result under normal conditions of vision in the fusion of two disparate images-forms of a single visible object, as received by each of the eyes of the observer, and of being unified in the brain through the agency of the optical nerves, the common optic *chiasma*, and by way of exercising cognition in effecting sight.

Discussions about these optical directives in underpinning the legitimate methods of constructing perspective were animated by Alberti and Ghiberti (in terms of their varying levels of adapting Ibn al-Haytham's *oeuvre* and its reception by mediaeval and Renaissance perspectivists). These elements of debate continued to also preoccupy figures like Piero della Francesca in his *De Prospectiva Pingendi*, and with applications in his *Flagellation* painting (1455–1460; Urbino) that rendered it exemplary of perfected perspectival constructs. Celebrated linear perspectives were also associated with Masaccio's *Santa Trinità* (in Santa Maria Novella, Firenze), Donatello's *Banquet of Herod*, or Raphael's remarkable *Scuola di Atene* (in the *Stanza della Segantura*, Vatican apostolic palace). Investigations that focused on the perfection of the depicted pictorial representational spaces, in the projections and constructions of linear central perspectives, combined with in-depth studies in geometric optics, resulted eventually in perspectival approaches to Euclidean geometry, which culminated in the seventeenth century in advanced legacies of geometric perspectivism, as for instance embodied in Girard Desargues' *Œuvres mathématiques*, and in his projective geometry.[12]

PICTORIAL ART AND TECHNO-SCIENCE

The historical focus in this exordium, on the relationships between the pictorial arts and the exact sciences in the Renaissance, illustrated some of the principal aspects of the development of perspective as a method of visual representation that was firmly grounded on adaptations from research in classical optics. The rupture from mediaeval modes of depicting a pictorial space, and consequently of sketching and drawing, was gradual, and it witnessed variegated efforts in perfecting the methods of geometric projection and construction, as furthermore aided by thorough analyses of optical and geometric studies. The development of perspectives as structuring forms of pictorial representation revolutionized the technical depiction of representational space in drawing, sketching, and painting. This in itself came as a creative response to the integration of the sciences within the visual arts of the Renaissance, and the use of novel techniques and equipment that were inspired by scientific installations and instruments. This episode in reshaping European visual arts was retained within the sphere of manipulating and perfecting the precision of spatial pictorial depictions in paintings, drawings, and sketches. One could even dare to state that this form of rethinking the visual arts also manifested novel modes of organizing paint and drafting lines on two-dimensional surfaces, as these were later undertaken through the avant-garde arts, which enacted novel experiments in the nineteenth century, and intensified such creative experimental endeavours and impetuses in the modern pictorial arts of the first half of the twentieth-century. The most profound shift in European pictorial art in the Renaissance, and the revolutionizing avant-gardism of more recent times, retained a close connection with the materiality and physicality of the pictorial object; be it as a paper, a canvas, a wooden board, a metallic sheet, a sketchbook, and in the manner these received various materials in terms of paint, charcoal, ink, etc. The manipulation of the structural order of pictorial depiction was still handy and corporeal in its physical materiality, and in the tangible concreteness of its objective presence. The contemporary challenges of our age, in terms of the unfolding of the essence of modern information processing and communication technologies, with their complex electronic and digital equipment, do not necessarily result in novel modes of manipulating the pictorial realm in its inner visual structuring characteristics, albeit bringing to it high instrumental precision in graphical execution (algorithmic), and also in generating within it the occurrence of the special effects of complex cinematic motions. This state of affairs reflected the variegated challenges that faced traditional art in its pictorial orders through the development of photography and more poignantly of cinematography and sound-film. Such conditions contrasted the cameraman with the painter, and the theatre-performer with the movie-actor, in terms of permeating reality via the agency of mechanical equipment at the turn of the twentieth century. At the time, a thinker like Walter Benjamin assessed such circumstances as being underpinned by a change in reactionary attitudes, like in a Picasso painting, which aimed at resonating with the progressive public reactions towards a Chaplin movie, albeit with the additional fact that painting was simply in no position at all to present 'an object for simultaneous collective experience',[13] namely like film, theatre or architecture would do.

While the impetus of Renaissance pictorial art emerged from encounters with the classical mathematical and optical sciences, and by way of shifting away from the stylised mediaeval *representation* to a more realistic aim in achieving perfected *similitudes*,[14] it was the machine as a reproductive tool in printing, and then in photography and ultimately of cinematography that drove the next most radical shift in pictorial art at the hands of the avant-garde. A similar state of affairs in our own epoch, which is spaced by almost one century from the latest early-twentieth-century major displacement in art, is being witnessed as a result of novel technology that is exemplified in our era by electronic equipment. It is not science *per se*, but more the essence of technology that is dominating the opening up of new horizons and forcing more habituated and past practices to a receding withdrawal from the mainstream of praxis and thought. Nonetheless, the essence of technology is also being adopted within the folds of established artistic practices, or at times used as a phenomenon of tangency for some contemporary artists, rather than merely pushing traditional media into recession. For instance, there might be a given painter who no longer uses traditional media to handle colouration and pictorial shaping, but rather manifests colours and shapes through videography.

The more fundamental *rupture*, which we have been witnessing in our entry into the new millennium of the hyper cybernetic technique, is resulting in the effacement of possibilities for a direct experiencing of materiality, physicality, corporeality, handiness, and tangible concreteness of the *matrix* that receives the epiphany of a drawing or a sketch. We lost touch with the uniqueness of the presence in space-time of the authentic artwork and its 'aura'.[15] The semblance of colour and of a graphical trace becomes particularly a phenomenon of artificial luminosity, which is digitally-induced within a complex machine that technologically processes and communicates information from behind a glass screen. This technological instrument and equipment can appear as *an electronically-set sketchbook*, but, altogether it is what exceeds the realm of sketching and drawing as a computerized machine executing far reaching commands in the manipulative manifestation of manifold layers in virtual cybernetic representational space with great visualization accuracies. It is against this backdrop that the chapters of the present edited volume advance their clusters of investigation and meditations in rethinking the horizons and impasses that face the future of the sketchbook, while taking into account the spheres of threat that confront its pedagogic, curatorial, and practical status as what may disappear from mainstream new aided-modes of *sketching/drawing* in the pictorial and graphical arts.

BIBLIOGRAPHY

Benjamin, Walter. 'The Work of Art in the Age of Mechanical Reproduction,' trans. Harry
    Zohn in *Film Theory and Criticism*, eds. Gerald Mast and Marshall Cohen. Oxford: Oxford
    University Press (1976): 612–34.

Carman, Charles H. "Albert and Nicholas of Cusa: Perspective as Coincidence of Opposites," in *Explorations in Renaissance Culture*, Vol. 33 (2007): 196–219.

Carpo, Mario. *Architecture in the Age of Printing*. Cambridge Mass.: MIT Press, 2001.

Cusanus, Nicolaus. *De coniecturis*, in *Nicolai de Cusa Opera omnia*, Vol. 3, eds. J. Koch, C. Bormann, and I. G. Senger. Hamburg: Felix Meiner, 1972.

Da Parma, Biagio Pelacani. *Quaestionis perspectivae*, ed. G. Federici Vescovini. Paris: Vrin, 2002.

Da Vignola, Giacomo Barozzio. *Le Due Regole della Prospettiva Pratica*. Roma: Camerale, 1611. With a comentary by Egnatio Danti.

Damisch, Hubert. *Théorie de la peinture*. Paris: Seuil, 1972.

_____. *Ruptures/Cultures*. Paris: Minuit, 1976.

_____. *L'origine de la perspective*. Paris: Flammarion, 1987.

Desargues, Girard. *Manière universelle de Monsieur Desargues pour pratiquer la perspective par petit-pied comme le géométral*, Paris: Imprimerie de Pierre des Hayes, 1647.

El-Bizri, Nader. "La perception de la profondeur: Ibn al-Haytham, Berkeley et Merleau Ponty," in *Oriens-Occidens: sciences, mathématiques et philosophie de l'antiquité à l'âge classique (Cahiers du Centre d'Histoire des Sciences et des Philosophies Arabes et Médiévales, CNRS)*. Vol. 5 (2004): 171–84.

_____. "A Philosophical Perspective on Ibn al-Haytham's Optics," in *Arabic Sciences and Philosophy*. Vol. 15 (2005): 189–218.

_____. "Imagination and Architectural Representations," in Mario Frascari, Jonathan Hale, and Bradley Starkey (eds.), *From Models to Drawings: Imagination and Representation in Architecture*. London: Routledge, 2007: 34–42.

_____. "In Defence of the Sovereignty of Philosophy: al-Baghdadi's Critique of Ibn al-Haytham's Geometrisation of Place," in *Arabic Sciences and Philosophy*. Vol. 17 (2007): 57–80.

_____. "Creative inspirations or intellectual impasses? Reflections on relationships between architecture and the humanities," in *The Humanities in Architectural Design: A Contemporary and Historical Perspective*, eds. S. Bandyopadhyay, J. Lomholt, N. Temple, and R. Tobe. London: Routledge, 2010: 123–35

_____. "Classical Optics and the *Perspectiva* Traditions Leading to the Renaissance," in *Renaissance Theories of Vision*, eds. C. Carman and J. Hendrix. Aldershot: Ashgate, 2010: 11–30.

_____. "The Conceptual Bearings of the Intercultural Roles of Architecture," in *The Cultural Role of Architecture*, eds. Paul Emmons, John Hendrix, and Jane Lomholt. London: Routledge, 2012: 199–207.

Foucault, Michel. *Les mots et les choses: une archéologie des sciences humaines*. Paris: Gallimard, 1966.

Ibn al-Haytham, al-Hasan. *Kitab al-Manazir*, 2 vols., ed. A. I. Sabra. Kuwait: National Council for Culture, Arts and Letters, 1983.

_____. *The Optics, Books I-III, On Direct Vision*, 2 vols., trans. A. I. Sabra. London: Warburg Institute, 1989.

Kemp, Martin. *The Science of Art: Optical Themes in Western Art from Brunelleschi to Seurat*. New Haven: Yale University Press, 1990.

Maynard, Patrick. *Drawing Distinctions: The Varieties of Graphic Expression*. Ithaca: Cornell University Press, 2005.

Raynaud, Dominique. "Une application méconnue des principes de la vision binoculaire: Ibn al-Haytham et les peintres du *trecento* (1295–1450)," in *Oriens-Occidens: Sciences, mathématiques et philosophie de l'Antiquité à l'Âge Classique. Cahiers du Centre d'Histoire des Sciences et des Philosophies Arabes et Médiévales*. Vol. 5 (2004): 93–131.

_____. "Le tracé continu des sections coniques à la Renaissance: Applications optico-perspectives, héritage de la tradition mathématique arabe," in *Arabic Sciences and Philosophy*. Vol. 17 (2007): 299–345.

Rose, Paul L. "Renaissance Italian Methods of Drawing the Ellipse and related Curves," in *Physis*. Vol. 12 (1970): 371–404.

Vescovini, Graziella Federici Vescovini. "La fortune de l'*Optique* d'Ibn al-Haytham: le livre *De aspectibus* (*Kitab al-Manazir*) dans le Moyen Age latin," in *Archives d'histoire des Sciences*. Vol. 40 (1990): 220–38.

_____. "Ibn al-Haytham vulgarisé. Le *De li aspecti* d'un manuscrit du Vatican (moitié du XIVe siècle) et le troisième commentaire sur l'optique de Lorenzo Ghiberti," in *Arabic Sciences and Philosophy*. Vol. 8 (1998): 67–96.

NOTES

1   See for instance some of the works of the French philosopher Hubert Damisch, such as his *Théorie de la peinture* (Paris: Seuil, 1972), *Ruptures/Cultures* (Paris: Minuit, 1976), and *L'origine de la perspective* (Paris: Flammarion, 1987). Refer also to the works of the art historian Martin Kemp, like his *Science of Art: Optical Themes in Western Art from Brunelleschi to Seurat* (New Haven: Yale University Press, 1990); or furthermore, see: Mario Carpo, *Architecture in the Age of Printing* (Cambridge, Mass.: MIT Press, 2001) and Patrick Maynard, *Drawing Distinctions: The Varieties of Graphic Expression* (Ithaca: Cornell University Press, 2005).

2   I investigated complementary themes on the elements of optics and geometry that underpinned the Renaissance debates around linear central single-point perspectives in the pictorial arts of the *Trecento*, *Quattrocento*, and *Cinquecento*. These are represented in the following selected publications: Nader El-Bizri, 'Imagination and Architectural Representations', in M. Frascari, J. Hale, and B. Starkey (eds.), *From Models to Drawings: Imagination and Representation in Architecture* (London: Routledge, 2007), 34–42; Nader El-Bizri, 'Creative inspirations or intellectual impasses? Reflections on relationships between architecture and the humanities', in *The Humanities in Architectural Design: A Contemporary and Historical Perspective*, eds. S. Bandyopadhyay, J. Lomholt, N. Temple, and R. Tobe (London: Routledge, 2010), 123–135; Nader El-Bizri, 'Classical Optics and the *Perspectiva* Traditions Leading to the Renaissance', in *Renaissance Theories of Vision*, eds. C. Carman and J. Hendrix (Aldershot: Ashgate, 2010), 11–30; Nader El-Bizri, 'The Conceptual Bearings of the Intercultural Roles of Architecture', in *The Cultural Role of Architecture*, eds. Paul Emmons, John Hendrix, and Jane Lomholt (London: Routledge, 2012), 199–207.

3   Nicolaus Cusanus, *De coniecturis*, in *Opera omnia*, Volume 1 (Paris, 1514), folio 46, and in *Nicolai de Cusa Opera omnia*, eds. J. Koch, C. Bormann, and I. G. Senger (Hamburg: Felix Meiner, 1972), Volume 3, p. 46. For a discussion of this phenomenon in connection with Nicolaus Cusanus and Leon Battista Alberti, refer to: Charles H. Carman, 'Albert and Nicholas of Cusa: Perspective as Coincidence of Opposites', *Explorations in Renaissance Culture*, Vol. 33 (2007): 196–219.

4   Ibn al-Haytham. *Kitab al-Manazir*, 2 vols., ed. A. I. Sabra (Kuwait: National Council for Culture, Arts and Letters, 1983); Ibn al-Haytham, *The Optics, Books I-III, On Direct Vision*, 2 vols., trans. A. I. Sabra (London: Warburg Institute, 1989).

5   This is particularly the case with Pelacani's *Quaestionis perspectivae*. See: Biagio Pelacani da Parma, *Quaestionis perspectivae*, ed. G. Federici Vescovini (Paris: Vrin, 2002).

6   Known also as Franciscus Barocius. This aspect figures mainly in his *Admirandum illud Geometricum Problema tredecim modis demonstratum*. Regarding some elements of the adaptive assimilation by Renaissance theorists of Arabic mathematical sources on conics and their applications in optics, I refer the reader to: Dominique Raynaud, 'Le tracé continu des sections coniques à la Renaissance: Applications optico-perspectives, héritage de la tradition mathématique arabe', *Arabic Sciences and Philosophy*, Vol. 17 (2007): 299–345. See also: Paul L. Rose, 'Renaissance Italian Methods of Drawing the Ellipse and related Curves', *Physis*, Vol. 12 (1970): 371–404.

7   Graziella Federici Vescovini, 'La fortune de l'*Optique* d'Ibn al-Haytham: le livre *De aspectibus* (*Kitab al-Manazir*) dans le Moyen Age latin', *Archives d'histoire des sciences*, Vol. 40 (1990): 220–238; Graziella Federici Vescovini, 'Ibn al-Haytham vulgarisé. Le *De li aspecti* d'un manuscrit du Vatican (moitié du XIVe siècle) et le troisième commentaire sur l'optique de Lorenzo Ghiberti', in *Arabic Sciences and Philosophy*, Vol. 8 (1998): 67–96.

8   Giacomo Barozzio da Vignola, *Le Due Regole della Prospettiva Pratica* (Roma: Camerale, 1611), with a commentary by Egnatio Danti.

9   I investigated related aspects on Ibn al-Haytham's theory of vision and the geometrization of the notion of place in critique of Aristotle's conception of *topos* in Book *Delta* of the latter's *Physics*. See for instance: Nader El-Bizri, 'Le problème de l'espace: Approches optique, géométrique et phénoménologique', in *Oggetto e spazio*, op. cit., 59–70; Nader El-Bizri, 'In Defence of the Sovereignty of Philosophy: al-Baghdadi's Critique of Ibn al-Haytham's Geometrisation of Place', *Arabic Sciences and Philosophy*, Vol. 17 (2007): 57–80; Nader El-Bizri, 'La perception de la profondeur: Ibn al-Haytham, Berkeley et Merleau-Ponty', *Oriens-Occidens: sciences, mathématiques et philosophie de l'antiquité à l'âge classique (Cahiers du Centre d'Histoire des Sciences et des Philosophies Arabes et Médiévales, CNRS)*, Vol. 5 (2004): 171–184. Nader El-Bizri, 'A Philosophical Perspective on Ibn al-Haytham's *Optics*', *Arabic Sciences and Philosophy*, Vol. 15 (2005): 189–218.

10   See also: Dominique Raynaud, 'Une application méconnue des principes de la vision binoculaire: Ibn al-Haytham et les peintres du *trecento* (1295–1450)', *Oriens-Occidens: Sciences, mathématiques et philosophie de l'Antiquité à l'Âge Classique. Cahiers du Centre d'Histoire des Sciences et des Philosophies Arabes et Médiévales*, Vol. 5 (2004): 93–131.

11   Raynaud, 'Une application méconnue des principes de la vision binoculaire: Ibn al-Haytham et les peintres du *trecento* (1295–1450)', 109–10.

12   See for instance Girard Desargues, *Manière universelle de Monsieur Desargues pour pratiquer la perspective par petit-pied comme le géométral* (Paris: Imprimerie de Pierre des Hayes, 1647).

13   Refer to Section XII of Walter Benjamin, '*Das Kunstwerk im Zeitalter seiner technischen Reproduzierbarkeit*', in *Zeitschrift für Sozialforschung*' (Frankfurt am Main: Suhrkamp Verlag, 1977), originally published in 1936; Walter Benjamin, 'The Work of Art in the Age of Mechanical Reproduction', trans. Harry Zohn in *Film Theory and Criticism*, eds. Gerald Mast and Marshall Cohen (Oxford: Oxford University Press, 1976), 612–34.

14   Michel Foucault argued that a shift in '*épistémè*', as indicative of the truth conditions that change within an overarching epistemic discourse, reveal a movement form classical representation to Renaissance emphasis on resemblance and similitude, which itself is dismantled in our era – This was central to his arguments in *Les mots et les choses: une archéologie des sciences humaines* (Paris: Gallimard, 1966).

15   See Sections II and IV of Benjamin's '*Das Kunstwerk im Zeitalter seiner technischen Reproduzierbarkeit*'.

2

Parerga – Carnet de Croquis: 'ni oeuvre, ni hors d'oeuvre'

Nader El-Bizri

I

In what way can thinking about the *sketchbook* in view of what we stated in the *Overture* (Chapter 1) of this edited volume offer tangential occasions for reflections on key philosophical leitmotifs? In this present chapter, I examine the possibilities of reflecting on the *sketchbook* from the standpoint of positing it as a *supplement* with respect to the pictorial and architectonic artworks. Consequently, I start by asking whether we can indeed think about the theoretical dimensions that surround the *sketchbook* from the viewpoint of reflections on the conceptual aspects of notions like the ancients referred to as: *parergon*. This entails thinking about the relativity of the *supplement* in signification and its presupposition of *what lacks*, in addition to positing the graphical trace (*le trait*; *Riss*; [rift]) that underpins the *ergon* (grasped herein as *the work*) as a *subordinate detached accessory*.

II

What resides outside the *ergon* (specifically conceived as an artwork) whilst also en-framing it (*l'encadrer*; *Ge-Stell*)? The state of affairs that can be disclosed from behind this question implies that displacements occur when thinking about that which is 'neither *in* nor *out*' ('*ni dedans ni dehors*'), in the sense of being that which is marked by 'placelessness' (ἀτοπία; *atopia*), by way of being 'neither the work *per se*, nor something outside it' ('*ni oeuvre, ni hors d'œuvre*') – neither internal nor external; neither above the work nor below it ('*ni dedans, ni dehors ; ni dessus ni dessous*').[1] This refers to the situation of what is: '*beside the point!*' described by Jacques Derrida as being of the order of 'an atopic insistence' of the πάρεργον (*parergon*): '*l'atopique insistante*'![2]

Derrida's line in thinking in this context resonates with Gaston Bachelard's reflections in the *Poetics of Space* (*La poétique de l'espace*) on the dialectics of the outside and inside (*la dialéctique du dehors et du dedans*). This is especially accentuated in architectural terms by way of the unease that we at times experience when dealing with doors, whether in opening or closing them. This evokes the phenomena of hospitality, of welcoming or of being welcomed, and of being admissible in the first place. It can also signal enclosure and sheltering, or even the hostility of inadmissibility by demarcating what amounts to trespassing. The unease that arises herein is situational in the manner we find ourselves located with regard to the openness of doors or their closed-ness, as we stand within the internality of a given space or in an externality with respect to it, or of being situated all along in the liminal place of the doorway that is ajar; 'l'entr'ouvert'![3] This also brings to mind what Maurice Merleau-Ponty notes in the *Phenomenology of Perception* (*Phénoménologie de la perception*) about the 'body-subject' (*le corps propre*), or my own subjectivity as it is inherent in the hold of my body through its kinaesthetic motion unto the world (*la prise sur le monde*); namely, what he refers to as '*le corps propre*', which is itself sensed and sensing, like my own hands when they touch each other, or my body as that which is spatialized and spatializing (*spatialisé et spatialisant*).[4] These commentaries refer to tendencies in philosophical thinking that highlight experiential fields in which the logic of non-contradiction, the law of identity and difference, of sameness versus otherness, is altogether non-dominant. This creates situations that exceed the binary and disjunctive conditions of the either/or in view of thinking about what is neither this nor that *per se*, but that is both at the same time in a mysterious uncanny way. The question that arises here is that: if such use of language seems to surpass the meaningfulness of utterances as they happen by way of the workings of *logos*, then would they be readily only inscribable within the narrative space of the *muthos*?[5]

III

The *sketchbook* (*carnet de croquis*) signals the *ergon* (the work) that has a potentiality to be (*dunamis*) instead of being that which exists in actuality *per se* (*energeia/entelecheia*). This is the case in spite of the *object-character* of the physical *graphèmes* that the *sketchbook* receives by way of registering the motions of the forms of presentation and of the figurative outline as a movement of the *Darstellung* (the portraying depiction of a shifting representation), which remains concealed within the pathways of the unfurling of the realized *ergon* (the work).

In what sense would responses to the interrogations we advanced so far assist us in rethinking the place of the *sketchbook* in pictorial, architectonic, and spatial modes of thinking-in-making? How would the design-determinants become interwoven with the intimate biographical facets of interestedness in the cultivation of the architect, the artist or the designer, through the productive engagement with artworks, objects and thoughts? Moreover, in what ways can the supplementary/accessorial nature of the *sketchbook* safeguard its future within the variegated modes of *praxis* of architects, artists and designers in our epoch of *Information–Technology Processing and Communication*, as it is unfolding against the horizons of modern techno–science?

IV

In addressing some of the motifs that call for thinking as highlighted above, I will further mediate my reflections through a deepening of the critical engagement in interpreting selected aspects from Derrida's philosophical analyses of art in *La vérité en peinture* (*Truth in Painting*). In doing this I will also refer to some of the remarks that he made in *De la grammatologie* (*On Grammatology*).[6] This line of inquiry will be undertaken against the background of Derrida's metaphysical critique of the fundamental ontological presuppositions that underpinned Martin Heidegger's later reflections on truth in art, in the latter's commanding essay: '*Der Ursprung des Kunstwerkes*' ('*The Origin of the Work of Art*'; '*L'origine de l'oeuvre d'art*').[7]

The irreducible specificity of the objective presence of a pictorial work of art, a drawing or a sketch, lies outside the spheres of mere reproducibility, even in terms of mimetic copying by way of retracing. The depiction of a given artwork through the agency of painting or drawing is itself marked by uniqueness, whereby reproduction is a non-identical repetition that individuates while copying an archetype or an exemplar. It belongs to the structure of analogy, *mimesis, homoiosis,* and *adaequatio*, while pointing to exemplarity, uniqueness, and originality. Individuated singularity is secured through the objective material presence of the copy as a thing. Nonetheless, one wonders about what distinguishes an artwork from being simply an object or a thing (*l'être œuvre, l'être objet, l'être chose…*). This question was central to Heidegger's meditations on the essence of the artwork as *a thing* in terms of thinking about the origin of the work of art. This evokes that which may be referred to as the 'thingness', or the 'thingly' (*Dinglish*) character of a thing (*l'être-chose d'une chose… sa choséité*).

Singular, individual, and as a definite article closed unto itself, the copy is individuated even when set within a repetitive series. Each drawing within the mimetic chain that reproduces a generic model has its specificity in depiction, representation, and in its mode of imitation. It defies the serial in repetition; it is '*hors série dans la série*'.[8] Having stated this, one ought to also indicate that in the age of not only the mechanical reproductions, but of digitized reproducibility *per se*, what Walter Benjamin cautioned about with truism still holds, namely that:

> Even the most perfect reproduction of a work of art is lacking in one element: its presence in time and space, its unique existence at the place where it happens to be. This unique existence of the work of art determined the history to which it was subject throughout the time of its existence.[9]

Benjamin adds that 'the presence of the original is the prerequisite to the concept of authenticity' (*Das Hier und Jetzt des Originals macht den Begriff seiner Echtheit aus*), which is external to the spheres of technical reproducibility. This *authenticity* points to what he takes to be of the order of the 'aura' of a work of art (without a parapsychological connotation). This is brought forth from its uniqueness as it is imbedded in the fabric of the art traditions (*Die Einzigkeit des Kunstwerks ist identisch mit seinem Eingebettetsein in den Zusammen-hang der Tradition*) and their ritualistic cult-praxis within its specific situational location and its original use.[10]

V

The repetitive depiction of an archetypal exemplar, a model, occurs in sequences of progressive tracing that are accompanied by regressive erasing. This state of affairs hints at the hesitancy in marking the trace, in the removal of what was noted, and in its editing effacement while retaining its original incisive mark, as entailed by 'sous-rature'. This notion is evoked by Derrida in connection also with Heidegger's crossing-over, striking through, the words: 'Sein', or 'Seyn', as 'being', ('~~Sein~~' / '~~Seyn~~') or as indicative of the verbal 'to be' ('~~to be~~') that need not be uttered when thinking about being, as 'there is', 'il y a', that 'it gives being', 'es gibt Sein'. 'Sous-rature' is an un-doing of a trace, the un-doing of what is written, drawn, depicted (or painted): 'de raturer', 'de dépeindre'. The tracing is retreated, pulled away in the sense of how a trace is withdrawn through effacing: 'le trait en retrait par rature'. This phenomenon of 'raturer' entails also 'dessiner à la gomme' (drawing with an eraser [being / ~~being~~ / …]), as Derrida for instance remarked on the artwork of Valerio Adami, Le voyage du dessin' (in 1975), when he stated: 'il dessinait à la gomme, le voici qui rature'; he draws with an eraser.[11] And yet, in this act of 'raturer', the trace is also intensified ('sous-rature — de l'archi-trace'),[12] but not as it is the case with the presence of 'le trait' in the 'por<u>trait</u>', as an essential outline. The trace is set in the retrograde movement or displacement of 'le trait en retrait par rature'. It returns to itself in being re-traced by retreat, while being also crossed over. 'Retrait' is here a retreating by way of re-tracing.

The trace is progressive and regressive, it brings something forth by outlining it, while it also retraces by way of turning back on itself. It does not merely progress by way of linearity, as it is the case with writing. It is not simply progressive, but rather offers flexibility in the manner it is enacted. The pictorial trace is not strictly spatial, like it is the case with the oeuvre of the plastic arts. We are not displaced spatially-temporally around it. We rather face it frontally as we do with a book or a letter, and yet it does not have the structural rigidity expected in reading, in terms of the sequential ordering of the way it offers itself in appearing to visual perceptibility. It can be approached from multiple directions on the surface receiving it; varying in the speed of our ocular survey of its outlines and contours, the levels of contemplation, of rest and motion, of shifting directionality, disruption, dislocation, optical-visual re-tracing. This depicts an unchained energy in production, reproduction, tracing and retracing, moving and shifting, being situated and displaced, in a oneness of the fragmented manifold, the 'membra disjecta'.

VI

Sight, speech, and gesture are co-entangled ('du regard, de la parole, du geste').[13] A manual motion in writing releases the audio-phonetic energies of silent private speech, the gaze in sight and the gesture of the hand ('la motricité manuelle qui délivre le système audio-phonique de la parole, le regard et la main pour l'écriture').[14] This aspect highlights the gestures of the hand, in the flow of handwriting and

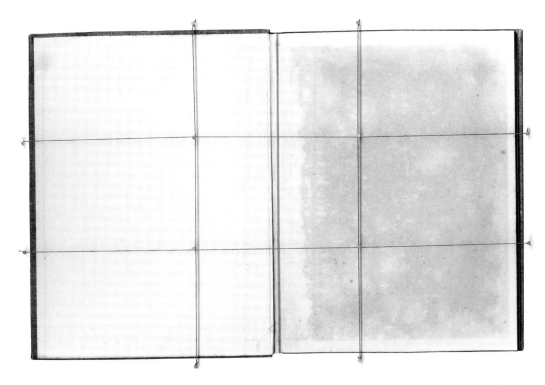

drawing, as contrasted with the pressing of buttons on typewriters, the sliding of fingertips on the glass screen of the highly-sensitive digital equipment of information processing and communication technology. Writing and drawing are brought nearer in the movement of fingers on the computer keyboard ('*appuyer sur des boutons*'), on interactive screens, in the relationships that emerge between ideograms and pictograms.[15] Algorithms and codes substituting calligraphy, lettering, and freehand drawing, or drafting with the aid of instruments that engage bodily motion and postures in relation to the drawing board, the stretch of the T-Square, the agility and handiness in manipulating compasses, triangles, projections, etc.

The 'trace' is imbedded in the forming of letters, in discourse and painting ('*ce trait dans la lettre, le discours, la peinture*').[16] The notion of '*ductus*' is evoked in this context, as derived from '*ducto*' (to lead, conduct, command, draw), and '*ductio*' as what conducts. In technical terms, the *ductus* serves herein as a chart that displays the geometric ordering and directionality of the number and sequence that orient the strokes and tracings, which form the calligraphic hand lettering of a given script tradition with its embellishment and spacing on the parchment, vellum, or paper that receives it. The type of *ductus* is connected with the speed of execution of individual letterforms or ligatures, which can be slow or cursive, and is measured in terms of modulating the number, sequence and direction of individual pen-strokes that structure the lettering. A *ductus* apportions and measures the execution by the hand of a calligraphic trace. Its derivative term 'duction' carries a technical ophthalmological significance in terms of referring to the various forms of the

2.1   The Thing Itself. Source: Courtesy of Heather Dawn Miller, www. heathermiller.co.uk

eye's rotation. The motion of the hand is thusly closely interconnected with the movement of the eye, and in the coordination between them when in motion renders the hand slightly second to the eye in neurological impulses through which a physical response to thought gets enacted. Moreover, 'duction' refers to a broader idiomatic usage in designating the acts of leading, bringing, or conducting as entailed by the Latin root expression *'ductio'*. Furthermore, 'duction' figures at the root of concepts denoted by terms like: introduction, deduction, induction, production, reproduction, seduction, etc. These describe a system of *'duction'* (*'un système de duction'*).[17] This etymological analytic of 'ducting' belongs also to the notion of draft, or draught, as in the sayings: 'draftsman', or 'draughtsman'; namely as what pulls or infiltrates an enclosure, a space, and runs through it like a current. The idea of trace as traction, as a friction that draws nearer, pulls. The trace as a trajectory: *'un trait'*, *'un trajet'*, *'une trajectoire'*. It spatially articulates a kinaesthetic manual bodily gesturing: *'de tirer'* (to draw [nearer]), *'un tiroir'* (a drawer).

In drawing, the occurrence of *'ductio'* is a hand-eye coordination that conducts the line along a given trajectory, which gives an actualized sensible manifestation of a potential trace that was latent in anticipatory imagination – an undrawn line, as imagined in its virtual essence prior to the act of sketching it. It is a potentiality to be that gets actualized and comes into appearance and presence (albeit, and at times also with unpredictability) through the trajectory that the hand–eye coordinative conduction executes in a progressive gesture by way of making a material trace on a given physical sketchpad.

VII

The sketch belongs to the realm of inquiry, and the sketchbook itself can be seen as a codex. Hence, it can be subjected to the studies that animate codicology and palaeography, in looking at it as a set of handwritten manuscripts and illuminations, and of examining their graphical traces, and even their glosses and marginalia, in view of deciphering the happening of their contents. They also offer us materials for archival curating. And yet, the notion of an archive brings to mind the idea of *origin* as entailed by the utterance *'arkhê'*, which names not only a beginning but also a commandment (*nomme à la fois le commencement et le commandement*). After all, it designates growth within nature and commencements in history, in being that which points at *origins*, whilst also figuring in the narrations of commands as a site of authority and nomology from within which laws are given.[18]

Sketching can be an investigative and freed mode of revealing that lets something be brought forth into appearing. We entangle hereon the idiomatic and the pictorial, discursive textuality with sketching (*'l'écriture discursive avec la peinture représentative … le langage et le tableau'*).[19] Is the *sketchbook* then a corrective additional artifice that replaces a missing part, fills a gap, points to a lack, a deficiency, hence that also supplements? Is it a form of *prosthesis*? However, the supplement does not replace or displace what it supplements, it is neither a signifier nor a representative, since it does not take the place of a signified or of what is represented ('*le supplément qui n'est simplement ni le significant ni le représentant, ne prend pas la place d'un signifié ou d'un représenté*').[20] The sketchbook can also be a problematic supplement for an artist who is led by concepts and ideas, as these become housed within its folds, and upon which precious qualities are bestowed, whereby they become sheltered from extraneous influences, which are other than the simple manifestation of these concepts and ideas in the manner they get guarded and registered within the sketchbook.

In an analysis of Diego Vélasquez's *Las Meninas* (1656) Michel Foucault hinted that the relation of language to painting borders on being *infinite* in its horizons ('*le rapport du langage à la peinture est un rapport infini*'),[21] and that such visual language also relates potentially to other art media, such as sculpture. He took language and painting (or the artwork) to be irreducible unto each other when we cross from the space of what we say to the spatiality of what we see. And yet, what we see is never fully contained in what we say, and we do show what we mean by what we say in terms of images, as well as making what we see clearer by what we utter about it and name in connection with it. This reveals the extent of the intertwining of text with image, the word and the icon, and more essentially, it also points to the development of a new worldview that is detached from the orders of classical representation and the Renaissance cultivation of realist similarity in their *épistémè*. The image moves deeper into the realm of *what is said* as 'conceptual modern art', which itself is no longer aiming at showing what it contains as narrative, rather it is silent in its pictorial quality, and necessitates a discourse for letting what it aims at appear and become unconcealed.

VIII

The *parergon* as supplement, which is 'neither a work *per se*, nor something outside it' ('*ni* oeuvre, *ni hors d'œuvre*') — Neither in or out ('*ni dedans, ni dehors*'),[22] situates itself in-between, in the rift, the cleft, or cleavage that separates and unites at the same time. It is like the liminal threshold, in the situational standing in front of a doorway, of what opens and closes in an admissibility of hospitality or in a hostility of inadmissibility, as we face what is ajar '*entr'ouvert*'![23] This depicts its inherent indeterminacy and incompleteness as what supplements.

The sketchbook as '*ni* oeuvre, *ni hors d'œuvre*' is detached while being re-attached and annexed. It is in a state of detachment as being dispatched as a messenger, a delegate, or as what is transmitted. It is a surplus, a remainder (*ce qui reste*); an additive accessory that the one dealing with it is also obligated to receive ('*un accessoire qu'on est obligé d'acceuillir*' [*à-côté; à-bord; à l'extrémité*]). It appears as a detachment that is badly detachable, as hard to detach ('*Un détachement mal détachable*').[24] It is '*ni propre ni impropre*' (neither proper nor improper), '*entre l'œuvre et l'absence d'œuvre*' (posited between the work and its absence).[25] And yet, such attributes that were associated with the sketchbook in its tangible handiness, its concrete objective presence, its physical materiality, are all further accentuated in the manner they get manifested through the screens of digitized instrumentality as exemplified by the manifestation of the graphic trace and the luminous colour on the screens of information processing and communication machines. Such accessories remove the experiencing of drawings, sketches, and the letters in their physicality as they traditionally occurred on material *matrices* (parchment, vellum, paper, metal, wood, textile, cloth, glass, etc.). They furthermore distance us from their texture as they are sensed by touch, or even the scent of their materiality, be it that of the receiving physical pad, or the pigment, ink, charcoal, crayon that once came to be traced upon it. Such pronouncements are not meant to be nostalgic, reactionary, or regressive, but rather point to what withdraws from our world and experiential realms in their multi-sensorial contents. Even if they retain a trace of its happening as supplements to the accessories, and thus as what is far removed from the hub of making and thinking in art, they occur at several degrees of separation at the peripheries of the peripheral margins of what is marginal.

Our electronic digitized accessories that contain what is so-called 'e-notebook/ e-sketchbook' challenge us forth with their complicated machinations. They are set upon us in such a manner that they are hard to become detached from. Their demands upon us are not neuter. They rather oblige us to respond to their calling, to receive through our own commands what orders us about in their execution of such commanding acts. They refer to what imposes itself upon us as what cannot but be received as it is transmitted unto us harassingly. Human beings drive such ordering will to power, albeit by being themselves challenged forth, orderable, and made reportable, and by being also already and always on-call, and at a distance,[26] to respond to this destined mode of *en-framing* that has been sent our way. This reflects a movement from concealment into un-concealment, from unveiling to veiling that is associated with the switching *on/off* of what retains a latent presence as active machinery mastered through the destined unfolding of the essence of technology (*das Wesen der modernen Technik*). Nonetheless, and having stated that by way of a radical critique, it remains to be the case that *tele-techno-science* has also its own promising horizons in terms of enabling wider forms of societal and cultural benefit at epistemic and communicative levels. Even though it is at work in facilitating and rooting the over–dominance of en-framing in its abstractive modes of determining human identity in reductive terms as standing reserves of power and energy, which are objectless in their determination, and lacking in character as things, let alone as embodied (en-souled) living beings.

IX

The idea of a supplement is connected with the notion of framing, of en-framing, '*le cadre, le cadrage, et l'encadrement'*. Such concepts were also pivotal in Heidegger's reflections on the unfolding of the essence of modern technology, with its mode of revealing by way of *en-framing* that he names '*Ge-Stell'*. Heidegger's reflections on the notion of the '*Riss'*, as a rift, a cleft, a cleavage (*Die Zerklüftung*), in–between two opposing regions or entities, which opens up a gap that holds them together while setting them apart in separation. It is not a mere rifting that ripped open; rather it is the intimacy in which opponents belong to one another, carrying them into the source of their unity and common ground. The rift–design draws together into unison, through outline, figure and *Gestalt*, set in the hardness of stone, in wood, in the trace of ink and lead (bringing to mind a visual manifestation in artistic/architectural terms, such as the 'splitting' in Gordon Matta-Clark's work). In such shaping, the rift is emplaced by way of a particular mode of placing (*Stellen*) and en–framing (*Ge-Stell*),[27] and not simply as a tearing open that incises. Reflections on en–framing (*Ge-Stell*) belong to meditations on the question of being (*Seinsfrage*) in connection with the unfolding of the essence of modern technology and the dominance of its mode of revealing truth by turning beings into a standing-reserve (*Bestand*). En–framing veils the 'objectivity' of objects, let alone further concealing their 'thingly' (*Dinglich*) character as things that gather the 'fourfold' into an essential oneness of 'earth, sky, divinities, mortals' (*Erde und Himmel, die Göttlichen und die Sterblichen*).[28] If Heidegger saw in this a threatening danger, he hinted at a sphere from within which the reflection on *the essence of technology* must happen; namely in terms of being a realm that is akin to *the essence of technology* whilst being also fundamentally different from it. He saw this as the calling of art. While similar sentiments arose at a relatively earlier epoch than Heidegger's, and within a distinct intellectual mood, the hopes pinned on the arts were called into question by Walter Benjamin, as expressed in the last foundational three sentences in his '*Das Kunstwerk im Zeitalter seiner technischen Reproduzierbarkeit*' ('The Work of Art in the Age of Mechanical Reproduction'). Benjamin stated therein that 'self-alienation has reached such a degree that it can experience its own destruction as an aesthetic pleasure of the first order' (*Ihre Selbst-entfremdung hat jenen Grad erreicht, der sie ihre eigene Vernichtung als ästhetischen Genuß ersten Ranges erleben läßt*). This was the basis for what he also saw as the making of politics aesthetic by Fascism, and the rendering of aesthetics political by Communism.

BIBLIOGRAPHY

Bachelard, Gaston. *La poétique de l'espace*. Paris: Presses universitaires de France, 2008.

Benjamin, Walter. "The Work of Art in the Age of Mechanical Reproduction," trans. Harry Zohn in *Film Theory and Criticism*, eds. Gerald Mast and Marshall Cohen. Oxford: Oxford University Press, 1976: 612–34.

Derrida, Jacques. *De la grammatologie*. Paris: Les éditions de Minuit, 1967.

———————. *La vérité en peinture*. Paris: Flammarion, 1978.

———————. *Khôra*. Paris: Galilée, 1993.

———————. *Mal d'archive, une impression freudienne*. Paris: Galilée, 1995.

———————. *Foi et Savoir*. Paris: Editions du Seuil, 1996.

El-Bizri, Nader. "Qui-êtes-vous Khôra? Receiving Plato's *Timaeus*," in *Existentia Meletai-Sophias*. Vol. XI, Issue 3–4 (2001): 473–90.

———————. "*ON KAI KHORA*: Situating Heidegger between the *Sophist* and the *Timaeus*," in *Studia Phaenomenologica*. Vol. IV, Issue 1–2 (2004): 73–98.

_____. "Being at Home Among Things: Heidegger's Reflections on Dwelling," in *Environment, Space, Place*. Vol. 3 (2011): 47–71.

_____. "The Conceptual Bearings of the Intercultural Roles of Architecture," in *The Cultural Role of Architecture*. Eds. Paul Emmons, John Hendrix, and Jane Lomholt. London: Routledge, 2012: 199–207.

Foucault, Michel. *Les mots et les choses: Une archéologie des sciences humaines*. Paris: Gallimard, 1966.

Heidegger, Martin. *Holzwege*. Frankfurt am Main: Vittorio Klostermann, 1950.

_____. *Vorträge und Aufsätze*. Pfullingen: Günther Neske, 1954.

_____. *Die Technik und die Kehre*. Pfullingen: Günther Neske, 1962.

_____. *Poetry, Language, Thought*. Trans. Albert Hofstadter. New York: Harper & Row, Publishers Inc., 1971.

_____. *Basic Writings*. Ed. David Farrell Krell. New York: Harper Collins Publishers, 1993.

Merleau-Ponty, Maurice. *Phénoménologie de la perception*. Paris: Gallimard, 1945.

Plato. *Timaeus, Critias, Cleitophon, Menexenus, Epistles*. Ed. and trans. R. G. Bury. Cambridge Mass.: Loeb Classical Library, 1960.

NOTES

1   Jacques Derrida, *La vérité en peinture* (Paris: Flammarion, 1978), 14.

2   Derrida, *La vérité en peinture*, 14.

3   Gaston Bachelard, *La poétique de l'espace* (Paris: Presses universitaires de France, 2008), 200–1.

4   Maurice Merleau-Ponty, *Phénoménologie de la perception* (Paris: Gallimard, 1945), 281–2.

5   This is what Derrida notes with respect to thinking about χώρα (*Khôra*; namely what is conventionally rendered in English as 'space' [in French as '*espace*', in German as '*Raum*', etc.], and yet in being that which exceeds the notion of spatiality in terms of its ontological significance and the ineffable character of attempting to account for its attributes. The name '*Khôra*' (also at times written in a simplified form as '*Chora*') is derived from Plato's *Timaeus* dialogue. It points to a 'third kind' or 'third genus' (48e4) besides the Platonic forms and their imitations in the realms that are apprehended by the senses. It is neither intelligible nor sensible *per se*; hence, it defies the logic of the either/or. It is an underlying, everlasting substratum that serves as a receptacle of becoming for the entities that enter it and withdraw from it (*Timaeus* 49e7–8, 50c4–5, 52a4–6). It is characterless in itself, and yet taking upon itself the character of what enters into it. For further reflections on this matter, refer in this context to: Jacques Derrida, *Khôra*, Paris: Galilée, 1993; Plato, *Timaeus, Critias, Cleitophon, Menexenus, Epistles*, ed. and trans. R. G. Bury (Cambridge, Mass.: Loeb Classical Library, 1960). I also analyzed elsewhere what is entailed by thinking about *Khôra* in relation to Plato, Heidegger, and Derrida, mainly in the following articles: Nader El-Bizri, '*Qui-êtes vous Khôra?*: Receiving Plato's *Timaeus*,' *Existentia Meletai-Sophias*, Vol. XI, Issue 3–4 (2001), pp. 473–90; Nader El-Bizri, '*ON KAI KHORA*: Situating Heidegger between the *Sophist* and the *Timaeus*,' *Studia Phaenomenologica*, Vol. IV, Issue 1–2 (2004), 73–98.

6   Jacques Derrida, *De la grammatologie* (Paris: Les éditions de Minuit, 1967).

7   The essay 'Der Ursprung des Kunstwerkes' appeared in: Martin Heidegger, Holzwege
     (Frankfurt am Main: Vittorio Klostermann, 1950); Gesamtausgabe, Band 5 [GA 5].
     For the English translation see: Martin Heidegger, 'The Origin of the Work of Art', in
     Poetry, Language, Thought, translated by Albert Hofstadter (New York: Harper & Row,
     Publishers Inc., 1971).

8   Derrida, La vérité en peinture, 229.

9   Refer to Section II of Walter Benjamin, 'Das Kunstwerk im Zeitalter seiner technischen
     Reproduzierbarkeit', in Zeitschrift für Sozialforschung (Frankfurt am Main: Suhrkamp
     Verlag, 1977), 40–66, originally published in Vol. 5, Issue 1 of the 1936 edition of this
     yearbook; Walter Benjamin, 'The Work of Art in the Age of Mechanical Reproduction',
     trans. Harry Zohn in Film Theory and Criticism, eds. Gerald Mast and Marshall Cohen
     (Oxford: Oxford University Press, 1976), 612–34.

10   Benjamin, 'Das Kunstwerk im Zeitalter seiner technischen Reproduzierbarkeit' ('The Work
     of Art in the Age of Mechanical Reproduction'), Sections II, IV.

11   Derrida, La vérité en peinture, 171.

12   Derrida, De la grammatologie, 132.

13   Derrida, De la grammatologie, 126.

14   Derrida, De la grammatologie, 127.

15   Derrida, De la grammatologie, 127.

16   Derrida, La vérité en peinture, 13.

17   Derrida, La vérité en peinture, 14.

18   Jacques Derrida, Mal d'archive, une impression freudienne (Paris: Galilée, 1995), 11.

19   Derrida, La vérité en peinture, 182–3.

20   Derrida, De la grammatologie, 429.

21   Michel Foucault, Les mots et les choses: Une archéologie des sciences humaines (Paris:
     Gallimard, 1966), 25.

22   Derrida, La vérité en peinture, 14.

23   Bachelard, La poétique de l'espace, 200–1.

24   Derrida, La vérité en peinture, 63–7.

25   Derrida, La vérité en peinture, 73–4.

26   This is what Derrida refers to as 'l'appelation à distance' in evoking what we might call:
     'tele-techno-science'. See: Jacques Derrida, Foi et Savoir (Paris: Seuil, 1996), 15.

27   I discussed this elsewhere in: Nader El-Bizri, 'ON KAI XΩPA: Situating Heidegger
     between the Sophist and the Timaeus', Studia Phaenomenologica IV (2004): 73–98.

28   Martin Heidegger, Die Technik und die Kehre (Pfullingen: Günther Neske, 1962), 5–36; and
     Vorträge und Aufsätze (Pfullingen: Günther Neske, 1954), 13–44. See also: 'The Question
     Concerning Technology', from Martin Heidegger, Basic Writings, ed. David Farrell Krell
     (New York: Harper Collins Publishers, 1993). I discussed this elsewhere in detail in:
     Nader El-Bizri, 'Being at Home Among Things: Heidegger's Reflections on Dwelling',
     Environment, Space, Place, Vol. 3 (2011): 47–71; Nader El-Bizri, 'The Conceptual Bearings
     of the Intercultural Roles of Architecture', in The Cultural Role of Architecture, eds. Paul
     Emmons, John Hendrix, and Jane Lomholt (London: Routledge, 2012), 199–207.

3

Palimpsest

John Hendrix

The sketchbook continues to be important for the *parti* in the design process in architecture. The computer is a vital tool in the development and execution of the design, and can also be important in the *parti*, for example when forms are generated from number sequences, but certain functions of the sketchbook cannot be replaced by the computer. The sketch can more completely represent the relation between the human mind, thought and psyche, and the architectural design. The best example of this is the quality of palimpsest in the sketchbook, where layers of forms and ideas overlay layers, and traces of partially erased layers rise to the surface and become part of the form. The quality of palimpsest can be found in drawings by Francesco Borromini in the seventeenth century, and Peter Eisenman in the twentieth century. The quality of palimpsest can be found in urban landscapes, Rome being the best example, where buildings or streets are composed of traces of past buildings or streets. Most importantly, the quality of palimpsest can be found in the human mind, where layers of consciousness are composed of traces, of memory fragments of visual and aural forms, and of previous layers. Through palimpsest the sketch can emulate the human mind, and be a tool in urban design and architectural composition, which connects the built environment to the human mind. The sketch should thus continue to be a mechanism to produce increasingly creative, insightful, and meaningful design.

This chapter examines a drawing by Francesco Borromini, Albertina 173 (1638), for San Carlo alle Quattro Fontane, in its symbolic, schematic, and geometrical content, to illustrate how palimpsest can operate on multiple levels in a sketch or drawing. The analysis discusses the incorporation of diagrams from Nicholas Cusanus and Athanasius Kircher, and the evocation of Humanist, Neoplatonic, and Hermetic philosophies in the drawing. The essay illustrates how the drawing anticipates elements of Freudian psychoanalysis, in the palimpsest of traces in human consciousness, the memory traces of perception, and the formation of dream images as traces of mechanisms in a palimpsest of forms. The essay then examines projects and writings by Peter Eisenman (Friedrichstadt, Long Beach, Wexner Center) in the twentieth century, to give further examples of how palimpsest is operative in architectural composition, in urban site conditions, the use of architectural typologies, and "scaling," the manipulation of the proportional relations of the composition, again in relation to the dream work of Sigmund Freud. The palimpsest of traces reveals the unconscious as an absence in the presence of conscious reason and perception. Palimpsest, whether in the sketch, drawing, building or city, can express elements of human identity and experience in art and architecture.

FRANCESCO BORROMINI

Francesco Borromini's drawing for the plan of San Carlo alle Quattro Fontane (Drawing 173; dated in 1638; Figure 3.1) in the Albertina Museum in Vienna, illustrates the potential for palimpsest in the drawing or sketch. The plan is a combination of three main operative geometries, the circle, octagon, and cross, as observed by Leo Steinberg.[1] The circle represents the divine, in its infinity and perfection, the octagon represents the Spirit as creation, and the cross represents the body of Christ. The shape of the plan of the worship space is an unrecognizable and apparently unjustifiable geometric configuration, although it has been shown that it is the result of a rational geometric construction. Borromini chose to keep the construction of the shape a secret, in the tradition of the medieval guild, which he would have learned in his training in Lombardy. The geometries are now understood through analysis of the drawings collected after his suicide.

Borromini's logical geometrical progression, disguised in an unrecognizable form, is a reflection of the syncretic thought of the Renaissance, and, I would argue that it acted as a precursor to a quality of the Freudian construction of dream space in the twentieth century. In the Freudian dream space, the manifest content of the dream, the pictorial content, appears as an irrational collage of images, while the underlying dream thoughts structure the dream in a syntactical manner analogous to linguistic structures. According to Sigmund Freud in *The Interpretation of Dreams* (1899), 'The dream thoughts are entirely rational and are constructed with an expenditure of all the psychical energy of which we are capable'. While 'little attention is paid to the logical relations between the thoughts, those relations are ultimately given a disguised representation in certain formal characteristics of dreams'.[2] In the plan of San Carlo, the relations between the three manifest geometrical shapes are given a disguised representation in the formal character of the plan. The plan is composed of a deep structure, an underlying conceptual or linguistic structure manifested geometrically, and a manifest content, its visual appearance.

In the construction of the plan, the architect begins with intersecting equilateral triangles inscribed in an oval; a geometric scheme published by Borromini's friend Athanasius Kircher to represent the concept of the coincidence of light and dark in the process of creation. The oval is generated from an ellipse created by the intersecting arcs of two circles, from whose centre-points the intersecting triangles are drawn. The architect then draws a rectangle tangent to the oval, then draws another rectangle halfway between the oval and the diamond on the minor axis, draws arcs on the tips of the diamond with the edges of the circles as midpoint, locates columns at the intersection of the arcs and rectangles, draws lines parallel to the triangle from the columns and locates columns at the intersection of that line with the rectangles, and draws lateral arcs from the opposite points of the diamond. But then he stops short at the midpoint between minor axis and column, and draws another arc from the intersection of axes. The lines drawn from

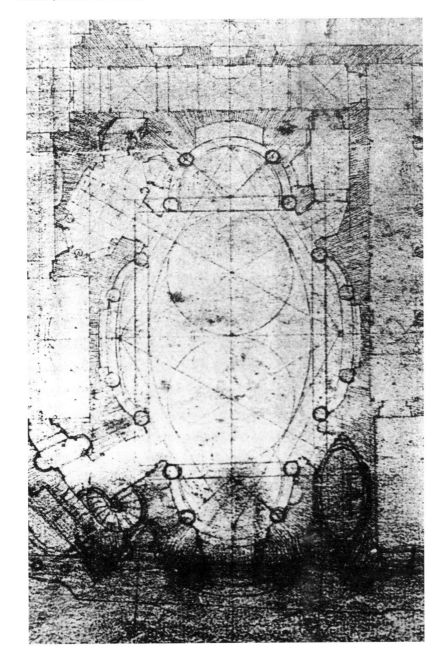

3.1   Francesco Borromini, AZRom173, Albertina, Vienna, 1638

the column parallel to the triangles cut the corner of the rectangle. Borromini was called a *tagliacantone*, or corner-cutter, by Gianlorenzo Bernini.[3]

The plan can be read in a variety of ways: as an undulating oval, an elongated octagon, or a circular Greek cross. As in a perceived image, or dream image, or word in language, a single form can be interpreted in multiple ways, as a palimpsest. An irrational form disguises a rational process, as in dream images or forms in nature. The construction of the plan is in keeping with the Albertian use of Pythagorean ratios of numeric harmony and *eurhythmia* or proportion. It therefore corresponds to the laws of nature, as manifest in the structure of the mind, so that the mind is a microcosm of the universe. The construction of the plan is in keeping with the Albertian notion of *concinnitas* as well. According to Leon Battista Alberti in his *De pictura* (1435): 'it is the task and aim of *concinnitas* to compose parts that are quite separate from each other by their nature, according to some precise rule, so that they correspond to one another in appearance.'[4]

NICOLAS CUSANUS AND ATHANASIUS KIRCHER

A diagram of intersecting triangles, or pyramids, appeared in the *De coniecturis* (1443) or *On Conjecture* of Nicolas Cusanus, and in manuscripts by Athanasius Kircher. The *De coniecturis* of Cusanus was well known to Kircher, who copied passages from it in his own writing. Cusanus described the intersecting pyramids as *figura paradigmatica*, paradoxical figures of light and dark, representing the progression from unity to alterity and alterity to unity. In *De Visione Dei* (1453), Cusanus said 'when I behold God in Paradise, [He is] supported by the wall of the coincidence of opposites.'[5]

The base of the pyramid of Cusanus is the darkness of primordial origin, while the apex is the infinite oneness and light of God. In between the base and the apex is found all created matter, which is divided in the intersecting pyramids into the regions of the universe, the terrestrial, celestial and supercelestial realms, corresponding to the body, soul and mind of the human being. As the pyramids intersect, unity is everywhere contained in alterity, and alterity is everywhere contained in unity. In the plan drawing of San Carlo, multiple geometrical forms are combined to produce a simple though unrecognizable shape; the final shape is composed of multiple symbols in a unitary form. The process of knowledge, represented by multiple forms, corresponds to divine creation, represented by unitary form, though the creation is unattainable by that knowledge. In the plan drawing of San Carlo, the unitary form is seemingly unattainable by the multiple forms from which it is generated in palimpsest.

Intersecting triangles of light and dark inscribed in a circle or oval appear in Kircher's *Prodromus Coptus Sive Aegyptiacus* (1636), *Obeliscus Pamphilius*, and *Musurgia universalis*. The diagrams of intersecting triangles correspond to the creation myth of Pimander from the *Corpus Hermeticum*; a group of writings compiled by Marsilio Ficino and translated into Latin in 1471, thought to be the writings of Hermes Trismegistus. Hermes is invoked as the most ancient source of wisdom in Ficino's *Theologia Platonica*. Ficino's translation of the *Corpus Hermeticum*, entitled the *Pimander* after the first of the Hermetic dialogues, had a widespread influence in Renaissance art and philosophy. The creation myth in the *Pimander* describes the ascension of light and the descent of darkness in the formation of the four elements. The ascension in the realm of air and fire is nutritive, while the descent in the realm of earth and water is generative. Matter has the power of generation, as represented in the intersecting pyramids and oval, or egg of the universe. Light is the word of God that forms an ordered world perceptible only in thought in a palimpsest, revealing in the mind an archetypal form prior to creation, the *exemplaria intelligibilis*. The elements are copies of the archetypes, thus the sensible cosmos is a copy of the eternal cosmos.

The scheme of intersecting triangles first appears in Kircher's writings inscribed in a circle in the *Prodromus Coptus Sive Aegyptiacus*, while Borromini was designing San Carlo in 1636. Kircher describes this figure, the *Sphaera Amoris* or *Sphere of Love*, as being composed of the Phi letter, a symbol of the material world; the letter V, showing love moving towards God; the upside-down V, showing love coming from God; and the letter O, expressing progression towards the material world. According to Kircher, 'The force of love flows through unity to multiplicity. The first point or apex is God, and it progresses through the world divided into three levels, eventually arriving in matter, connecting the infinity of the heavens with the strength of matter through all intermediate levels of nature'.[6] This description of love comes from an ancient Egyptian tablet called the Bembina Tablet, according to Kircher, and it is an element of Hermetic philosophy, combined with the Celestial Hierarchies of Pseudo-Dionysius and the Platonic elements. In *Oedipi Aegyptiaci*, Kircher identifies the pictogram of intersecting triangles inscribed in an oval as the root of the thirteenth letter of the Egyptian alphabet, the name for which is love, through which the mechanisms of the universe are put into motion, as represented in the diagram. Kircher then superimposed the intersecting triangles onto a geometrical representation of the Celestial Hierarchies conceived by Cusanus, which corresponds to the vertical organization of Borromini's San Carlo.

The themes developed by Kircher in his Hermetic and Neoplatonic writings are translated by Borromini into a palimpsest of architectural forms, through the use of symbols, diagrams and geometrical transmutations, which correspond to the philosophical themes as represented in the texts. Borromini subjects geometries in the plan to fragmentation, juxtaposition, reversal, and distortion, as in images in dreams. As Freud describes in *The Interpretation of Dreams*, 'dreams feel themselves at liberty…to represent any element by its wishful contrary; so that there is no way of deciding at a first glance whether any element that admits of a contrary is present in the dream-thoughts as a positive or as a negative'.[7] Such is the quality of the Baroque in the apparent proliferation of the signified or interpretation beyond the simplicity of the signifier or form, to represent the mind as a complex of interrelated significations, prefiguring the structuring of the unconscious through dreams by Freud in the twentieth century.

SIGMUND FREUD

Freud defined psychical structures as a dynamic continuum of causal relationships in a palimpsest, as enacted in the plan drawing of San Carlo. According to Freud, dreams 'are to be explained on a dynamic basis—by the strengthening and weakening of the various components of the interplay of forces, so many of whose effects are hidden from view while functions are normal'.[8] The psychical structure is to be explained in terms of the dynamic interplay of forces, but in an enigmatic representation, as the underlying rationale is unavailable to consciousness. Such is the nature of Baroque *stupefazione*, the inaccessibility of the unconscious as expressed by the unknowability of God in the structure of thought, as related by the Humanist notion of *concinnitas* and the Neoplatonic account of *nous* in the higher level of the Soul with access to the divine Mind.

In the dream work of Freud, as a result of the complex network of psychical relationships which produce the dream images, and the mechanisms of condensation and displacement, dreams are composed of disconnected fragments of visual images, syntactical structures in language, and thoughts, the *Sachvorstellung* or thing presentation, and the *Wortvorstellung* or word presentation, which are seen in a variety of logical relations to each other in a palimpsest of traces that is difficult to unravel, and which can appear to be irrational. The irrational appearance of a palimpsest of layers of rational relations between traces can be seen in Borromini's plan drawing. The palimpsest of dream images is seen by Freud as the condensation and displacement of figures and spatial relationships, such as foreground and background, and the coincidence of opposites, as in the *coincidentia oppositurum* of the pyramids of light and dark.

The network of logical relations, which contribute to the composition of dream images, is too complex to be unravelled in dream analysis. Displacement, condensation, fragmentation, substitution and the *coincidentia oppositorum*, are products of the complex network of logical relations, or the mnemic residues of such, in the *Vorstellungsrepräsentanz* in dream thoughts, which is too complex to correspond to any logical structure. The *Vorstellungsrepräsentanz* is the dream image, which is a representation of a mnemic residue or memory trace of perception, which is itself a representation of the perceived object. The simple image itself is a palimpsest of traces, which are processed to produce it. In the process of the dream formation, the logical links that hold the psychical material together are lost. It is the task of analysis to restore the logical connections that the dream work has destroyed, as dreams are seen as the royal road to knowledge of the unconscious activities of the mind, as Freud wrote in *The Interpretation of Dreams*.

The relation between the dream image and the dream thought, or manifest content and latent content, the surface aspect and the deep aspect, can be seen in the relation of the thinking subject to language, and to forms in art, like the geometries in the sketch. The dream image responds to the dream thought, the latent content, in the *Vorstellungsrepräsentanz*, as a form of psychical activity in response to perceptual activity. The content of perception is anticipated and rearranged, as the subject is anticipated in language; the word represents the image to another word as the signifier represents the subject to another signifier, and it is that series of relations, which make both the dream and language intelligible. The representation of the image by the word, of the subject by the signifier, is a tool for intelligibility in architectural composition.

PETER EISENMAN

In composing a building on a site, the architect may incorporate actual traces in the site of past conditions, axes from previous planning into the architecture. This can be seen in a project for the Friedrichstadt competition (1980–81) in Berlin by Eisenman Robertson Architects, which incorporates the absent city wall of the eighteenth century, foundation walls from the nineteenth century, remnants of a proposed twentieth-century grid, and the Berlin Wall, for the purpose of combining a series of opposites: memory traces and traces of the absence of memory, unity and fragmentation, and addition and subtraction, as described in Eisenman's *Cities of Artificial Excavation*. The layering of traces in the palimpsest involves traces of presence as well as traces of absence. A drawing, or a building, can contain 'not only presences, but the memory of previous presences and the immanences of a possible presence'.[9] Thus, according to Eisenman 'the introduction of this trace, or condition of absence, acknowledges the dynamic reality of the living city'. Sigmund Freud, in *Civilization and Its Discontents* (1929), uses the city of Rome, with the presence of traces of past presences woven into its fabric, in a palimpsest, to illustrate the survival of the memory-trace in the mind. 'Now let us make the fantastic supposition that Rome were not a human dwelling-place, but a mental entity with just as long and varied a past history: that is, in which nothing once constructed had perished, and all the earlier stages of development had survived alongside the latest'.[10]

The survival of the memory-trace in the mind depends, as does the ruin in the city, on the health of the mind over time. 'Even for mental life, our assumption that everything past is preserved holds good only on condition that the organ of the mind remains intact and its structure has not been injured by traumas or inflammation'. Freud admits of the limitations of 'mastering the idiosyncrasies of mental life…by treating them in terms of visual representation', because more than one content cannot occur simultaneously in space, but in fact it can be seen that the unconscious is both structural and spatial, and the overlapping of forms in space has the same consequences as cathexis and condensation in language. The palimpsest of traces of past presences on a site or drawing is then transferred to architecture as a reflection of the structure of the unconscious, and can enact the entering of the unconscious into conscious thought, in the absences of the trope or the rhetorical figure, or the visual signifiers.

A project for a university art museum at the California State University at Long Beach (1986) by Eisenman was intended to conceive of a building as 'an architectural artifact, a palimpsest of its own history',[11] as described in *Cities of Artificial Excavation*, so that the architecture can tell a story or a narrative of history, and can record 'the traces of a lost and future civilization'. The building is seen as 'layered and shifting, continually exposing different surfaces', in a series of superimpositions that reveals previously unseen relationships and contrasting scales. Pieces of information become 'marks of intelligence' or glimpses of the ways through which culture organizes itself. The reproduction of the traces is then purposefully dislocated from the site, to be seen as a conceptual construct in relation to real space and history. A palimpsest of traces in a city or site or drawing can only be a mental construction, the temporal and geometrical logic of reason superimposed on perceived space, as in the *a priori* intuition of Immanuel Kant, revealing the relation between the human mind, in perception, memory, and cognition, and the real world as defined by space and time.

Representation in dreams, according to Freud, is often facilitated by replacement, as in a *coincidentia oppositorum*, or a condensation in a palimpsest of dream thoughts. 'When a common element between two persons is represented in a dream, it is usually a hint for us to look for another, concealed common element whose representation has been made impossible by the censorship. A displacement in regard to the common element has been made in order, as it were, to facilitate its representation'.[12] As Jacques Lacan has shown, this is precisely the mechanism of metaphor, in the eliding of the signified, which produces the anchoring point, the point at which signification is produced, and the point at which the unconscious is made present as an absence. Displacement has also been seen to be a mechanism in architectural composition. This is one of many examples in Freud's dream interpretation which points to the linguistic structuring of dream images.

The two principal mechanisms of the formation of dream images are displacement and condensation. Displacement is responsible for the fact that dream images do not correspond to conscious reason, and causes the dream to be seen as nothing more than a distortion, or perversion, of reason, a deceptive façade, as in architecture. Lacan has shown that displacement is a primary mechanism of both metaphor and metonymy in language, and that it results in a figurative or poetic signification or effect in language that goes beyond its literal function and introduces the unconscious. In such a mechanism, the dream can be seen as a form of tropic language whose logical sense is removed from rational discourse.

The other principal mechanism in dream formation is condensation, which involves the *coincidentia oppositorum*, as well as the diachronic combined into the synchronic, and 'collective and composite figures'. Condensation is the most active mechanism in dream formation, as 'in dreams fresh composite forms are being perpetually constructed in an inexhaustible variety', as described by Freud in *On Dreams*.[13] In condensation, the dream image is over-determined by material in the dream thoughts. A single dream image may constitute a combination of several pictorial or linguistic forms that have no apparent relation to each other, as in the compositions of Peter Eisenman. The condensation and displacement, which Freud observes as characteristics of the dream image, lend to the theory that the dream is a pictorial language, that the unconscious is structured like a language, in a palimpsest.

Condensation and displacement are the mechanisms of the compositional strategy of 'scaling' in Eisenman's architecture. Scaling involves 'the formal superposition of analogous material at different scales', as described in *Barefoot on White-Hot Walls*,[14] as in dream work, 'which reveals previously hidden relationships', those repressed relationships that are uncovered by unconscious mechanisms. The process of scaling, 'like Freud's dream work, is one of condensation and displacement: displacement of scale, condensation by superposition'.[15] This can be seen in the Wexner Center (1980–86, Figure 3.2). Eisenman seeks to use the mechanisms of dream work as introduced by Freud in architectural composition, in scaling, in order to reveal relationships between architectural forms, which have been repressed by the conscious discourse of classical or traditional architecture, in the same way that dream work reveals elements of the constitution of the subject, which have been repressed by rational discourse, by the illusion of consciousness and the *cogito* in the constitution of the subject. Such a strategy introduces into architecture something which is not architecture, something which is other to it, as dream work introduces into conscious reason something that is other to it.

For the Wexner Center, 'the superposition of two scaled grids was registered on crucial points to determine overlaps, strange disjunctions and arbitrary figures in order to produce latent configuration and new meanings without conscious motivation',[16] in a palimpsest. The latent configuration corresponds to the latent content of the dream for Freud, the retroactive signification which is produced through the analysis of the dream in dream work. The composition, structure, and significance of the dream are all given by conscious thought in analysis, while the particular quality of the relationships between images in the dreams

3.2   Peter Eisenman, Wexner Center. Source: Image: John Hendrix

is created by mechanisms which can be compared to linguistic mechanisms, which are uncensored by conscious thought. Eisenman is interested in producing an architecture that represents the role of dream work, between image and representation. The unconscious is introduced into conscious discourse, as represented by the condensation and displacement of dream work, as well as the traces and absences in a palimpsest of forms and in the structure of language.

Though there is a direct correspondence between the dream thought and the dream image for Freud, the construction of the dream entails a more complex relationship between the thought and the image. As is seen in condensation and displacement, 'just as connections lead from each element of the dream to several dream thoughts, so as a rule a single dream thought is represented by more than one dream element; the threads of association do not simply converge from the dream thoughts to the dream content, they cross and interweave with each other many times over in the course of their journey'.[17] These complex relationships can be seen in the palimpsests of the compositions by Borromini and Eisenman.

The displacement that occurs in dreams is responsible for distorting, more than anything else, the 'psychical intensity' of the thoughts, which correspond to the dreams, according to Freud. The psychic intensity is described as the significance or 'affective potentiality'[18] of the thought or perceptual trace; the system of differences between the traces is a system of intensities as much as a system of signifiers, or more, because of the nature of the relation between the memory image and perception; some images or words are perceived at a different level of intensity than others, more clearly or more loudly, etc., and it stands to reason that the variations in intensities would be translated in the composition of the dream images, and that those variations would be illegible in relation to any conceptual structure. 'In the course of this process…the psychical intensity, significance or affective potentiality of the thoughts is, as we further find, transformed into sensory vividness'.[19]

As a result of the complex network of psychical relationships which produce the dream images, and the mechanisms of condensation and displacement, dreams are composed of traces of 'disconnected fragments of visual images, speeches and even bits of unmodified thoughts', which 'stand in the most manifold logical relations to one another', which are seen for example as 'foreground and background, conditions, digressions and illustrations, chains of evidence and counterarguments',[20] conditions which Eisenman seeks to enact in architecture. The architectural sketches and compositions contain a palimpsest of logical relations, which contribute to a composition, as in the composition of dream images. The displacement, condensation, fragmentation, and substitution found in dream images are found in the palimpsest of the sketch. Palimpsest can be a quality of a sketch, drawing, building, city, perception, memory, or idea. Applied to art and architecture, it can contribute to work of meaning and consequence, in the expression of human identity and experience.

BIBLIOGRAPHY

Alberti, Leon Battista. *On Painting*, translated by C. Grayson. London: Penguin Books, 1991.

Cusanus, Nicolaus. *Unity and Reform, Selected Writings of Nicholas de Cusa*, edited by J.P. Dolan. Notre Dame, IN: University of Notre Dame Press, 1992.

Eisenman, Peter. *Cities of Artificial Excavation*. Montreal: Canadian Centre for Architecture/ New York: Rizzoli International Publications, 1994.

_____. *Eisenman Inside Out*. New Haven and London: Yale University Press, 2004.

_____. "Architecture and the problem of the rhetorical figure," in *Eisenman Inside Out*. New Haven and London: Yale University Press, 2004.

_____. *Barefoot on White-Hot Walls* (*Barfuss Auf Weiss Glühenden Mauern*). Edited by P. Noever. Ostfildern: Hatje Cantz Verlag, 2005.

Freud, Sigmund. *On Dreams, the Standard Edition*. Translated and edited by J. Strachey. New York: W.W. Norton, 1952.

_____. *The Interpretation of Dreams*. Translated and edited by J. Strachey. New York: Avon Books, 1965.

_____. *Civilization and Its Discontents*. Translated by J. Riviere. NewYork: Dover Publications, Inc, 1994.

Hendrix, John. *The Relation Between Architectural Forms and Philosophical Structures in the Work of Francesco Borromini in Seventeenth-Century Rome*. Lewiston, NY: Edwin Mellen, 2002.

_____. *Architecture and Psychoanalysis*. Peter Eisenman and Jacques Lacan. New York: Peter Lang, 2006.

Kircher, Athanasius. *Prodromus Coptus Sive Aegyptiacus*. Romae: Propaganda Fide, 1636.

Steinberg, Leo. *Borromini's San Carlo alle Quattro Fontane: A Study in Multiple Form and Architectural Symbolism*. New York: Garland Publishing, 1977.

NOTES

1   Leo Steinberg, *Borromini's San Carlo alle Quattro Fontane: A Study in Multiple Form and Architectural Symbolism* (New York: Garland Publishing, 1977), 93.

2   Sigmund Freud, *The Interpretation of Dreams*, trans. and ed. James Strachey (New York: Avon Books, 1965), 544–45.

3   Steinberg, *Borromini's San Carlo alle Quattro Fontane*, 127.

4   Leon Battista Alberti, *On Painting*, trans. Cecil Grayson (London: Penguin Books, 1991), 71.

5   Nicolaus Cusanus, *De Visione Dei*, translation in John Patrick Dolan, ed., *Unity and Reform, Selected Writings of Nicholas de Cusa* (Notre Dame, IN: University of Notre Dame Press, 1962), 152.

6   Athanasius Kircher, *Prodromus Coptus Sive Aegyptiacus* (Romae: Propaganda Fide, 1636), 256. The Latin text reads as follows: '*Unde, meo quidem iudicio, Amorem rectissime statuas, ut desiderium quoddam boni pulchrique, vel bonitatis per*

pulchritudinem ipsam conferendae vel accipiendae, videlicet, cuius potestas veluti unius sit magnitudinis dima natio, cuius punctum vel apex sit primus in Deo, progressus per mundum triplicem tripliciter distributum, finis autem in ipsa materiae, cuius denique quaedam sit infinitudo circa verticem, potentiae merae infinitudo circa meteriem, conexionis virtus infinita per omnes naturae intermedios gradus'.

7   Freud, *The Interpretation of Dreams*, 353.

8   Freud, *The Interpretation of Dreams*, 649.

9   Peter Eisenman, 'Architecture and the Problem of the Rhetorical Figure', in *Eisenman Inside Out* (New Haven and London: Yale University Press, 2004), 207.

10   Sigmund Freud, *Civilization and Its Discontents*, trans. Joan Riviere (New York: Dover Publications, Inc., 1994 [1930]), 6.

11   Peter Eisenman, *Cities of Artificial Excavation* (Montreal: Canadian Centre for Architecture / New York: Rizzoli International Publications, 1994), 132.

12   Freud, *The Interpretation of Dreams*, 357.

13   Sigmund Freud, *On Dreams, The Standard Edition*, trans. and ed. James Strachey (New York: W. W. Norton, 1952), 30.

14   Peter Eisenman, *Barefoot on White-Hot Walls (Barfuss Auf Weiss Glühenden Mauern)*, ed. Peter Noever (Hatje Cantz Verlag, 2005), 108.

15   Eisenman, *Barefoot on White-Hot Walls*, 110.

16   Eisenman, *Barefoot on White-Hot Walls*, 116.

17   Freud, *On Dreams*, 32.

18   Freud, *On Dreams*, 34.

19   Freud, *On Dreams*, 34.

20   Freud, *On Dreams*, 40.

4

The Ontological Sketchbook

Robert Clarke

INTRODUCTION

This chapter considers the wordless nature of absorbed experience which arises in the practice of drawing, but which might be said to exist in all practices. This absorption occurs in privileged moments when consciousness is deeply immersed in the process of practical activity itself, where the internal and external worlds appear to merge in a form of deeply engaged reverie and a loss of 'self.' Such moments form an integration in the imaginative consciousness of the drawer that appear in their midst to be timeless. However, these attentive experiences are as momentary as they are unpredictable, for they cannot be willed or premeditated, but are evidence of a pre-reflective awareness of practical involvement. It will be argued that this evolves or unfolds in a dialectical relationship between what Martin Heidegger calls 'calculative thought' [*berechnen*] (when the drawer steps out of the work to reflect upon the next move), and William James' 'stream of consciousness,' which recognizes a deferral of inhibitions so that drawer and drawing become undivided in an '…inextricable interfusion.'[1] The discussion that follows draws selectively on the philosophies of Arthur Schopenhauer, William James, DT Suzuki, Martin Heidegger, Ludwig Wittgenstein, among others, in order to offer a contextualization of the mental state of absorption and the ineffable nature of aesthetic consciousness as it arises in the practice of drawing. That practice not only leaves the physically externalized traces of a drawing itself, but discloses an internal source which the author describes as the 'ontological sketchbook.'

I

What can be said about drawing that is not already known by the drawer? For what is known is not so much about drawing itself, but about what is expressed *through* drawing about the ontological relationship between the drawer and their lived experience. It is an existential space where the activity of drawing seizes hold of consciousness and draws from within itself as an unformed potentiality of whatever a drawing becomes.

To draw requires one who is the drawer. It requires something to be drawn – a world, a life-world [*Lebenswelt*]. It involves a surface and something to draw with; it calls for an intended purpose, even when what that is, is not known exactly; perhaps it is better that it is not. Drawing involves making an inscribed semblance of sorts, a summoning of presence and a conjuring with what shows up.

Although drawing is of our consciousness, once it is 'drawn out' into a shared world it is no longer in consciousness as such, but is of a practical involvement that '…differs from the speculative order because in practice man tends to something other than mere knowledge.'[2] In practice, knowledge is being put to use for the sake of making something present to us. According to Maritain '…art belongs to the practical order. Its orientation is towards doing … and not to what he calls "the pure inwardness of knowledge."'[3]

The practice of anything involves transcendence of the body in which action or activity is aimed at some purpose or end. Thus, for now, we can say that drawing relates both to itself as a practice brought to light in practical ends but is also reflexive because it is a turn away from the practical action which engendered it and so returns us the immanence of thought and feeling. This is a double *telos* as an emanation from the interior of the body and yet which arrives in the shared spaces of inter-subjectivity and the world of human relations and experiences. Thus, each encounter with drawing is the radical encounter we share with others. It enters the space in which meanings arise and are debated in accordance with the cultural contest to occupy temporal status within whatever there is among what is known to be settled into whatever the future makes of tradition. The object of any endeavour seems always to be aimed at a stable occupation or reoccupation of culture. Touch is the mark of the texture of the world. In the most immediate sense it is a relation between the body and the material fact of the world. Although in touching we become unified, touch is also a reassurance of difference too. I touch a surface to verify what I see is there. That difference is signified by the particularity with which properties inhere in substances and in part can come to define them. Texture is part of the necessary differentiation of beings marked out by surfaces and boundaries beyond, or within, which there is perhaps an unreachable interior; an interior which marks out subdivision and travels into the unseen where the essential nature of things might be disclosed if only we could grasp them. It is as though what we are after in such enquiries is the immanence, not of our own selves, but of the world as something potentially instructive and revealing. Put another way, there is always a desire (however latent) to unify the transcendent space of the world with the immanence of our consciousness of it. A drawing in pencil on a piece of paper is a primordial instance of this aim in where, among an infinite multitude of choices available to us as human practices, we try to unify, or at least, to align, subject and object, as though they were wholly separate in us. Such are the real, necessary or, at least, historical preoccupations with the trans-temporal possibilities of expression. But the beginning of action can be seen as a fresh start, almost as if in the light of a wish, what is done might define a primordial connection we have to our individual existence and the ways we co-opt to configure meanings that become our way of being. Making sense of the world is a way of settling (for the moment) what can be shown so that we might work with that and differentiate between what is or is not significant for us. In the sense that we are what we do, we are the accumulation of our practices and it is in attempting to express our practical orientation to the world that interests the artist.

II

Motivations often lay hidden from view and we progress through a series of strategies drawn from unconscious experience, as rational preferences and emotional affects. A drawing unfolds, and goes on unfolding, even when we step back to reflect on the next move. The endeavour is always fraught with uncertainty. That which appears obvious is never a sufficient cause by which to steer away from the comfort of the knowledge we already possess. The soft and hard spots of vulnerability spinout in ruffled creases and ruptures that will not lie flat; and yet a habitual momentum grows from returning to the visibility of what is there in the improvisation of an image from within. Mindful awareness, indistinct and peculiar, encourages a direct meditation on the dialogue between what is known internally and what is exposed without. The critical voice of the mind acts as form of surveillance, at times it is disparaging, at others, it drives us to press on down the track. Conviction and correction go hand-in-hand and carry with them the inseparable binding of sensations. At times, a linguistic inadequacy shows up in a loss for words. The gestural body inhabits itself in the moment of intimacy to connect a network of possibilities that might lie ahead. What is clearer is the spontaneous push of feeling, always susceptible to critique that threatens to unravel what have been accomplished so far.

Undoubtedly, the drawer is an intermediary of authentic and inauthentic translations of thought and feeling, both vital and necessary. For only through their transitions can the drawing be worked upon and transformed. There is a declared intentionality, underwritten by an awareness that we started out with the need to make drawing necessary. The necessity of drawing is propelled by a cultural spirit in which it has its place already validated by tradition. Elaborations weave together a visualized comprehension of decisive actions and movements, and the drawing proceeds. The logic of drawing is verified by the existence of all other drawings, of drawing itself as a sufficiently valid discipline worth the endeavour. The history of drawing is a cultural resource; and everything we now draw, and how, is determined by what already exists. However, the limitless potential of drawing is never exhausted by what already has been done. Steiner substantiates this as follows, '…within the boundless substitutable weave of textuality, everything and nothing have already been said definitively.'[4] Drawings are as much texts as symphonies, statues and silhouettes are – as all is, as Barthes reminds us, for it involves '…formally limitless tissues of quotations, drawn from innumerable clusters of preceding and surrounding cultures.'[5]

Yet the text is also part of the 'language-game' which gets us caught up in the restrictions of the rhetoric of rules, syntax and utterances; they point to signification, rather than what is actually there in resolute silence of an image-forming process such as drawing. Wittgenstein noticed that when faced with a work of art, we resort to adjectives such as 'fine,' 'beautiful' and 'good.' He believes that this is by no means necessary and adds a cautionary note that identifies the problem that adjectives, as words, '…don't tell us what words are about, what their real subject is, so that the adjectives deployed play hardly any role at all.'[6] This has profound implications, not only for aesthetics, but is also of consequence for all makers of artefacts. The restrictions of language are evasively ambiguous, and Wittgenstein shows how when we become immersed in a practical skill, words retreat, so that where they occur (either internally, or spoken aloud) they are uttered in stark concision not normally typical of everyday communication. He demonstrates this with the example of a skilled tailor:

> Suppose I went in for tailoring and I first learnt all the rules, I might have on the whole, two sorts of attitude. (1) Lewy says "This is too short." I say "No. It is right. It is according to the rules." (2) I develop a 'feeling' for the rules. […] Here I would be making an aesthetic judgement… according to the rules in sense (1). On the other hand, if I hadn't learnt the rules, I wouldn't be able to make an aesthetic judgement.[7]

Wittgenstein points out that learning the 'rules' actually changes the judgement of what we are about. In other words, there is always a resort to laws, drills and established processes which we refer to when we draw. Further on in the discussion, Wittgenstein returns to the analogy of the tailor in which the concision of language, as short-hand, comes to the fore:

> If a man goes through an endless number of patterns in a tailor's [and] says: "No. This is slightly too dark. This is slightly too loud" etc. he is what we call an appreciator of material. About this he remarks: It is not only difficult to describe what appreciation consists in, but impossible. To describe what appreciation consists in we would have to describe the whole environment.[8]

Why might this be a problem to an artist? Because there are an infinite number of cases of appreciation and so, in a sense, the fecundity of art practice is that it must decide which path to take from among them. What unfolds in a drawing are an extraordinary number of potential decisions to be taken at each moment of the encounter. Even in the most pedestrian or rudimentary drawing, such as, for instance, in making 'exact' copy of some pre-existing work, the artist is beset with a labyrinth of possible approaches as ways in. However, Wittgenstein illuminates the linguistic terseness, just referred to, as in action '…a good [pattern] cutter won't use any words except words like "too long," "All right." When talk of a symphony of Beethoven we don't talk of "correctness". Entirely different things matter.'[9] A danger we can fall into is what Wilde called '…careless habits of accuracy.'[10] The matter in question is that language involves a wholly different set of rules to that of a silent practice such as drawing. When we are concentrated upon the activity we are engaged in a kind of absorption, when the linguistic extension of thought into sentences and paragraphs, becomes curiously redundant. At best we call upon single words or short expressions, rather than those we use when we read, write or talk. It is as though consciousness gets wrapped up in practical involvement in the immediacy of what is happening in front of our eyes, and thus is freed from the structures of language and what Heidegger calls 'calculative thought.' Instead, what floats below the surface of linguistics is a *bodily* stream of consciousness; it is of the whole body, rather than solely a preoccupation of the mind; the body as the dynamic source of all movement and sense, response and gesture. That much is axiomatic to Merleau-Ponty's phenomenology developed with assiduous originality from Heidegger's ontology who had encapsulated it somewhat in the neologism *Zuhandenheit* or, the 'ready-to-hand.'

However, we need to return to the pragmatism of William James who, in his researches into psychology, famously coined the familiar term 'stream of consciousness.' James first arrived at this insight in his book *Psychology,* which appeared in 1892. There at its birth he speculated that '…consciousness, then, does not appear to itself chopped up in bits… It is nothing jointed; its flows. A "river" or a "stream" are the metaphors by which it is most naturally described. In talking about it hereafter, let us call it the stream of "thought", of consciousness.'[11] What is pertinent to our argument is the connection suggested by James' discovery that words, as isolatable units of expression, are strung together, and by that token are bits that can be chopped up. They are governed by the rules of language articulated through grammar, syntax and cultural expectation of appropriate linguistic expression. When words are strung together, like beads, we string them along as we go. A linear temporality is embedded there, about which we say by its very nature it is sequenced by a predetermined logic through which meaning can be conveyed and anticipated and interpreted. A counter to this – though as equally temporal as logic – is, for example, the Dadaist poetry that set out to disrupt logical progression and unsettle the accepted forms by which meaning typically arises. That, and the parapraxes of Freudian theory, shake up the liquid unconscious, and come close in interpretation to what we might make sense of automatic drawing as well as the absurd weird uncanny nature of words. The stream of consciousness, as indivisible flow provided a method used by Beckett and Joyce, among many others. Yet, even these attempts to break the rules of language, as they were then understood, replaced one set of rules for another.

It seems that it is impossible to dispense with rules altogether, for only in their light can we know how to break them apart. The prospects this subversion affords, is, of course, essential to what goes by the name of 'originality.' But for now, we must return to James' stream of consciousness for its windings seem to pin down what flows and bubbles in the ripples of the processes of making art.

The labels and equivalences of language spoken and thought, is disrupted and put in abeyance when we involve ourselves in practical activity; something mysteriously analytic, gets pleasantly freed-up and deferred. For in moments of complete absorption, for example when drawing, we become released from ourselves, where we place ourselves in the striving to reform the pattern of which we have little knowledge before it appears. This sustains uncertainty, and we must learn to live with the unknown. Schopenhauer expresses experience in *The World as Will and Representation*:

> When, however, an external cause or inward disposition suddenly raises us out of the endless stream of willing, and snatches knowledge from the thraldom of the will, the attention is now no longer directed to the motives of willing, but comprehends things free from their relation to the will.[12]

Notice how he *detaches* the will (which we might aver is substantiated not only by action, but by language) and moves away from the ego towards the suggestion that released from it, there is a blind, yet vigorous, sense of the intuition. Language *is* as logical as it is wilful and a differentiating sign of our humanity. As with the making of images, we can become lost in it. Yet, it can have the detrimental effect of diminishing no-discursive acts, and the readiness of other forms of feeling as shown by Susan Langer in *Philosophy in a New Key*. Schopenhauer seems to have got there first:

> Then all at once the peace, always sought but always escaping us on that first path of willing, comes to us of its own accord, and all is well with us. Then in contemplation, being is lost in the object, forgetting all individuality, abolishing the kind of knowledge which follows the principle of sufficient reason [i.e. our propensity to a logical disposition] and comprehends only relations.[13]

That 'being is lost' can be interpreted as our individual awareness of our separate egos. For Schopenhauer, something ultimately unnecessary to us dissolves in a meditative or absorbed encounter with the arts, but what is it that dissolves? Many things, but among them, is *language*. In the presence of special experience, initially, are we not speechless? That wordlessness tells of more than the flapping chatterbox tongue is used to cope with. This occurs, I argue, in precious moments of absorption in practical purposes like drawing and making art. Such moments cannot be willed nor predicted. They are fleeting and we do our best work because of their presence. I shall go further and suggest that their existence is necessary to the practices of art. Yet, remarkable though they are, by and large they go on unremarked. How few descriptive examples of the immediacy of the creative process actually exist to get shared about and reinforce us! Too few have I discovered. Our future depends on their luminous existence. In paying attention to the heart of practices, we can express what it feels like, as well as why it is significant, to become momentarily one of Schopenhauer's 'timeless subjects of experience.'[14]

Soapboxes are only modest enclosures that, if they are lucky, end their days as matchwood. But, are we not these days giving too much credence to the intellectualization of art? Today, doing is not enough: the practical must be accompanied now by positioning statements and plagiarized misunderstandings of philosophy itself. Picture-book philosophy (viz. 'Deleuze for Beginners,' for example) skimmed for a gravitas that fools no one but artists themselves.

THE ONTOLOGICAL SKETCHBOOK 57

James' pluralistic researches were miles ahead of their time, yet remained prescient. He saw parallels between the stream of consciousness and the Buddhist notion of *viññāna-sota,* which reflects the first of the '…three universal characteristics of existence.'[15] In the midst of purposeful of activity, the stream of consciousness mainly '…passes unrecorded or unobserved…'[16] and James goes on to add, as if in passing, '…in general all our non-rational operations come from… the source of our dreams…in it arise whatever mystical experiences we may have… our supra-normal cognitions, if such there be… it is the fountainhead of much that feeds our theology.'[17] This moves us from consciousness to substantiation of the mystical and of metaphysics, concerns that run counter to the mainstream of the scientism of much contemporary thought.

The perspicacity of James' project is its concern to defining the framework of the subliminal pre-conceptual aspects of consciousness; and these are deeply relevant to how we might arrive at an understanding of the engaged nature of art practice, and hence, to attend to what occurs in the wordless, indivisible, moments there in the creative process. James' research is helpful because it offers a challenge to the dominance of intellectualism in contemporary practice. The following is taken from James' *The Pluralistic Universe* of 1909, where he discriminates the radical differences there are between concept formation and language:

> Intellectualism's edge is broken, it can only approximate to reality, and its logic is inexplicable to our inner life…May you and I be confluent in a higher consciousness, and confluently active there, tho we know it not? I am tiring myself and you, I know, by vainly trying to describe by words what I say at the same time exceed conceptualisation or verbalisation. As long as one remains talking, intellectualism remained in undisturbed possession of the field. The return to life can't come by talking. It is an act.[18]

As are, indeed, all practices, for to make art is to *act.* James' distrust of language chimes with the precepts of Zen Buddhism, which applies techniques or *dos* ('ways') that seek to disrupt the customary modes and uses of language. These ways include *kōan,* verbal paradox, calligraphy, humour, sounds and even ridicule. All of which are 'intended to undermine what James calls the tyranny of 'intellectualism,' 'conceptualization' and 'verbalization.'[19] According to James,

> …when the reflective intellect… in the flowing process… distinguishes its elements and parts, it gives them separate names… The flux no sooner comes than it tends to fill itself with emphases, and these salient parts become identified and fixed and abstracted; so that now flows as if shot through with adjectives and nouns and prepositions and conjunctions.[20]

James' assertion acknowledges the difficulty of matching up the speechless experiences of immersed involvement, such as when drawing, with the structures of language. For words, arrest the flow of the practical when what occurs is constantly changing and responsive in the dynamics of movement and the interiority that is of equivalence to the Aristotelian concept of *phusis* [φύσις] (a budding growth, forcing its way into fulfilment, to spring forth), or the Latin 'nasci' (to be born, to progress, to grow, to be produced).

James believes that below the surface of consciousness, is a substratum that can, if permitted, surface in what he calls 'pure experience'. James states that '...the name I give to the immediate flux of life which furnishes the material to our later reflection with conceptual categories [...] an experience pure in the literal sense of 'that' which is not yet any definite 'what', though ready to be all sorts of whats.'[21]

If 'pure experience' exists (and some think it does not) then it does so as pre-reflective when in the moment of its experience it is not aware of itself, it simply *is*. 'It is a 'that' rather than a 'what' object.'[22] For Heidegger it is the experience of 'presence and presence-at-hand [*Anwesenheit und Vorhandenheit*] Here, the 'what' is the analytic of ascribing words to experience; it is language. In Heidegger's ontology, language is 'calculative thought' which enables us to reflect and to weigh up options and utterances. It is the moment that theory takes over from action, out of which we return to practical tasks.

CONCLUSION

This chapter has attempted to throw light upon the particular nature of absorbed immersiveness that occurs, unwilled yet yearned for, right at the centre of practice. Though rarely discussed, it is a universal experience that is not particular to drawing or art, but can occur in all activities in which we are able 'to lose ourselves.' Maritain's idea of the 'practical intellect,'[23] which he derived from Aristotle, also substantiates the special quality and elusive mysteries of immersed moments in practical experience, in life itself.

It is helpful to quote in full a resonant passage in Schopenhauer, which recognizes the wordlessness of immediate perception, in its pre-categorical stages:

> ...we do not let abstract thought, the concepts of reason, take possession of our consciousness, but, instead of all this, devote the whole power of our mind to perception, sink ourselves completely therein, and let our whole consciousness be filled by the calm contemplation of the natural object actually present, whether it be a landscape, a tree, a rock, a crag, a building, or anything else. We lose ourselves entirely in this object, to use a pregnant expression; in other words, we forget our individuality, our will, and continue to exist as pure subject, a clear mirror of the object, so that it is as though the object alone existed without anyone to perceive it, and thus we are no longer able to separate the perceiver from the perception, but the two have become one...[24]

Is this not what happens to us in the midst of immersed experience when the drawing, or artefact we are making, becomes inseparable from us, when fugitive time and space dissolve, so that there is no longer any distance and we are as speechless as are the materials? It is the return to the things in *ourselves*, that is the path to experiencing the presence of the ontological intuition and the vital way in which it absorbs us into an impermanent totality of being here. What we can learn from experience of drawing is to find ourselves capable of sustaining the uncertainty that makes growth possible for, '…what we learn from experience is how to have unknown experiences.'[25]

Finally, the psychoanalyst, Marion Milner has written many phenomenological descriptions of drawing, a method she deployed in her treatment of a child, and published as *The Hands of the Living God* (2011). Adam Phillips believes that for Milner, '…psychoanalysis is the attempt to make that paradoxical thing, a secular theology; which means for Milner – after Blake, Darwin and Freud – a body-based theology that tries to describe the body's forms of attention.'[26] Milner states in the preface that '…thus it was against a background of preoccupations both with the nature of the creative process and the nature of internal perception that I began my work.'[27] In her conclusion Milner reviews the discoveries she'd helped her patient make through drawing stating that '…we had even seen the struggle leading right up to her [the patient] battles over the nature of creative thinking, up to her slow recognition of that opposite of her conscious thinking that is unconscious, the gap in the consciousness that consciousness has to relate to itself to, the something not there, the Cloud of Unknowing, the empty circle.'[28]

The source of everything given is referred to by philosophers as 'sense data.' It is all that we gather through our senses as something within and beyond us that matches both into what Heidegger calls '…the meaningful dimension of the environing world.'[29] We must learn not to theorize without understanding its origin in *life* as an embodied logos. This is examined by Merleau-Ponty and Kitaro Nishida (both Heideggerians), who sought to show that theoretical attitudes had a habit of atomising experience into dualistic categories. To counter this, Nishida proposes 'acting-intuitively' wherein we see (through practice) what works

> The artist goes through process of seeing things step by step; a process of improving the totality. Therefore we can say, with Bergson that even the artist does not know how the work will turn out…[30]

We are all of us practical theorists who understand theory most cogently through what emerges first in our work. This is no self-evident platitude, for experience shows it gets missed in the miasma of justification and 'analysis,' rather '…the compass of the priority of created form over its reception of its intelligible presence needs to be spelt out.'[31] As Steiner reminds us, '…the poem comes before the commentary. The construct precedes the deconstruction,'[32] as he explains here:

> There have been instances, though few, though suspect in their artifice, in which a picture, a literary text, a musical composition, have been realized in calculated response to some theoretical, critical, programmatic expectation […] But normally, the bringing into being of the work of art is prior to all other modes of its subsequent existence. It has precedence; it has right of way.[33]

We need to ensure that theory does not lose touch with the primacy of practice that attunes us to an unfolding awareness of lived experience gathered in the making process itself. The humility of this position seems authentic to lived

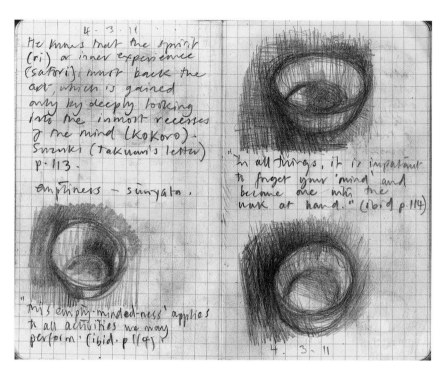

4.1   Sketchbook pages. Source: Drawing: Robert Clark

4.2   Sketchbook pages. Source: Drawing: Robert Clark

experience and creativity, and therefore well suited to encourage holistic ways of understanding the primordial ontology of practices.

Therefore, the ontological sketchbook is not made from paper pages but is the source of our being which is the accumulation of a lived experience immersed in cultural discourses. Taken into ourselves they await the moment when they will be brought back into the light, changed, mediated by the fleeting nature of our knowledge and the surprising awareness that we know more and less than we imagined we would.

So, with that in mind, may the path into theory be directed by the light of the clearing opened up by the practical search first, for '…therein something moves following its own course.'[34]

BIBLIOGRAPHY

De Beistegui, Miguel. *The New Heidegger*. London: Continuum, 2005.

Franck, Frederick., ed. *The Buddha Eye: An Anthology of the Kyoto School and its Contemporaries*. New York: World Wisdom, 2004.

Harper, Ralph. *On Presence: Variations and Reflections*. Baltimore: The John Hopkins University Press, 1991.

Heidegger, Martin. *Being and Time*. Oxford: Blackwell, 1997.

James, William. *Psychology*. New York: Macmillan, 1892.

_____. *A Pluralistic Universe*. London: Longman, Green, 1909.

_____. *The Varieties of Religious Experience*. London: Routledge, 2008.

Langer, Susanne. *Philosophy in a New Key*. Cambridge, Massachusetts: Harvard University Press, 1979.

Maritain, Jacques. *Art and Scholasticism with Other Essays*. New York: reprinted by Kessinger Publishing (Undated), 1924.

Merleau-Ponty, Maurice. *Phenomenology of Perception*. London: Routledge, 2002.

Milner, Marion. *A Life of One's Own*. London: Virago, 2000.

_____. *The Hands of the Living God*. London: Routledge, 2011.

Nishida, Kitaro. *Fundamental Problems of Philosophy: The World of Action and the Dialectical World*. Tokyo: Sophia University Press, 1970.

Olkowski, Dorothea. *Merleau-Ponty, Interiority and Exteriority, Psychic Life and the World*. New York: State University of New York Press, 1991.

Schopenhauer, Arthur. *The World as Will and Representation*. Vol.1. New York: Dover Publications, 1969.

Scott, David. "William James and Buddhism: American Pragmatism and the Orient," in *Religion* 30 (2000): 333–352.

Steiner, George. *Real Presences*. Chicago: Chicago University Press, 1989.

Suzuki, Daisetz T. *Zen and Japanese Culture*. Princeton: Princeton University Press, 2010.

Taylor, Eugene and Wozniak, Robert, eds. *Pure Experience: the Response to William James.* Bristol: Thoemmes Press, 1996.

Wilde, Oscar. *The Decay of Lying: Pen, Pencil and Poison; the Critic as Artist; the Truth as Masks.* New York: BiblioBazaar, 2009.

Wittgenstein, Ludwig. *Lectures and Conversations on Aesthetics, Psychology & Religious Belief.* Oxford: Blackwell, 1978.

NOTES

1   William James, *A Pluralistic Universe* (London: Longman, Green, 1909), 254.

2   Jacques Maritain, *Art and Scholasticism with Other Essays* (New York: reprinted by Kessinger Publishing (Undated), 1924), 3.

3   Maritain, *Art and Scholasticism with Other Essays*, 3.

4   George Steiner, *Real Presences* (Chicago: Chicago University Press, 1989), 118.

5   Steiner, *Real Presences*, 118.

6   Ludwig Wittgenstein, *Lectures and Conversations on Aesthetics, Psychology & Religious Belief* (Oxford: Blackwell, 1978), 3.

7   Wittgenstein, *Lectures and Conversations on Aesthetics, Psychology & Religious Belief,* 5.

8   Wittgenstein, *Lectures and Conversations on Aesthetics, Psychology & Religious Belief,* 7.

9   Ludwig Wittgenstein, *Lectures and Conversations on Aesthetics, Psychology & Religious Belief,* 8.

10   Oscar Wilde, *The Decay of Lying: Pen, Pencil and Poison; the Critic as Artist; the Truth as Masks* (New York: BiblioBazaar, 2009), 144.

11   William James, *Psychology* (New York: Macmillan, 1892), 152.

12   Arthur Schopenhauer, *The World as Will and Representation,* Vol.1 (New York: Dover Publications, 1969), 196.

13   Schopenhauer, *The World as Will and Representation*, 196–197.

14   Discussed in Schopenhauer, *The World as Will and Representation*, 179.

15   David Scott, "William James and Buddhism: American Pragmatism and the Orient," in *Religion* 30 (2000): 339.

16   James, *A Pluralistic Universe*, 462–463.

17   James, *A Pluralistic Universe*, 462–463.

18   James, *A Pluralistic Universe,* 288–289. Words in italics are the author's emphasis and not James.

19   Scott, "William James and Buddhism: American Pragmatism and the Orient," 340.

20   Scott, "William James and Buddhism: American Pragmatism and the Orient," 340.

21   James, *A Pluralistic Universe*, 93.

22   Scott, "William James and Buddhism: American Pragmatism and the Orient," 341.

23   See Maritain, *Art and Scholasticism with Other Essays*.

24 Schopenhauer, *The World as Will and Representation*, 178.

25 Adam Phillips introduction to Marion Milner, *The Hands of the Living God* (London: Routledge, 2011), xxiii.

26 Phillips in Milner, *The Hands of the Living God*, xxxi.

27 Phillips in Milner, *The Hands of the Living God*, xlvii.

28 Milner, *The Hands of the Living God*, 451.

29 Martin Heidegger, *Being and Time* (Oxford: Blackwell, 1997), 68.

30 Kitaro Nishida, *Fundamental Problems of Philosophy: The World of Action and the Dialectical World* (Tokyo: Sophia University Press, 1970), 184.

31 Steiner, *Real Presences*, 150.

32 Steiner, *Real Presences,* 150.

33 Steiner, *Real Presences,* 150. Words in italics are the author's emphasis and not Steiner's.

34 Daisetz T. Suzuki, *Zen and Japanese Culture* (Princeton: Princeton University Press, 2010), 123.

5

Plotting the Centre: Bramante's Drawings for the New St. Peter's Basilica

Nick Temple

METAPHYSICAL AND MATERIAL REFERENCES

> … the world does not have a [fixed] circumference. For if it had a fixed center,
> it would also have a [fixed] circumference; and hence it would have its own
> beginning and end within itself, and it would be bounded in relation to
> something else, and beyond the world there would be something else and space
> (locus). But all these [consequences] are false. Therefore, since it is not possible for
> the world to be enclosed between [a physical] center and physical circumference,
> the world – of which God is the center and the circumference – is not understood.
> And although the world is not finite, it cannot be conceived as finite, because it
> lacks boundaries within which it is enclosed.[1]

Nicolaus Cusanus' (Nicholas of Cusa) meditation on the nature and meaning of centre and circumference in the divine world pre-occupied not just Renaissance humanists and theologians, but also architects.[2] In particular, the idea that divine infinitude could somehow be 'circumscribed' as an architectural concept in religious buildings, with their bounded/enclosed spaces and geographically/topographically defined centres, concentrated the minds and imagination of architects. The quest for spatial and geometric coherence of divine centre finds expression in the myriad of architectural drawings that have been preserved from the fifteenth and early sixteenth centuries.

The tools and techniques deployed by the Renaissance architect to communicate this Cusanian idea drew upon a complex array of references, both symbolic and practical. In particular, through the agency of the sketch and presentation drawing it is possible to witness how these multiple references were negotiated and registered as a discursive framework of relationships to give spatial definition to the received onto-theological order of the cosmos. A salient feature of this objective is the manner in which the search for geometrical and mathematical precision, in the articulation and connectivity of spaces, was informed by an equal concern for their visual coherence and persuasiveness (through the techniques of perspective and orthographic projection) and their accommodation within a pre-existing urban context and cultural milieu. The drawing served as a contemplative datum in which to reconcile these relationships here, whereby the marks on paper – with their references to certain exemplary models – provided indicators, or gestures, for more concrete relationships that were as yet undefined but nevertheless open to possibility and ultimate realization.

This chapter explores an aspect of this process through an examination of a selection of drawings for the new St. Peter's Basilica by Donato Bramante (1444–1514) and his assistants Baldassare Peruzzi (1481–1536) and Antonio da Sangallo the Younger (1484–1546). The drawings focus on the relationship between principal and secondary spaces and their supporting structural elements, highlighting how the design of St. Peter's was conceived as a constellation of spaces that emanate from the crossing of the basilica. Bramante was seeking to convey in these drawings spatial and symbolic continuity between the old and the new basilica, through their transparent and diaphanous superimposition. The many changes and revisions made by Bramante and his assistants, in the design of the crossing and its subsidiary spaces, highlight uncertainties about the methods and processes deployed in redefining the centre(s) of the building – in both a physical and metaphysical sense. Interestingly, these methods sometimes involved recto-verso and mirrored relationships, whereby the two faces (or two halves) of a drawing convey mutual dependence.

The study considers how Bramante sought to reconcile philosophical/theological notions of centre in terms of a broadly Christian/Platonic outlook in early sixteenth century Rome, with the requirements to accommodate existing spatial and topographical conditions, as they relate to the location of the tomb of St Peter. This chapter explores how these potentially conflicting conditions were reconciled by suggesting that Bramante sought to resolve in architectural terms theological and philosophical challenges by a combination of drawing, numerical ordering and geometric reckoning.

NUMERICAL ORDERING/GEOMETRIC RECKONING

Initial clues to Bramante's treatment of the scheme for the new St. Peter's Basilica, as a discursive problem between physical and metaphysical, real and ideal, earthly and heavenly, can be found in an unexpected work; the *School of Athens* fresco in the Stanza della Segnatura in the Vatican Palace. Executed around 1509 by Raphael, the scene of discoursing philosophers, set in a monumental architectural ensemble with representations of Plato and Aristotle at its centre, forms part of a larger cycle of frescoes in the Stanza. Reference to the *School of Athens* in this study is justified in part by claims that Bramante was the author of the perspective construction of the fresco.[3] For the purposes of the present argument, the investigation of the fresco will be limited to specific features that indicate a particular thinking about orientation and centring of ideal space, which I contest also informed Bramante's scheme for St. Peter's.[4]

The location of the fresco, on the east wall of the chamber and oriented towards the *Disputa* on the west wall, tells us something about a key aspect of the iconography of the fresco cycle; namely that philosophical knowledge 'prepares the way' for the revealed truth of divine knowledge, the principal theme underpinning the *Disputa*. The 'destination' of this spiritual journey, as defined by the orientation of the two frescoes, is the new St Peter's Basilica, located to the west of the Stanza, which at the time was under construction. The investigation extends Manfredo Tafuri's argument that the frescoes of the Stanza constitute a 'manifesto' of the architectural projects of Julius II in Rome.[5] The *Disputa* could be said to serve in Augustinian terms as an expression of *civitas* (the community of citizens), highlighted by the dominance of pious/holy figures at the expense of conspicuous architectural elements, whereas the *School of Athens* represents *urbs* (the physical city), indicated by its more concrete reference to building (in the form of a central coffered vaulted structure redolent of Bramante's scheme for St. Peter's).

The transformation, moreover, from painted scenes to actual building (the new basilica) is unleashed through the properties of number and geometry – the 'building blocks' of the Christian/Platonic cosmology. This connection, as I will demonstrate, entailed a translation from Pythagorean number and Euclidean geometry to the perspective construction of pictorial space. Initial clues to this relationship can be found in two *tabulae* (chalk-boards) located in the foreground of the *School of Athens*; on the extreme right and left hand sides that face the *Disputa* opposite. Rather like Bramante's preparatory sketches for the new basilica, these tablets could be said to serve as a conceptual 'record' of the project. To the left, we see the tablet represented in the form of an abacus, with various numerical symbols highlighted on its black surface. The meaning of these symbols is easy to determine; the triangular configuration of the *Tetractys* in Roman numerals is superimposed on a representation of the musical ratios (*diatessaron, diapente, diapason*) highlighted in Greek letters. The tablet, which is held by an admiring youth in the fresco, is partly inclined and oriented within the perspectival grid of the paved floor. On his left is an elderly bearded figure with open book and pen in hand, and shown recording information from the abacus. Identified as a representation of Pythagoras, the figure provides a further clue to the symbolic meaning of this part of the fresco.

Balancing this arrangement is the other tablet, on the right hand side and laid flat on the pavement, with a figure shown bending over with dividers in hand and measuring its contents. Like the inclined tablet opposite, the identity of the figure (most probably Euclid) is informed by the contents of the tablet – two interlocking triangles in the form of a six-pointed star. It seems likely that this configuration is intended to complement the numerical representations on the other tablet, by invoking geometric reckoning. The precise meaning of the two triangles, however, is less certain given that its configuration is not completely accounted for in the propositions of Euclid's *Elements*. The uncertainty centres on whether the geometric figure is an equilateral hexagram (or six-pointed star), as some have argued, or some other 'hybrid' configuration.[6] For Simonetta Valtieri, the ratios of the intersecting sides of the superimposed triangles (with the inclusion of the

5.1   Raphael, *School of Athens* (c.1509). Vatican, Stanza della Segnatura, showing Euclid's diagram (from the right-hand tablet in fresco) superimposed according to Valtieri. Source: Photo: Scala, Florence © 1990

diagonal chords) match the Pythagorean numbers recorded on the Tetractys on the other tablet.[7] Valtieri further argues that the geometry may have been used to map the architectural background of the fresco. Further, Robert Haas has demonstrated that the foreshortening of the geometric figure on the 'Euclidean' tablet is more exaggerated than one would expect within the perspective projection of the fresco.[8] What is important however to recognize in this configuration is what Enrico Guidi describes as '... a knowledge of irrational, i.e. immeasurable numbers: numbers which cannot be measured by mathematics, but only by geometry.'[9]

It seems therefore that Raphael was trying to communicate a double meaning in the relationship between both *tabulae*: firstly to reconstruct the shift from Pythagorean whole numbers, and their cosmic associations, to the status of irrational numbers in Euclidean geometry, and consequentially the 'perspectival' transformation of geometry itself. Indeed, the content and pictorial relationships between both tablets in the fresco conveys this translation; from the virtual uprightness of Pythagoras' tablet, of 'elemental' whole numbers, to the exaggerated foreshortened tablet of Euclid (laid flat on the gridded floor) invoking 'optical' geometry, and finally to the larger perspective of the whole fresco. This translation is further amplified by the likelihood that the figure representing Euclid, shown holding dividers in hand over the right hand tablet, is a portrait of Bramante himself ('*Prospettico melanese depictore*').[10] Given Bramante's probable authorship of the background architectural ensemble of the fresco, this double identity is compelling evidence of an intentional connection between Greek philosophical thought and humanism.[11]

The question of how number and geometry (and by implication Greek thought and humanism) were intended to be understood in the *School of Athens* finds a useful precedent in Leonardo da Vinci's *Last Supper*, as examined by Leo Steinberg.[12] In his argument, Steinberg makes the case that both number and geometry are conceived not as competing or conflicting systems, but 'rather as expressions of the same unified cosmological order, albeit revealed through different modes of understanding.'[13] He uses the term 'duplexity' to explain how perspective provides the visual armature for disclosing this dialogue between the traditions of numerical ordering and geometric reckoning.[14] We will see shortly how this understanding informed Bramante's drawings for the new St. Peter's Basilica. It seems evident that by the early part of the 16th century, as the *School of Athens* demonstrates, this duplexity takes on more explicit terms of reference, reflecting a conscious attempt to conceive humanism (and Julius II's Pontificate in particular) as the inheritor Greek learning.

As I have suggested elsewhere, the relationships between number and geometry, in the two *tabulae*, are ultimately reconciled by the presence of Plato in the fresco.[15] In particular, Plato's left hand, which holds a copy of the *Timaeus*, coincides with the vanishing point of the perspective, from which the paved floor radiates out to 'meet' the groups of figures gathered around the two tabulae.[16] Here, visual coherence conveys, in rhetorical terms, continuity between ancient Greek philosophy and Renaissance humanism.

Seen in this context, the iconography of the *School of Athens* could be said to reveal, at one level, a form of 'handing down' of philosophical principles, which in turn present the first glimmerings of Christian Trinitarian symbolism. The triad of classical thinkers (Pythagoras, Plato and Euclid) provides therefore the basis for conceiving a humanistic rendering of the mystery of the Trinity variously prophesied through numerical ordering and geometric reckoning, and culminating in the representation of the Host at the vanishing point of the *Disputa* opposite.

This rather compressed (and simplistic) interpretation of the symbolism of the *School of Athens* I believe provides a useful backdrop to Bramante's design for the new St Peter's Basilica, in the way the fresco articulates a transmission from Christian-Platonic cosmology to pictorial space, from metaphysics to the representations of practical life. If we accept Valtieri's argument, then this transmission is effectively codified in the two *tabulae*; their inscribed configurations constitute the recto (Pythagorean number) and verso (Euclidean geometry) of a unified cosmological system. At the same time, they communicate in symbolic terms the orientation and 'centring' of the *School of Athens* in relation to the *Disputa*, the expression of divine knowledge.

THE IDEAL IN THE REAL

By the time Raphael executed the *School of Athens*, in 1509, the construction of the new basilica was already underway. The ground was broken on 18th April 1506 for the foundation stone and construction of the first corner piers of the crossing. Most of the drawings to be examined here probably predate the construction of the new basilica.

Two works that have a particular bearing on the original design and foundation of the basilica will serve as a starting point here. The first is the famous parchment plan of the basilica which gives us a picture of Bramante's vision for the building. The second is the foundation horoscope for the new basilica, which was thought to register the planetary positions on the day of the basilica's foundation. The layout of the new St Peter's Basilica, as indicated in the parchment plan, has been the subject of intense debate.[17] It was almost certainly used as a presentation drawing to Julius II and his court in early 1506. It is likely that models accompanied the drawing, as was usual practice for design projects during the Renaissance.[18] The significance of the plan lies in its description of only half of the basilica. This arrangement is likely to reflect in part uncertainty at the time about whether the new building should be centralized or longitudinal. The drawing further demonstrates Bramante's focus on resolving the crossing as the principal generator of the whole scheme, reinforced by the fact that the construction of the new basilica actually began in this area. In most modern reconstructions of Bramante's original design, the parchment plan is handed to convey a centralized scheme. Recognising the ambiguity of the plan, was it intended to be seen as a working drawing, to relay practical information, or an 'iconic' work endowed with specific symbolic meanings? It seems plausible that it served both purposes, given the probable expectations of such a drawing of a revered building to explain the layout of spaces, and at the same time to convey a sense of the symbolic significance of the site of St. Peter's burial.

The idea of mirroring the half-plan, to reveal its complete form, tells us something about the role of drawing at this time, as a form of revelation; parallel to the recto-verso relationship (as seen for example in numismatics), the mirrored image renders the idea of representation as being in possession of a hidden counterpart (or 'other'), redolent of the two faces of Janus – an analogy moreover that has a particular bearing on the possible symbolism of Bramante's scheme.[19]

The question of how the form and layout of the new St. Peter's Basilica would have been understood by Julius II and his court would no doubt have been influenced by the revised interest in Platonic thought during the Renaissance.[20] This assumption, however, has recently received some criticism, on the basis that it ignores a broader understanding of the reception of antiquity in the Renaissance.[21] Notwithstanding these disputes, Rudolf Wittkower's interpretation will serve as an initial reference in this examination of Bramante's drawings for the new St. Peter's, recognising also the evident importance of this tradition in the *School of Athens*. One of the more common geometric configurations, associated with the Pythagorean/Platonic tradition in architecture, is the rotational square (the so-called 'quadrature' or 'Roriczer' series) as we see in ecclesiastical buildings and in

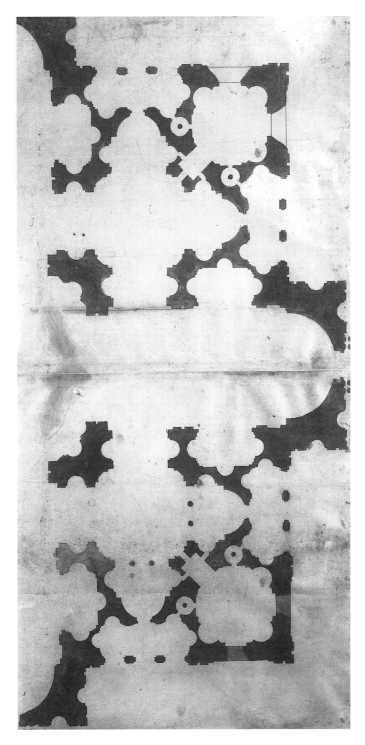

5.2   Donato Bramante, Parchment Plan of New St. Peter's Basilica (Summer, 1505?), Florence, Galleria degli Uffizi, Gabinetto Disegni e Stampe, Uff.1A

the design of urban spaces from the Late Middle Ages. Examined recently in Marvin Trachtenberg's *Dominion of the Eye*, the quadrature can also be traced in Bramante's plan for the new St. Peter's Basilica, whereby major and minor spaces are informed by this rotating geometry.[22] Probably derived from the famous problem posed by Socrates to the slave boy in Plato's dialogue, the *Meno*, the rotational technique conveys not just the proportional relationships between spaces, in the plan of the new St. Peter's, but also their translation into the three dimensional volumes of the whole building a feature that would probably have been highlighted in the supporting models of the building presented to the Pope.[23]

This brings us to the second work to be considered here; the foundation horoscope of the new Basilica, where we see the same geometry applied.[24] Whilst the use of the rotational square in horoscopes, to highlight the twelve zodiacal signs, is not without precedent, its appearance here may have been a conscious acknowledgement of the layout and symbolism of the new basilica. Traditionally, as Rachel Ann Seely states, 'The temple is oriented toward the four world regions, or cardinal directions, and to various celestial bodies such as the polar star.'[25] We can see how this principle was enthusiastically adopted by Bramante in his scheme for St Peter's, in part to emulate the Temple of Jerusalem. At one level the mirrored plan of the parchment drawing reveals Bramante's Greek cross plan, set on the cardinal points, with the east-west axis as the primary orientation to the tomb of St. Peter and the altar. This beautifully echoes the alignments of the horoscope, organized around each rotating square quadrant. One can see how the horoscope could be construed as a celestial 'mirror' of Bramante's plan of the basilica, in the way the hierarchy of constellations is reflected in the spatial treatment of primary and secondary zones. The mirroring between the spatial footprint of the building (articulated in the handed parchment plan) and its 'reflected' cosmological diagram (the geometrized horoscope) could be further understood as a recto-verso relationship, in the way actual and ideal, terrestrial and celestial, visual and metaphysical are inextricably paired and oriented either earthbound or skyward. We will probably never know for certain if the author of the horoscope directly drew inspiration from Bramante's scheme, nor indeed to what extent Bramante was consciously alluding to the cosmological meanings and astrological associations of the *quadrature* in his design. It would seem unlikely however that such connections were not an underlying factor in the intended symbolism of the new basilica; the 'fulcrum' of the Roman Catholic Church.

Notwithstanding the importance of this geometry, in the conception of the design, it is a general misunderstanding that proportional and geometric principles were applied as readymade systems in the design process; that architecture was effectively 'generated' from these arrangements. James Ackerman alludes to this when he states: 'Perhaps the character of Renaissance architecture owes much to the fact that its monuments started, not from a complete idea, fixed in the symbolism of the blueprint, but from the flexible impressions constantly susceptible to change.'[26] This misunderstanding, moreover, also has much to do with a misreading of the role of architectural drawing, as Marco Frascari argues: 'Architectural lines create a *graphesis*, a course of actions based on factures by

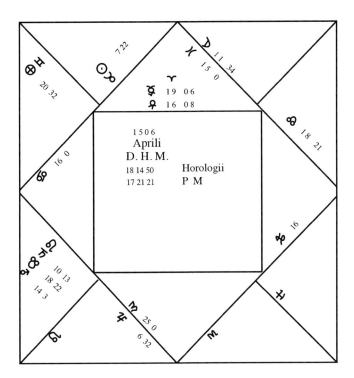

5.3   Foundation Horoscope for New St. Peter's Basilica, 1506 (published 1552), Luca Gaurico (redrawn by Stephen Calcutt)

which architects actualize future and past architecture into representations. Architectural drawings must not be understood as visualizations of building, but as essential architectural factures.'[27] Frascari's notion of 'facture' lies, I believe, at the heart of Bramante's design process for the new St. Peter's Basilica; the drawings are not technical or instrumental recordings, in the modern sense, but are rather heuristic expressions of possible (albeit incomplete) scenarios of the scheme. This attribution of drawing is especially revealing when we consider the issue of whether Bramante envisaged the new basilica to be centralized or longitudinal in plan. As Meg Licht argues: whilst 'some attention is paid to both the outer perimeters of the building and its internal spatial divisions', the question of the overall configuration of the building is largely 'left in suspense.'[28] This ambiguity should not be viewed as indicative of indecisiveness, on the part of the architect and his patron, but rather as reflecting an implicit recognition of the temporality of architecture (and by implication of the design process), whereby the memory of the old St. Peter's Basilica is permanently embedded in the emergence of the new. To put it another way, architectural drawing at this time was guided by a sense of the symbolic meanings of spaces, in which design (*disegno*) constituted a form of creative 're-enactment' of a pre-existing onto-theological order. We can see this for example in Uffizi A 20r where Bramante superimposes a version of the plan of new St. Peter's over the layout of the old Constantinian basilica; as if the old and the new co-exist. This idea permeated the design and construction of the new basilica for almost a hundred years, most clearly exemplified in Tiberio Alfarano's famous 1571 drawing of St Peter's.[29]

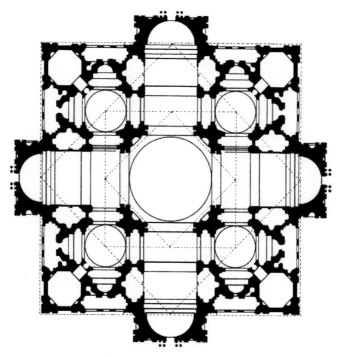

5.4   Plan of New St. Peter's Basilica, indicating application of the 'Rotating Square'. Source: Drawing: Nick Temple

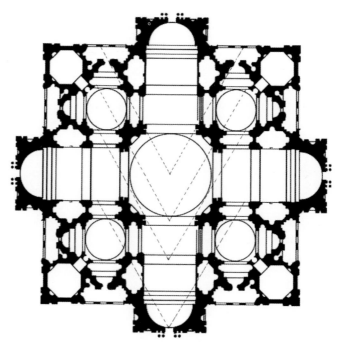

5.5   Plan of New St. Peter's Basilica, indicating sequence of 60 degree angles of vision, Gretta Tritch. Source: Drawing: Nick Temple

PERSPECTIVIZING CENTRE

Bramante's pre-occupation with the plan, as the principal mode of representation in the design process, was accompanied by a new innovation, the supporting perspective sketch. As Ann C. Huppert argues, Bramante's drawings for the new St. Peter's Basilica reveal for the first time an attempt to combine the practices of orthographic projection – principally the plan – with perspective renderings of parts of the building.[30] This is demonstrated in Uffizi A20r, 20v and A7945v, where thumb-nail perspective sketches are used to convey parts of the interior, notably the transition from supporting piers to the spandrels and domed vaulting above. In each case the sketch is located alongside or within the plan (to which it directly refers), and serves as a quick approximation of the architectural conjunctions. In these supporting sketches, however, there is no evidence that Bramante was particularly concerned with the detailed application of the architectural orders, and their relationship to the ornamental treatment of surfaces. Instead we are presented with perspective renderings that express the broad geometric volumes of the spaces, in which classical architectural elements are only sparsely represented as abbreviated references. We have to wait until Antonio da Sangallo the Younger to find examples of drawings for the new St. Peter's (such as Uffizi A 70r) that more systematically explore the full vocabulary of classical architecture through sectional details and elevations.[31]

What is evident in Bramante's drawings is a sense in which the geometric layout of the plan, and its proportional arrangement of spaces, was consciously translated into three-dimensional foreshortened snap-shorts, by means of the techniques of freehand perspective. The combination moreover of perspective sketch and measured plan is especially revealing since the inscribed spaces attempt in various ways to redefine relationships between centre and periphery; between void and supporting structure. Interestingly, this process often entailed retracing building outlines through the use of recto-verso drawings. We can see this for example in Uff.107, which shows different solutions for the south-east corner of the basilica.[32] Bramante's attempt to define these peripheral zones, as 'satellite' spaces of the nucleus of the Basilica, is demonstrated in the way he includes on the recto an outline of the circular dome above (no doubt to serve as a microcosm of the principal dome of the basilica) and the inclusion of a supplementary perspective view of part of the internal elevation of the space (to echo the articulation of the main crossing). Through the visible trace of the drawings on both recto and verso sides, which registers the thickness and porosity of the paper, we are given a greater visceral sense of the spatial/volumetric features of the plan.

Bramante's adoption of perspective drawing, to explore elements of the scheme, may have had a more direct bearing on the design of the building. This idea relates to an assertion made by Gretta Tritch that Bramante's design for St. Peter's was more indebted to Aristotelian principles, since the plan of the Basilica was conceived with the experiences of the spaces more in mind than their metaphysical properties.[33] Tritch argues that the layout was partly conceived perspectively, using the 60 (rather than the 90) degree field of vision. This, she suggests, is indicated by the progression through the spaces (from east to west), where the locations of supporting piers (many of which are recorded in Bramante's perspective sketches) frame a sequence of 60 degree views.[34] This argument, however, should be treated with some caution, given that, as Alberto Pérez-Gómez states: 'It was impossible for the Renaissance architect to conceive that the truth of the world could be reduced to its visual representation, a two-dimensional diaphanous section of the pyramid of vision.'[35]

Considered in the context of the translation from number and geometry to perspective, it seems clear that the 'altering' (or reconstructing) of reality through perspective formed part of a still pervasive onto-theological (transcendent) order, in which pictorial space represented a more perfect – other-worldly – domain. But can we speak of perspective in the same symbolic terms when comparing Bramante's thumb-nail sketches for the new St. Peter's with his likely authorship of the design of the architectural background of the *School of Athens*? More generally, can the representational techniques adopted in painting and architectural design at this time be treated in the same way? This touches on a more extensive debate, beyond the scope of this present study, concerning the principles of perspective codified in Alberti's famous *de pictura* and their relevance to architecture.[36]

We know that by the early sixteenth century perspective drawing becomes much more integrated in architectural design, evidenced in the various schemes for St. Peter's Basilica from Bramante onwards. My comparison between the *School of Athens* and Bramante's designs for the St. Peter's touches on the more specific issue of centring and orientating of both real and imaged space, and the manner in which perspective was deployed to achieve this goal. Steinberg's term duplexity, as applied to Leonardo da Vinci's *Last Supper* described earlier, comes to mind here in the way perspective is deployed to bring into dialogue the real and the ideal, number and geometry. Departing from Albertian principles of perspective as an independent and codified form of pictorial representation, we can see how it served a 'supplementary' role in Bramante's design of the new St. Peter's. This is demonstrated in Uff.107 A (referred to earlier) and Uff.7945 A. In the first, the

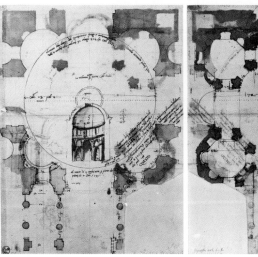
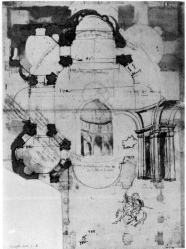

5.6   Donato Bramante, Sketch (plans and perspectives) of New St. Peter's Basilica (Summer, 1505?), Florence, Galleria degli Uffizi, Gabinetto Disegni e Stampe, Uff.107A. (recto & verso).]

sectional perspective sketch (on the recto side), with the shadowed opening of the oculus clearly visible, is drawn within the central domed space, so that it extends between the perimeter structure and the domed centre of the plan. In a rather different vein, Bramante used the verso side Uff.7945 to explore the main crossing of the basilica, by highlighting through a combination of plan, perspective and outline geometries, the relation between the volume of the new basilica and the location of the apse and altar of the old. In both drawings therefore, plan and perspective are intended to be read together as a single composite drawing to redefine spatially the idea of centre through its vertical and horizontal alignments.

The resulting tension between the reality of built form and its exemplary model pervaded Bramante's design for the new basilica. At one level we are given an impression of this tension in the celebrated parchment plan, where the search for both symbolic and aesthetic expression, in the articulation of spaces, resulted in compromises in the structural integrity of the building, in particular the insufficient size of the four piers at the crossing to bear the significant loads of the superstructure above.[37]

CONCLUSION

Implicit in Bramante's drawings for the new St. Peter's Basilica is a sense that the 'entire project, at every stage, unfolds from its nucleus.'[38] This point is reinforced by Ackerman in reference to both the drawings of the new St. Peter's and the competition entries for San Giovanni dei Fiorentini (executed under Julius II's successor, Leo X), in which he states: 'In churches the great trend toward the central plan was accompanied by a method of design that can be described only as centrifugal. The architect starts drawing in the centre and works outwards, and it is not until he has reached a final solution that he begins to consider what the outer face should be.'[39] It seems that this pre-occupation with centre pervaded architectural thinking during this period and reflected a desire to 'situate' actual (sacred) spaces within a pre-ordained Christian-Platonic cosmological order.

The resulting progression from centre to periphery in the design process meant that many subsidiary spaces of churches were treated as constellations of the principal centre, namely the crossing. Through drawing we can see how this progression entailed an on-going negotiation between figure-ground, geometric and proportional relationships and perspective reconstructions, of which the sheet of paper or parchment provided a physical datum for redefining the notion of the 'ideal in the real' as it pertains to the techniques of reflective or recto-verso relationships.

BIBLIOGRAPHY

Ackerman, James S. "Architectural Practice in the Italian Renaissance," in *Journal of the Society of Architectural Historians*, Vol. 13, No. 3 (October 1954): 3–11.

Cusanus, Nicolaus. *On Learned Ignorance*. Trans. Jasper Hopkins. Minneapolis: Banning, 1981.

Davies, Paul. "La Madonna delle Carceri in Prato," in *Architectural History*, Vol. 36 (1993): 1–18.

Frascari, Marco. "Lines as Architectural Thinking," in *Architectural Theory Review*, Vol. 14, No. 3 (2009): 200–12.

Goffi, Federica. "Drawing Imagination and Imagination of Drawing: The Case of Tiberio Alfarano's Drawing of St. Peter's Basilica," in *Interstices: A Journal of Architecture and Related Arts: The Traction of Drawing*, Vol. 11 (2010): 20–30.

Haas, Robert. "Raphael's *School of Athens*: A Theorem in a Painting?" in *Journal of Humanistic Mathematics*, Vol. 2, No. 2 (July 2012): 2–26.

Hall, Marcia (ed.). *Raphael's School of Athens*. Cambridge: Cambridge University Press, 1997.

Hankins, James. *Plato in the Italian Renaissance*, 2 vols. Leiden: E.J. Brill, 1990.

Harries, Karsten. *Infinity and Perspective*. Cambridge, Mass: MIT Press, 2001.

Hubbert, Ann C. "Envisioning New St. Peter's: Perspectival Drawings and the Process of Design," in *Journal of the Society of Architectural Historians*, Vol. 68, No. 2 (2009): 158–77.

Joost-Gaugier, Christiane L. *Raphael's Stanza della Segnatura: Meaning and Invention*. Cambridge: Cambridge University Press, 2002.

Lampugnani, Vittorio Magnago and Henry A. Millon. *The Renaissance from Brunelleschi to Michelangelo: The Representation of Architecture*. Milan: Bompiani, 1994.

Licht, Meg. "I Ragionamenti – Visualising St. Peter's," in *Journal of the Society of Architectural Historians*, Vol. 44, No. 2 (May, 1985): 111–28.

March, Lionel. *Architectonics of Humanism: Essays on Number in Architecture*. Chichester: Academy Editions, 1998.

Nesselrath, Arnold. *Raphael's School of Athens: Recent Restorations, Vatican Museums*, Vol. 1. Vatican City State: Edizioni Musei Vaticani, 1997.

Padovan, Richard. *Proportion: Science, Philosophy, Architecture*. London: Spon Press, 2001.

Pérez-Gómez, Alberto. "Questions of Representation: The Poetic Origin of Architecture," in *Architectural Research Quarterly*, Vol. 9, Nos. 3/4 (2005): 217–25.

_____. "Architecture as Drawing," in *Journal of Architectural Education*, Vol. 36, No. 2 (Winter, 1982): 2–7.

Quinlan-McGrath, Mary. "The Foundation Horoscope(s) for St. Peter's Basilica, Rome, 1506: Choosing a Time, Changing the *Storia*," in *Isis*, Vol. 92, No. 4 (December 2001): 716–41.

Rowland, Ingrid. *The Culture of the High Renaissance: Ancients and Moderns in Sixteenth Century Rome*. Cambridge: Cambridge University Press, 2001.

Sbacchi, Michele. "Euclidism and Theory of Architecture," in *Nexus Network Journal*, Vol. 3, Issue 2, (September 2001): 25–38

_____. "Projective Architecture," in *Nexus Network Journal*, Vol. 11, No. 3 (December 2009): 441–54.

Seely, Rachel Ann. "St. Peter's Basilica as *Templum Dei*: Continuation of the Ancient Near Eastern Temple Tradition in the Christian Cathedral," in *Studia Antiqua*, Vol. 4, No. 1 (Winter 2005): 63–80.

Tafuri, Manfredo. "Roma Instaurata," in *Raffaello Architetto*. Eds. C. L. Frommel, S. Ray, and M. Tafuri. Milan: Electa Editrice, 1984.

_____. *La ricerca del rinascimento*. Turin: Einaudi, 1992.

Temple, Nicholas. *Disclosing Horizons: Architecture, Perspective and Redemptive Space*.
London: Routledge, 2007.

_____. *Renovatio urbis: Architecture, Urbanism and Ceremony in the Rome of Julius II*.
London: Routledge, 2011.

Trachtenberg, Marvin. *Dominion of the Eye*. Cambridge: Cambridge University Press, 2008.

Tritch, Gretta. "Questioning the Philosophical Influence of Beauty and Perception in
Bramante's First Scheme for St. Peter's," in *Inquiry*, Vol. 6 (2005): 1–23.

Valtieri, Simonetta. "La Scuola di Atene," in *Mitteilungen des Kunsthistorischen Institutes in
Florence*, XVI (1972): 63–72.

Vasari, Giorgio. *Lives of the Painters, Sculptors and Architects*. Trans. A. B. Hinds. New York:
Dutton, 1963.

Wittkower, Rudolf. *Architectural Principles in the Age of Humanism*, London: Academy
Editions, 1977.

NOTES

1   Nicholaus Cusanus, *On Learned Ignorance*, trans. Jasper Hopkins (Minneapolis:
Banning, 1981), Ch. II of Book 2, 114. Quoted in Karsten Harries, *Infinity and Perspective*
(Cambridge, Mass: MIT Press, 2001), 47.

2   Rudolf Wittkower is quite explicit about the importance of the Cusanian geometric
model in Renaissance concepts of centre: 'The most perfect geometrical figure
is the circle and to it was given special significance. To understand fully this new
emphasis we must turn for a moment to Nicholas of Cusa who had transformed the
scholastic hierarchy of static spheres, of spheres immovably related to one centre,
the earth, into a universe uniform in substance and without a physical or ideal centre.
In this new world of infinite relations the incorruptible certitude of mathematics
assumed unprecedented importance. Mathematics is for Cusanus a necessary vehicle
for penetrating to the knowledge of God, who must be envisaged through the
mathematical symbol. Cusanus, developing a pseudo-hermetic formula, visualises Him
as the least tangible and at the same time the most perfect geometrical figure, the
centre and circumference of the circle.' Rudolf Wittkower, *Architectural Principles in the
Age of Humanism* (London: Academy Editions, 1977), 28.

3   The claim largely derives from Vasari (1568); Giorgio Vasari, *Lives of the Painters,
Sculptors and Architects*, trans. A. B. Hinds (New York: Dutton, 1963), Vol. 2, 187. Ralph
E. Lieberman however argues the contrary, since Bramante's extensive and laborious
design of the crossing piers of the new St. Peter's Basilica could not compare with
'so unconvincing and irrational a passage as the one we see [in the fresco].' 'The
Architectural Background', in Marcia Hall (ed.), *Raphael's School of Athens* (Cambridge:
Cambridge University Press, 1997), 64–84, 73.

4   Literature on the *School of Athens*, and the fresco cycle in the Stanza della Segnatura
in general, is extensive. Recent studies include: Christiane L. Joost-Gaugier, *Raphael's
Stanza della Segnatura: Meaning and Invention* (Cambridge: Cambridge University
Press, 2002); Marcia Hall (ed.), *Raphael's School of Athens* (Cambridge: Cambridge
University Press, 1997), Nicholas Temple, *renovatio urbis: Architecture, Urbanism and
Ceremony in the Rome of Julius II* (London: Routledge, 2011), 214–63.

5   Manfredo Tafuri, 'Roma Instaurata', in C.L. Frommel, S. Ray and M. Tafuri, *Raffaello Architetto* (Milan: Electa Editrice, 1984), pp. 59–106, 63. See also, Temple, *renovatio urbis,* 214–63.

6   For a detailed investigation of the various theories, relating to the identity and meaning of the geometry, see Robert Haas, 'Raphael's *School of Athens*: A Theorem in a Painting?', *Journal of Humanistic Mathematics*, Vol. 2, No. 2 (July 2012), 2–26. The case for the hexagram is based on both geometric integrity and symbolic meaning (Magen David), the latter alluded to by the presence of hexagrams in the floor mosaics in the Stanza.

7   Simonetta Valtieri, 'La Scuola di Atene', *Mitteilungen des Kunsthistorischen Institutes in Florence*, XVI (1972), 63–72.

8   Haas, 'Raphael's *School of Athens*', 12–15.

9   Arnold Nesselrath, *Raphael's School of Athens: Recent Restorations, Vatican Museums*, Vol. 1 (Vatican City State: Edizioni Musei Vaticani, 1997), 29.

10   On Bramante as the 'Prospettico melanese depictore', see: Ingrid Rowland, *The Culture of the High Renaissance: Ancients and Moderns in Sixteenth Century Rome* (Cambridge: Cambridge University Press, 2001), 105–08.

11   Underlying this connection however is a controversy during the Renaissance, concerning the relationship between Platonic/Pythagorean number and Euclidean geometry. Michele Sbacchi makes the case that the relationship was never resolved, but instead resulted in a dichotomy that has its roots in an "epistemological difference" evidenced in Plato's *Meno*. (M. Sbacchi, 'Euclidism and Theory of Architecture', *Nexus Network Journal*, Vol. 3, No. 2, (September 2001), 25–38, 3). Sbacchi argues that the Quattrocento saw the primacy of numerical ratios over geometrical relationships in architectural theory and practice, an assertion largely echoed by Wittkower (*Architectural Principles,* 101–16). Sbacchi highlights Alberti's predilection for numerical relationships to support his argument (Sbacchi, 'Euclidism and Theory of Architecture', 3). Both Richard Padovan and Lionel March however take a very different stance on this point; the former by some evidence of the use of irrational numbers by Alberti, and later Palladio (Richard Padovan, *Proportion: Science, Philosophy, Architecture* (London: Spon Press, 1999), 83), and in the latter by an argument that Alberti's treatment of *lineamenti* was an attempt to "fuse the irrationals of the *ad triangulatum* with the whole number ratios of *ad quadratum*." (Nicholas Temple, *Disclosing Horizons: Architecture, Perspective and Redemptive Space* (London: Routledge, 2007), 43; L. March, *Architectonics of Humanism: Essays on Number in Architecture* (Chichester: Academy Editions, 1998), 200).

12   L. Steinberg, *Leonardo's Incessant Last Supper* (New York: Zone Books, 2001), 56–7.

13   Temple, *Disclosing Horizons*, 43.

14   Steinberg, *Leonardo's Incessant Last Supper*, 56–7.

15   Temple, *renovatio urbis*, 214–63.

16   As arguably the most venerated ancient philosophical text in the early modern world, Plato's *Timaeus* was also considered by some, such as Marsilio Ficino, to be prophetic of Christian cosmology, an attribution underlined by the fact that Plato was nick-named the 'Attic Moses' (a title not even the nearby figure of Aristotle was given). One can see how Renaissance humanists would have interpreted the *Timaeus* as both building upon the numerological principles of Pythagoras (Plato's 'predecessor') and anticipating the geometric ideas of Euclid (Plato's 'successor').

17   Christoph Luitpold Frommel, 'St. Peter's: The Early History', in Henry A. Mellon and Vittorio Magnago Lampugnani (eds.), *The Renaissance from Brunelleschi to Michelangelo: The Representation of Architecture* (Milan: Bompiani, 1994), 399–423.

18   On Renaissance architectural models see Henry A. Millon, 'Models in Renaissance Architecture', in Millon & Lampugnani, *The Renaissance from Brunelleschi to Michelangelo*, 19–73.

19   This relates to my argument that Bramante's design for St. Peter's was partly inspired by the Janus Quadrifrons. Temple, *renovatio urbis*, 201–07.

20   Wittkower's interpretation of Bramante's centralized scheme for the new St Peter's is based on the assumption that 'The Renaissance conception of the perfect church is rooted in Plato's cosmology.' *Architectural Principles*, 23. On Platonism in the Renaissance see in particular, James Hankins, *Plato in the Italian Renaissance* (Leiden: E.J. Brill, 1990), Vols. 1 & 2.

21   Manfredo Tafuri, *La ricerca del rinascimento* (Turin: Einaudi, 1992), pp. 3–32; Paul Davies, 'La Madonna delle Carceri in Prato,' *Architectural History* 36 (1993), 1–18.

22   Marvin Trachtenberg, *Dominion of the Eye* (Cambridge: Cambridge University Press, 1997) pp. 118–19. See also my *Disclosing Horizons: Architecture, Perspective and Redemptive Space* (London: Routledge, 2007), 112–22.

23   This expression of the proportional relationships of volumes, in the model of buildings, is inferred in Alberti's assertion that models should 'exclude decoration... show plainly and simply the parts to be considered...[and] focus attention on certain calculated standards of architecture rather than on the ingenuity of the fabricator of the model.' Millon, 'Models in Renaissance Architecture', 22.

24   Mary Quinlan-McGrath, 'The Foundation Horoscope(s) for St. Peter's Basilica, Rome, 1506: Choosing a Time, Changing the *Storia*', *Isis*, Vol. 92, No. 4 (Dec. 2001), 716–41. The study is based on a horoscope published in 1552, which Quinlan-McGrath claims is actually a rectified version of the original produced in 1506.

25   Rachel Ann Seely, 'St. Peter's Basilica as *Templum Dei*: Continuation of the Ancient Near Eastern Temple Tradition in the Christian Cathedral', *Studia Antiqua*, Vol. 4, No. 1 (Winter, 2005), 63–80, 66.

26   James S. Ackerman, 'Architectural Practice in the Italian Renaissance', *Journal of the Society of Architectural Historians*, Vol. 13, No. 3 (Oct. 1954), pp. 3–11, 9.

27   Marco Frascari, 'Lines as Architectural Thinking', *Architectural Theory Review*, Vol. 14, No. 3 (2009), 200–12, 200.

28   Meg Licht, 'I Ragionamenti – Visualising St. Peter's, *Journal of the Society of Architectural Historians*, Vol. 44, No. 2 (May, 1985), 111–28, 111.

29   Federica Goffi, 'Drawing Imagination and Imagination of Drawing: The Case of Tiberio Alfarano's Drawing of St. Peter's Basilica', *Interstices: A Journal of Architecture and Related Arts: The Traction of Drawing*, Vol. 11, (2010), 20–30.

30   Frascari, 'Lines as Architectural Thinking', 201.

31   Ann C. Hubbert, 'Envisioning New St. Peter's: Perspectival Drawings and the Process of Design, *Journal of the Society of Architectural Historians*, Vol. 68, No. 2 (2009), 158–77.

32   Ackerman mistakenly identifies the recto drawing as a plan of the crossing, which is clearly not the case given the representation of the east entrance portico at the bottom. 'Architectural Practice', 7, Fig. 8.

33   Gretta Tritch, 'Questioning the Philosophical Influence of Beauty and Perception in Bramante's First Scheme for St. Peter's', *Inquiry*, Vol. 6 (2005), 1–23. Tritch's assumption however of a direct (and exclusive) correlation between perspective renderings of space and Aristotelian thought is simplistic, given that perspective at this time was not a 'reconstruction' of reality, and humanity's experience of it. See Alberto Pérez-Gómez, 'Questions of Representation: The Poetic Origin of Architecture', *Architectural Research Quarterly (arq)*, Vol. 9, Nos. 3/4 (2005), 217–25.

34   One implication of this argument, which Tritch does not highlight, is that the conscious use of perspective, to define the arrangement of the physical spaces, was informed in some way by the 'optical' correction of building elements (such as the profile of the supporting piers at the crossing). This argument, however, challenges the view of most historians that the techniques of optical correction in design only became fully established in the seventeenth century, thanks to the development of stereotomy. Michele Sbacchi, 'Projective Architecture', *Nexus Network Journal*, Vol. 11 (2009), 441–54, 447.

35   Pérez-Gómez, 'Questions of Representation', p. 220. In addition: '... the symmetrical correspondence between the elements of real objects and those of their images was not recognized. Objects, as rendered in perspective, were considered altered (*digradati* was the term frequently used). Attention was indeed paid to what was changed by projection.' Sbacchi, 'Projective Architecture', 446–47.

36   As Pérez-Gómez states, 'The opening pages of *De Re Aedificatoria* contend that design consists "in a right and exact adapting and joining together the lines and angles which compose and form the face of the building." The role of design was "to appoint the edifice and all its parts their proper places, determine number, just proportion and beautiful order." Design, however, was in Alberti's mind "inseparable from matter", so that drawing was perceived as the embodiment of architectural ideas, distinct from perspectives that represented (in painting), the reality of a building.' 'Architecture as Drawing', *Journal of Architectural Education*, Vol. 36, No. 2 (Winter, 1982), 2–7.

37   '... the St. Peter's crossing piers had to be flattened, much to the detriment of the handsome profile. This lack of technical discipline may explain in part why the High Renaissance is one of the few great eras in architectural history in which a new style emerges without the assistance of any remarkable structural innovation.' Ackerman, 'Architectural Practice', 4.

38   Licht, '*I Ragionamenti*', 112.

39   Ackerman, 'Architectural Practice', 9.

6

The Relationship Between Sketching and Painting in Chinese Traditional Aesthetics

Li Wenmin

Artists engage in sketching when they have ideas or subjects in mind. They leave the marks or traces as a drawn record. In Western art history sketching has often been regarded as speedy, exploratory, spontaneous or unfinished. Many Chinese paintings seem to echo this description in several regards. It is therefore interesting to analyze how sketches serve the final pieces in Chinese traditional painting. The sketch, as a way of studying the subject from life and as preparation for future works, is not common to the Chinese tradition and is not generally carried out by Chinese artists as part of their practice. Indeed, it is difficult to find sketches of ancient Chinese 'masters.'

As such, this chapter presents an attempt to investigate the relationship between life sketching and painting in traditional Chinese aesthetics. It does not intend to be a historical review of Chinese traditional painting but, rather, a discussion upon the methodology used in Chinese artists' sketches. This analysis will help to develop an understanding of aesthetic approaches to life sketching and its relation to painting. This process of sketching may seem similar to that of the West, but the fundamental value of capturing the likeness and the essence of the object distinguishes the significance of the sketch in its preparatory function in Chinese painting. It will be argued that the way to convey likeness and the essence of the object can be a particular means of evoking emotions and perceptions, which happens during the act of observation in order to draw from imaginary images and for mark-making activities.

Exploring drawing and sketches in a Western context has made my position as a Chinese researcher particularly interesting, as I have realized that I cannot isolate my Chinese heritage and cultural background from this work. Therefore, this chapter will also suggest how a contemporary artist may apply and interpret this traditional method in their drawing practice. Specifically, I have been interested in exploring the possibilities for a contemporary artist to interpret and apply the way Chinese traditional artists conveyed the object, underpinned by an appropriate understanding of the subject.

I would like to provide some background about the status of sketching in contemporary Chinese art practice before I discuss its role in Chinese traditional painting. Born in the 1970s I was educated in a 'Westernized' art education system in China, specifically as an oil painter. Contemporary Chinese art stems from Westernized art education, which was established in the early twentieth century. Whilst studying contemporary art practice in China in the 1990s sketching was a common exercise in addition to engaging in intensive academic drawing courses. Generally, we sketched what we observed, and life sketching was important as a practical way to gaining skills and experience. We would pose for each other after class to make sketches and drawings, and also went out to the countryside to sketch people or landscapes as part of the learning process. We drew what we saw in front of our eyes and quickly responded to it. There would be consideration of tones, structure and emotional reaction depicted of the subject. Sometimes these sketches are translated onto canvases. However, due to the convenience and immediacy offered by photographs we often chose to use them as references for our paintings instead of sketches. However, we still believed that sketching from life was a fundamental practice for an artist. Many Chinese artists express the same belief and their sketches are often incorporated into their paintings as a result.

In contrast to the approach to contemporary training, traditional art education in China is completely different, as it does not stress great importance on sketching from life. Chinese traditional artists commonly believed that it was an accurate, yet empty representation of the subject if the likeness was captured only through life sketching and drawing. Chen Zao, in his book chapter *Jiang hu chang weng ji* (*The treatise of jiang hu long old man*),[1] states when the artist poses the life model (dressed up, sitting still and looking serious) and look up at the model and down at the paper to draw that the image appears like a reflection in a mirror and like a wooden puppet.[2] The same argument also appears in a treatise by Su Shi, who was an important scholar and artist in the thirteenth century.[3] He suggested that if a model is dressed up and sitting still with fixed sight, how can an artist convey the essence of that model when such a subject is so unnaturally serious and tense. Therefore, there have been few methods of this kind used for teaching beginners how to capture subject likeness through life sketching in traditional Chinese education.

However, these examples do not suggest that the Chinese rejected learning from life drawing and nature. In fact, Chinese artists considered nature as a Master tradition from which to learn, to understand, to perceive and to represent. Many Chinese artists in history traveled extensively to grasp the essence of mountains and the landscape in order to better understand nature as a subject. There are also stories and anecdotes that relate to the pursuit of understanding nature for these artists. For example, Teng Chang from the tenth century had many different plants and flowers from which to observe, sketch and draw. One of his followers Zhao Chang (tenth and eleventh century), who liked drawing from his garden in the early morning dew, described himself as 'painting from life Zhao Chang.' But this literal translation of life painting in Zhao Chang's title contains two meanings, one of which is to learn from nature and the other is to paint in life to show his respect

THE RELATIONSHIP BETWEEN SKETCHING AND PAINTING IN CHINESE AESTHETICS   85

for it. In clarification, Zhang Chang was from a particular period when Chinese painting reached the peak of realism in style. This constituted an important transitional period when artists searched for ways of perceiving and expressing nature through realism, while simultaneously maintaining the 'truth' and 'essence' of the subject in artworks, hence searching for ways to represent objectivity, and yet retain the implications of experiential subjectivity. This approach dramatically declined in the Yuan Dynasty (1271–1368) that followed when social changes triggered transformations in societal ideologies.

Chinese artists have established an individual approach in learning and studying nature in terms of painting, which has fundamentally determined the manner by which they consider sketching from nature in relation to their artworks. Beginners learning Chinese traditional painting techniques start their curriculum by copying and imitating the works of ancient masters, from which they obtain the necessary skills and knowledge for depicting objects. This approach also allows the development of observation skills. This process is painstakingly slow however, yet considered worthwhile, as copying and imitating is believed to lead to a successful mastery of required skills. Indeed, it is considered the foundation to becoming a 'good' artist. The requirements of a skilled hand coupled with a profound understanding of the world and a 'virtuous temperament' are believed to be the keys to producing good artworks in this tradition. To reach the *spirit* of this is of primary concern, as copying constitutes one of the principles that indicates the importance of the learning process as it unfolded from 'borrowing' to 'creating.' Almost every Chinese artist working in this tradition meticulously copies and imitates the work of earlier masters so that they would be confident in creating their own, more individual, paintings. This is a very distinctive feature of teaching and learning in the Chinese tradition, which can also be found in educational disciplines such as learning literature by reciting the poems and essays of masters. Therefore, in being different to the emphasis laid upon life drawing in Western education, Chinese painting traditions have not established similar pedagogies in teaching students how to sketch and draw from life.

There is another important method that Chinese students must perfect, which is to learn to observe correctly and accurately. Chinese theories emphasise accurate and sensitive observation. Observation is the first lesson any draftsperson must take seriously to become adept. Nonetheless, this is not a distinctive Chinese trait, since precise observation was highly emphasized in both the East and the West. For instance, Leonardo da Vinci was one of the most meticulous and faithful observers of nature. In da Vinci's sketches of the body the structure is presented as accurately as possible with all bodily details observed. As Moshe Barasch argues, da Vinci wished to represent all there is in nature, with no omission or selection, by transforming the figure into a mirror of reality.[4] The boundary between his work and scientific statement became blurred for da Vinci as a consequence. Having said that, it remains to be the case that in Chinese traditional painting systems this form of scientific knowledge is reliant on careful observation and visual representation of objects.

Zheng Xie's (1693–1765), who was a master of bamboo painting in the early Qing Dynasty, statement on painting bamboo shows the function of observation in Chinese painting. He summarized three types of bamboo in the process of painting: the bamboo in the heart, the bamboo in the eyes and the bamboo in the hand.[5] When seeing bamboo in the morning light, with a foggy, shadowy, and frosty atmosphere around it, the artist has *Yi* 意 (translated as 'the spontaneous and individualistic expression,[6] and hidden meaning of the image in the artist's mind'),[7] which echoes the sense of the bamboo in the heart. Therefore, the artist has the impetus and inspiration for expressing this *Yi*. The bamboo in his eyes is not the same as that in his mind, and likewise the bamboo in his work is not the same as that in his mind. Therefore, *Yi* must be in the artist's thoughts prior to the actual act of mark making. This is the key principle. Not only does it require the artist to observe the object carefully, but it is also meant to stimulate his or her feelings and emotions to the point of enacting the expression through some kind of communion with the depicted object. The object therefore functions as a trigger to evoke the artist's creative responses to it. However the resulting 'sketch' is not mentioned at all in this process.

Likewise, some Italian artists from the sixteenth and seventeenth century shared a similar understanding, namely, that the process of externalizing the internal workings of the intellect as a form of creation is considered to be at the heart of the nature of drawing. Giorgio Vasari argues that drawing is initiated in the artist's mind.[8] In other words, as Federico Zuccari also noted, that which is to be expressed must firstly appear in the artist's mind.[9] Consequently, the inner design or idea preceded the act of the outer design or physical drawing, which is seen as the visualized shape of the structured idea through various media.[10] Therefore after careful and inspiring observation, the artist paints what stays in their heart of the subject matter. This imagery 'in the heart' derives from that in the eyes, and through sketches made by the hand it is expressed outwardly.

To further highlight the particulars of Chinese art practices, two artists from China will be discussed in this chapter in order to better exemplify the processes mentioned above, as these are manifested through the relationship between their sketches and paintings. Both were active on the Chinese art scene in the first half of the twentieth century when China was undergoing great changes in art education. However, these artists represent two different groups that were at work in Chinese modern/contemporary art scenes. The first is Huang Binhong (1865–1955), an artist who has never travelled abroad, and the second is Fu Baoshi (1904–1965), who studied art and theory in Japan. Their life sketches are made in a similar way, but work differently for their paintings.

Huang is considered one of the leading masters in modern China, particularly as an artist who made efforts to revitalize Chinese painting by working within the framework of the traditional. He focused on learning from the ancient masters by travelling extensively and going deep into the mountains to make sketches from nature until he was seventy years old. His distinctive style of painting reached maturity around his seventieth birthday, and most of his most successful works were made in his eighties and nineties. His paintings of mountains, noted for their blackness, density and boldness, were considered revolutionarily when compared to traditional depictions.

Fu Baoshi, however, studied overseas and tried to combine both Chinese pre-modern traditions with modern Western techniques. He learnt painting by making copies of ancient works in a mounting shop, and later received the assistance of Xu Beihong to study in Japan. Fu adopted traditional Chinese painting techniques of classical themes and motifs in depicting landscape and figures. In addition however, his work reflects pronounced influences from his artistic training in Japan, which can be seen clearly in the reproductions of his artworks. In these images it is possible to trace how life sketches contributed to his paintings.

In Fu's sketches and paintings, it is possible to see the close relationship of composition, atmospheric depiction and detail of the objects studied. His sketches were created from observation, and his paintings were faithful to what they conveyed. So, even though his techniques and skills show his understanding of traditional medium and process, his methods of transforming observation to creative making are greatly determined by the sketches of what he experienced on site. There is a close traceable relationship between his sketches and his paintings, with very few changes occurring between them.

In contrast, Huang shows how he applies Zheng Xie's 'three bamboo' theory in his paintings. By putting Huang's sketches and paintings together, one can recognize shapes, marks of landscape objects, but not in the same process as that seen in Fu's work. Huang also did many draft studies for his landscape paintings, and his final pieces did not appear to be from any given single sketch, but rather more of an amalgamation of all his sketches and not specifically representing any particular mountain or place. When this artist paints a mountain, there appears to be hundreds of faces of that mountain in his mind. The image of the mountain the artist intends to make therefore is the complex perception of the object fused with feelings that arise from observation. That is the mountain in his heart and the one in his eyes. The purpose is to convey the *Yi*, the mountain as experienced in his heart. Before the artist begins the painting of the mountain by his hand, he integrates what he seen into an image, or several images in his mind. Wang Zhongxiu discussed that '…Huang demonstrated his understanding of an early art theory in that there are tens and hundreds of thousands of trees, but there is no stroke of a tree; there are tens and hundreds of thousands of mountains, but there is no stroke of a mountain; there are tens and hundreds of thousands of strokes, there is no stroke; having is not having and not having is just having.'[11] In Huang's sketches, the strokes do not convey the exact shape or appearance of the object. But, his evoked emotions or associated imagery becomes the objects in his heart for his painting.

Learning this as a starting point to understand how I can apply core issues in Chinese painting, I have interpreted and applied it in my own sketch-to-drawing process as an artist. Before I execute any mark making, I learn to observe objects from my daily life. John Berger uses '…ruthless observation…'[12] to explain how it turned Watteau into a great artist, because this is not only a question of artists using their eyes but also a result of honesty, of their fighting with themselves to understand what they see. From the action of observing with honesty what I see, I learn how to respond to the objects that I will later draw.

The intentional activity of observing everyday things from my life as subjects for drawing has provided me with a good opportunity to look at these things from different perspectives and viewpoints, by perceiving different faces at different times, and shaped by distinct surroundings or various personal experiences. For instance, when I look at a tree that I pass on my way to school, it shows me different characters in different seasons, with the change of weather or in the way it appears in this particular suburban environment or in another. Sometimes when I pause to look up at its body and leaves, I follow the force of the growth of its trunk, or I sense the tenderness and freshness of its leaves in the spring or the way they become in the autumn after having gone through the mill. Through this, I respond to its physical appearance. Meanwhile, the changes in the tree also draw my attention from time to time to the manifestation of how it 'is' in look and feel. In doing so, I intend to capture the outer likeness and the object's nature, which has a particular kind of interaction with me.

Many depictions of birds I have drawn are the Indian Myna, which can be found everywhere in Sydney. In Australia, the Indian Myna is considered an invasive pest. Compared with the native hollow-nesting species, the Indian Myna is extremely aggressive. This aggressiveness has enabled the Indian Myna to displace many breeding pairs of native hollow-nesters, thereby reducing their reproductive success. As a visitor to Australia, my life, including my art, is related to my belief in the world, and it is understandable that the Indian Myna's striking features have drawn my attention as a migrant breed on this continent, and that my drawings demonstrate my understanding of these particular species.

This understanding helps me with the action of observing an object. It also assists me in my drawing in many ways. After observing it from different perspectives, an image starts to form. It is the work of memory, but I see it more like a trace of an imaginative sketch made in my mind. I believe that, after training and practice, an artist will see and remember things in an *artistic* way. Matisse explained how different a tomato is to him when he sees it as an artist, rather than as a person not making art at that time. He sees a tomato as others do when he eats it, but he sees this tomato in a different way when he paints it.[13] This also relates to my experience, for when I intentionally seek to draw the bird in my mind I do not just keep the imagery as normal memory but as an imaginative sketch. This sketch changes all the time. Sometimes it is more representational and naturalistic in tones and proportions, sometimes less, with added suggestive lines and marks. These images in my mind will be realized when I start to draw in my studio, however the first stage of observation and imaginative sketching provides the references for my artwork. This process demonstrates how sketching connects to my drawing activity.

I no longer do sketches as I did at school, although from time to time I still make some studies of objects to find appropriate marks. However, careful and sensitive observation provides the reference to the trace of the object's likeness and the sketch in my mind becomes the preparation for the marks in the actual drawings. The process reinforces the role of observation in imaginative sketching for me. This has allowed the freedom to play with perceptions of the object, and has prompted the creation of many different imaginative images of the same object in my mind. Knowing I would emphasis certain aspects of the object, I pay more attention to the details in making different imaginative sketches in my mind from this particular perspective, with different chosen characteristics of the object in order to have the full range of imagery as references for later drawings.

In this chapter, I began by offering an attempt to briefly examine the roles of sketching in Chinese traditional painting, and to establish a link between Chinese art tradition and contemporary drawing as they unfold in practice. The emphasis on copy and reduced focus on life sketching and drawing has made traditional Chinese teaching and learning of art more distinctive in its philosophical orientation. With careful and sensitive observation, the imaginative sketches become traces of emotions and expressions in the artist's heart, but, more importantly, such ways of making artwork has been beneficial to contemporary artists in applying and interpreting selected traditional aesthetics within the current drawing practices in China.

BIBLIOGRAPHY

Barasch, Moshe. *Theories of Art: From Plato to Winckelman*. New York: New York University Press, 1985.

Berger, John. *Berger on Drawing*. Aghabullogue: Occasional Press, 2007.

Edwards, Betty. *The New Drawing on the Right Side of the Brain*. New York: Penguin Putnam Inc., 1999.

Fuller, Peter. *Rock and Flesh*. Norwich: Norwich School of Art Gallery, 1985.

Hay, Jonathan. *Shi Tao: Painting and Modernity in Early Qing China*. Cambridge: Cambridge University Press, 2001.

Li, L. L., ed. *The Historical Records of the Development of Chinese Ancient Art Theory*. Shanghai: Shanghai People's Arts Publisher, 1997.

Mei, R. L. M., ed. *Shuang Xing Hui Ying*. Shijiazhuang: Hebei Education Publisher, 2006.

NOTES

1   L. L. Li, ed., *The Historical Records of the Development of Chinese Ancient Art Theory* (Shanghai: Shanghai People's Arts Publisher, 1997), 147.

2   Li, *The Historical Records of the Development of Chinese Ancient Art Theory*, 147.

3   Li, *The Historical Records of the Development of Chinese Ancient Art Theory*, 98.

4   Discussed in Moshe Barasch, *Theories of Art: From Plato to Winckelman* (New York: New York University Press, 1985), 333.

5   The thorough collection of Ban Qiao (ban qiao quan ji) in Li, ed. *The Historical Records of the Development of Chinese Ancient Art Theory*. 347.

6   Jonathan Hay, *Shi Tao: Painting and Modernity in Early Qing China* (Cambridge: Cambridge University Press, 2001), 181.

7   The thorough collection of Ban Qiao (ban qiao quan ji) in Li, *The Historical Records of the Development of Chinese Ancient Art Theory*, 347.

8   Discussed in Peter Fuller, *Rock and Flesh* (Norwich: Norwich School of Art Gallery, 1985), 7.

9   Discussed in Fuller, *Rock and Flesh*, 7.

10   Fuller, *Rock and Flesh*, 8.

11   R. L. M. Mei, ed. *Shuang Xing Hui Ying* (Shijiazhuang: Hebei Education Publisher, 2006), 91.

12   John Berger, *Berger on Drawing* (Aghabullogue: Occasional Press, 2007), 39.

13   Discussed in Betty Edwards, *The New Drawing on the Right Side of the Brain* (New York: Penguin Putnam Inc., 1999), 4.

7

The Design Sketchbook: Between the Virtual and the Actual

Douglas Gittens

I

The design sketchbook appears as an inherently fluid transient space, since it functions as an in-between liminal threshold, as a portal through which creative intentions can find their fix in the world. It presents an immanent field of potentiality whereby the *virtual* can find expression in the *actual*. The sketchbook is a permeable membrane wherein design potentialities transfer from the human imagination to the actual world by means of the kinetic action of pen on paper when perceived in such a way. Between its sheets it channels the virtual[1] – the nearly as – into the world of ideas and objects, engaging the designer in a rediscovery of an imaginative network of ascribable possibilities. In turn, it enables the reclamation of a 'virtuality' of a kind quite other to the algorithmic 'virtuality' associated with digital design technologies, thereby realigning the virtual with the imaginative life of the designer.

This chapter explores the latent potential for the designers' sketchbook to perform as a dynamic, interstitial phenomenon, through which it is possible to evidence Gilles Deleuze's notion of the virtual and the actual. The contemporary use of the word 'virtual' almost exclusively binds its meaning to the world of digital technologies, becoming solely allied with the digital realm; its use reserved for describing virtual reality, virtual gaming, virtual friendships, virtual sex, virtual tourism, virtual communities and so on. However, in referencing Henri Bergson's theory of duration, Deleuze defines the virtual as a potentiality yet to be actualized, in essence the virtual is a real object only yet to be made material. For Delueze, the virtual is as real as the actual, for the '…virtual is fully real in so far as it is virtual… Indeed, the virtual must be defined as strictly a part of the real object – as though the object had one part of itself in the virtual into which it plunged as though into an objective dimension.'[2]

Through an examination of design praxis, this present chapter *represents* the sketchbook as an effective tool for formulating an alternate mode of a design-orientated process; a mode effecting a more instantaneous, vigorous, and intuitive engagement with the materialization of ideas, concepts, and new ways of thinking.

Moreover, the chapter champions the significance of the term 'virtual' as a central part of sketchbook-praxis, reasserting both the original meaning of the word and its theoretical importance to Deleuzian philosophy.

II

Akin to the artists, designers, and architects who use them as working documents, perceptions of the sketchbook are many and varied. However, irrespective of the demands of each discipline, and the manifold idiosyncrasies of tradition they incur, the majority of creative practitioners utilize the sketchbook as a storage vessel, whereby thoughts, observations, and ideas are deposited in one place. In turn, such habits affect the sketchbook's objectivity, transforming it into a versatile reference tool for the formation of more robust or complex expressions of an initial idea. Perceptions of the sketchbook are, in this sense, limitless. Likewise, there are no limits about what a sketchbook might become. The empty sketchbook can be considered as an engine of potentiality, the only restrictions placed upon it are those enshrined by the conventions that shape individual consciousness and the designer's praxis. It is this quality of virtual potentiality, coupled with the inherently private nature of the sketchbook, that draws the design practitioner to commit not only their embryonic ideas to paper, but also map out their observations, thoughts and questions concerning the world they operate within.

As each page of a sketchbook is turned, a profound sense of immanence emerges from somewhere behind the bleached surface of its plane, as if each sheet heralds the arrival of something new that has never existed before. The empty sketchbook presents its creative user with an untamed, unmapped field of possibilities, a vista into which the designer lays out new pathways and connections as circumstances allow. Overtime this topography is mapped and, as the last page is filled, the sketchbook's potential may take on a different trajectory as ideas re-emerge, sometimes many years later, becoming further iterations of dormant potentialities awoken once more.

III

The sketchbook of the creative, once perceived as field of immanent potential, produces a flexible dynamic space of interwoven possibilities that often evaporate during the production of more fixed or completed works. In its most flexible condition, the sketchbook is analogous with the conceptual metaphor of Gilles Deleuze and Felix Guattari's 'rhizome',[3] in that it seeks to form connections and extensions in ways that differ from more orthodox patterns of design development. Rhizomic plants bifurcate for Deleuze and Guattari, growing their roots in a fundamentally different manner to that of other plants, yielding shoots and grasses in unexpected locations. Their root networks split and divide, producing alternative and unexpected pathways through the darkness of the earth where normative boundaries and restrictions become irrelevant. The unknown and unplanned nature of this activity mirrors divergent thought and patterns commonly found in the sketchbook within a given creative orientation.

Utilising the metaphor of the 'rhizome' to generate a framework for a critical assessment of Western philosophy and associated socio/political strategies of power, Deleuze and Guattari developed an allegory that aligns Western philosophy with the structure of a tree. A tree, by comparison to a rhizome, is a root and branch configuration '…where everything branches out from a central trunk – the little twigs branch out from larger ones, and so on, back to the central core.'[4] Andrew Ballantyne confirms the use of this metaphorical image as an armature for the critical assessment of Western philosophy and its association with a methodical centralization of political power in the West.[5] Moreover, Deleuze and Guattari claim that the West in its entirety, its systems relating to language, semiotics, its power structures, its sciences, art, culture, and philosophy, have all been shaped by such 'tree like' patterns of thought. These qualities, for Deleuze and Guattari, develop *habits of thought* that are inherently 'tree like' (or arborescent) and transcendent by nature stating, '…it is odd how the tree has dominated Western reality and all of Western thought, from botany to biology and anatomy, but also gnosiology, theology, ontology, all of philosophy.'[6] By contrast, the Orient has generated contrasting modes of thinking more readily associated with the grasslands of the steppe and the seemingly haphazard meanderings of the nomad, an association nurturing modes of thinking that are characteristically immanent, rather than transcendent. Whilst Western philosophy has emerged from the lands of the forest, Eastern philosophy has evolved on the grasslands of the steppe and the rhizomic expanses of Oceania.[7] These qualities are important when considering the sketchbook because they possess a latent capacity for generating non-aborescent patterns of thought and practice. Sketchbooks are inherently more '*rhizomic*' by nature.

Moreover, Deleuze and Guattari maintain, the human brain does not function as an arborescent mechanism, for the configuration of our brains (being a network of synapses and micro-fissures over which arcs of thought vector out in as many unpredictable as predictable pathways) are more readily understood as rhizomic systems than logical root and branch type of structures.[8] The position Deleuze and Guattari assume is one of despair regarding Western habits of thought, stating, '…we're tired of trees. We should stop believing in trees, roots, and radicles. They've made us suffer too much. All of arborescent culture is founded on them, from biology to linguistics. Nothing is beautiful or loving or political aside from underground stems and aerial roots, adventitious growths and rhizomes.'[9]

When viewed from this position it becomes apparent that the designer's sketchbook has the potential for encouraging, even nurturing, rhizomic modes of design thinking and action. In its raw form, a sketchbook is not immediately predisposed to becoming an arborescent root and branch configuration, but rather, its inherent potentiality suggests the formation of the opposite kind of engagement, an approach to its surface more akin to that of the rhizome. Whilst there might be a passing resemblance to a homogenized structure whereby each idea is a further expression of the same exploration, these are passing moments in a far more expansive and interrelated network of ideas, observations, thoughts, statements, appointments, 'to do' reminders and even shopping lists.[10] Rather than a controlled catalogue of past or old works, the design sketchbook is a dynamic network that allows for the free flowing of theoretical and imaginative applications enfolded within a process of incubation.

IV

The creation of a completed design, irrespective of the discipline within which it is executed, is defined by the methodological constraints imposed upon it by the means of production. This is particularly true in the case of designed images and the realization of complex artifacts, buildings and machines. Commercial designers and architects, by the nature of their practice, have to conform to all manners of commercial influences and compromises that are normal to the production of designed items. The complexities and rigour of commercial production inevitably define and shape any initial design vision, for the needs of users, clients, budgets; and the modes of production always manipulate the final iteration of the designer's primary conception. In effect, the nature of production leads to the formation of pre-determined *habits of practice*; ones that are worthy, reliable, modes of production and as such can endure the rigours of the commercial environment.

The practice of keeping a sketchbook, however, engages the individual designer in a soupier, far messier affair than the systemic logistics of commercial production. They allow free thinking, sporadic and untimely propositions beyond the rigidity of the design 'for client' process. The contents of a sketchbook have a propensity for meandering, coupled with an inherent appetite for finding lines of flight steering away from fixed modes of thinking and doing. Engagement with the sketchbooks propensity for negotiating other, less rigid and confined avenues of thought encourages the development of unconventional modes of operation and eccentric forms of expression.

Helene Frichot, expanding upon Deleuze's analysis of Francis Bacon's sensorial engagement with painting, identifies comparable issues affecting the architect at the commencement of the design process. Deleuze claims that within the painter is a collective field of conscious/unconscious influences pertaining to memory and habit, which in turn are mixed with the external influences that surround the artist in their day-to-day lives.[11] These influences are of course, bought to bear upon the painting even before the first brush stroke is administered to the canvas, for '…the canvas is never a tabula rasa, but a noisy field of forces of habit, opinion and cliché.'[12] Frichot argues that the architect (and therefore the designer by association) carries with them a complex set of predetermined influences as they approach their own 'canvas'. She suggests that in using the 'diagram' (or sketch) as a form of 'interference' (being a literal intervention of the hand in the production of a diagram) this enables the architect to '…challenge pre-packaged codes, create surprises, and proffer the gift of the novel.'[13] Comparably, a sketch embodies the qualities identified within Frichot's analysis of the diagram. Essentially the act of sketching produces a kind of interference within pre-assembled design habits associated with established practices. This analysis also suggests that sketching encompasses a challenge to the limitations associated with commercial design, offering up a fresh exploration through the margins of commercial practice. Perceived as such, the sketch becomes a transgressor, undermining established design methodologies by questioning their value and purpose, which in turn offers up novel, divergent and often exigent modes of practical design engagement.

Following the hypothesis of Deleuze and Guattari's rhizome, the sketchbook produces eventualities, through arcs and vectors that follow unpredictable pathways. Such a perception of the sketchbook conjures the impression of a dynamic, even nomadic mode of operation, whereby sketchy interference with normative design practice occurs on a regular basis, causing eruptions to materialize in unexpected places. Locked into a rhizomic process, the ideas, creative moments, shifts in direction, and novel expressions commonly found in a sketchbook have a propensity for re-emergence on another page, another sketchbook, in a rebirth in the mind during a bus journey or walking down the street, sometimes weeks, months or even years into the future. Occasionally, (and here I write from personal experience) an idea explored a decade ago might inexplicably reappear, the rhizomic infrastructure of the sketchbook navigating time, allowing the idea to flourish in an unexpected location.

Sketchbooks incubate their contents, secretly replicating, mutating and multiplying the moments held deep within their folds. They incubate potentialities by nurturing and feeding apparently dormant expressions, whilst simultaneously sending out slow moving tendrils that negotiate the lumpy, sodden restrictions

7.1   Rhizomic doodling. Source: Drawing: Douglas Gittens 2012

of our consciousness, sending out strands that eventually arc out to find new opportunities for germination in unfamiliar landscapes. Given time, such networks become sprawling masses of the novel, making catalogues of provocative engagements within the discipline of design that are hidden away from the hungry gaze of clients, patrons and gallery audiences. Sketchbooks evolve secret webs, clandestine circuitry, and hidden networks that generate a creative agenda peculiar to the author. Whilst client and user probe completed objects, products, and buildings, the sketchbook secretly attends to the business of making connections, seeking out opportunities, and etching incantations into its surfaces assisting the complex alchemy of the creative endeavour.

V

'"Nomad thought" does not immure itself in the edifice of an ordered interiority; it moves freely in an element of exteriority.'[14] Fluid and adopting a state of dynamism, 'nomad thought' according to a Deleuzian interpretation prefers a situation conducive to movement, adaptation, reconfiguration and change. It is not, therefore, a root and branch assemblage; rather its free-flowing nature produces a metamorphosis of thought. A mutation characterized through the origination of the novel.

Arborescent models of thinking however, have their place and can be useful to designers, as they aid the solving of logistical problems, and they avoid ambiguity, as well as enable the commercial applications of a design to evolve. The designer spends much of their time wrestling with applied or practical endeavours that absolutely require arborescent thought-structures to occupy centre stage. Nevertheless, this is not the only way to think and, when time and willingness allow, the sketchbook furnishes the designer with an opportunity to engage with a fluid network of design possibilities. This liberates the designer from the normative aborescent habits associated with the design process; their sketchbook is often the sole means through which an alternative mode of operation is established. Enfolded within the surfaces of a sketchbook, a designer can rediscover their imaginative nomadic capacity, as their sketchbook enables them to think fluidly upon the dynamic interface that exists between the virtual and the actual.

VI

As outlined earlier, the term 'virtual' is now almost exclusively associated with the convoluted semantics of digital technology. The word is entangled within an increasingly commonplace reconfiguration of its original meaning and bound to the semantics of the digital; its use restricted to the computerized worlds of virtual reality, virtual gaming, virtual friendships, virtual sex, virtual tourism, virtual communities and so on. However, the root meaning and definition of the word 'virtual' is less tailored than that afforded to it through any association with the 'virtual' environment of digital technologies. The dictionary definition of the adjective is '...having the essence or effect but not the appearance or the form of.'[15] By examining the 14th century origins of the word, further insight clarifies its essential meaning, the term having evolved from the Medieval Latin 'virtualis' (effective), which in turn stems from the original Latin 'virtus' (virtue, and more specifically manliness, courage). The archaic use of the term 'virtue' refers to an effective, active, inherent power or force.[16]

There are two aspects concerning the origins of 'virtual' that warrant more examination in particular regard to the present discussion. Firstly, the virtual exists only in essence, or effect, whilst not being 'actual' or 'real' in the true sense. Secondly, the root meaning of the term suggests the presence of an inherent efficacy, power, or force. In the first instance, the implication is that the truly virtual is only ever such during a state of being not-yet-present, or has yet to be, and therefore does not possess any tangible existence in the world – yet. In this sense, the virtual *is* the realm of possibilities, a realm inherently other-to the material-world of concrete actualities. The second quality implies that the virtual possesses usefulness by merit of an inherent power, ability, or quality, encompassing a congenital expediency for producing a future result, action or thing.

By comparison, the *actual* is counterpoint to the virtual. Here the *Collins English Dictionary* definition describes the 'actual' as '1) existing in reality or as matter of fact, 2) real or genuine, 3) existing in the present time; current.'[17] This term has its origins in later Latin as 'actualis' (relating to acts, practical) and from the Latin 'actus' (act). *The Oxford Dictionary of Philosophy* reveals the evolution of the word within the discourse of western philosophy as, '...in modal logic the actual world is the world as it is, contrasted with other possible worlds, representing ways it might have been'.[18] Taking this evolution a step further, Deleuze's reading of the virtual interweaves his position with a philosophical mix comprized from Spinoza's work regarding *immanence*, and Henri Bergson's philosophy concerning the temporal nature of *duration*.[19] For Bergson, the *past* has an existence as real as the *present* and both are coexistent elements of time, however, they do not exist in the same way.[20] Bergson conceptualizes the past as being virtual in nature, as opposed to the actuality of the present.[21] This virtual quality of the past actualizes the present for Deleuze. Todd May clarifies the symbiotic relationship of the past and present in very straightforward terms:

> Thus my own past is a participant in, and at the same time a perspective on, the past itself. That past exists within me, and appears at each moment I am engaged with the world. It is in this engagement that the actualisation of the virtual occurs. A person, through action or memory or perception, brings the past to bear upon the present moment. An action may bring previous learning to bear in the discovery to of a solution to a puzzle...[22]

In Deleuzian theory, the virtual coexists with the actual, being an ever-present whole composed of two distinct fields in time.[23] The actual is that which we can perceive and conceive, while the virtual, as Helene Frichot has identified, is often interpreted as being the unseen, the invisible, and that which cannot be represented or conceived.[24] The creative sketchbook epitomizes this concept to some extent, as the holder of the private workings of an idea beyond the public eye.

For Deleuze, the virtual is an immeasurable field of intensity satiated with an infinite number of potentialities, often described by Deleuzian theorists and commentators as the *plane of immanence*. However, it is important to note that Deleuze in his work with Felix Guattari describes this virtual field as the plane of consistency, a model informing a core theoretical rhythm that underscores the philosophical adventure within their work *A Thousand Plateaus*.[25] Here, the plane of immanence contains every potential becoming of something that might exist: every idea, concept, cognitive revelation, object, animal, space, world everything. Moreover, every possible something that exists in the virtual is immanent to the actual for Deleuze. In this sense, anything is possible. As Andrew Ballantyne explores when he aligns Deleuze and Guattari's philosophical constructs of the *Body without Organs*, the *Plane of Immanence*, and the process of creativity experienced by designers at the start of the design process:

> The body without organs is pure immanence... having in it no conceptual
> apparatus that has been imposed from outside... The body without organs is
> a state of creativity, where preconceptions are set aside. It is the state before a
> design takes shape, where all possibilities are immanent, and one holds at bay
> the common-sense expectations of what the design should be.[26]

On one hand, there is the chaotic field of the virtual and the domain of things that might become, whilst on the other there is the territory of the actual, comprising that of consciousness, the body, and the world. The seemingly chaotic realm of the virtual does not actualize a chaotic world however. On the contrary, the actual world appears to be highly ordered. Pre-existing circumstances in the 'actual' manage the potentialities as they emerge from the virtual realm according to Deleuze, whereby the preconditions common to the actual world restrict a chaotic emergence of all virtual potentialities.

By means of Deleuze and Frichot, it is possible to see how immanence has a bearing on how we are to understand the purpose of the designer's sketchbook. Frichot, after Brian Massumi[27] contends that the plane of immanence is that which philosophers, artists, architects, and designers negotiate on a daily basis even though it 'overwhelms our senses, and our capacity to make sense... The plane of immanence leaves us with bloodshot eyes, ringing ears, ground down teeth, exhausted limbs and in a thorough state of perplexity.'[28] Frichot also suggests that the plane of immanence is a dynamic interface, or threshold, between the virtual and the actual.[29] As indecipherable and indiscernible as the virtual might be, the plane of immanence operates as a threshold through which actualization can punch into being, and as such forms an imperative schematic for understanding how creative practitioners operate. More precisely, Deleuze uses the notion of the fold (*le pli*) as a metaphor of how the virtual ceaselessly folds into the actual. For as incomprehensible as the virtual might be, it is probably best recognized as the whispering voice forever just beyond our perception that motivates our creative engagement and actions.[30]

VII

What I am proposing here by way of these notions and theories is that the humble sketchbook possesses a latent capacity to ride the interface between the twin dominions of the virtual and actual. The sketchbook, by merit of its relative independence from commercial pressure, social expectation, and design cliché, can surf the folding of the virtual into the actual via the plane of immanence. Essentially, I purport that the sketchbook functions as an interlocutor, making possible a conversation between the virtual and the actual, a conversation held in secret to some extent, which allows for free speech and honesty between the author and the page and thereby focussing a vast terrain of potentialities into concrete actualities.

When perceived as an interlocutor, the sketchbook is not simply an accumulator of ideas, or an index of creative reflection, but rather it appears as an interstitial device that facilitates a folding of the virtual into the actual. The sketchbook is a tool that manipulates the emergence of a virtual potentiality into the actual world, and, in this way, sketchbooks actuate and activate potential. They are mediators for the transference of the infinite possibilities immanent within the virtual.

A practical demonstration of how the process of transference works is achievable by conducting a simple drawing experiment with a small group of designers. Figure 7.2 shows a number of lines drawn with a pencil, on separate pieces of paper, by five designers. By instructing each to draw a line, it was possible to see that they all performed the task in a similar way. This was despite working entirely independently of each other, and none having observed the other whilst drawing their own unique line.

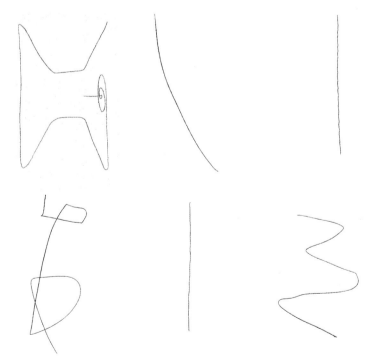

7.2   Line drawings executed by five designers. Source: Image: Douglas Gittens 2012

They had the freedom to draw any type of line in the task, and any variable of a line was possible. However, various circumstances occurred during the process, which in-turn determined the specific expression of the *potential* line that actually emerged onto the paper. It is fair to assume that each designer possessed individual preconceptions of what the line might be, pre-empting the actualization of each line, and no doubt, a plethora of various cultural, individual, and environmental pre-existent circumstances buzzed into action as each decided what kind of line to draw. Other conditions may have contributed to what kind of mark they made, for example the surface of the table, the type of drawing instrument they used, the grain of the paper and so on. Maybe they became excited or anxious by the task, or, by contrast, they may have experienced a demanding day and were tired and uninspired. Nevertheless, whatever the circumstances that characterized the emergence of each line, a given assembly of conditions acted together and organized the coming into being of each drawing. Irrespective of the circumstances that manipulated its becoming, a virtual line became an actual line, and the previously imperceptible became observable.

This simple exercise gives a real, demonstrable existence to the infinite kinds of lines that are possible in the process of making the virtual 'thought' an actual 'mark'. Actualization is the emergence of something born from a process left to run[31] and the circumstantial becoming of something wrought from the restless, ever folding and refolding plane of immanence – where all things are immanent – waiting for a coalescence of worldly circumstance that will generate their expression in the actual.

VIII

Following Deleuze's analysis concerning the virtual and the actual, it is possible to argue that actualization is a core process within the mystery of creative activity. This approach venerates actualization as the means whereby human beings generate ideas and thoughts, and, consequently, develop made-objects and designs. For Frichot actualization is the means whereby artists, designers, writers and the like make their creative moves.[32] It is a process in which we all have a part to perform,[33] and as Deleuze suggests '…evolution is actualization, actualization is creation'.[34] Actualization is the folding of the virtual into the actual. A becoming that sends the creative human being on a course of discovery through unexplored territory of the possible.[35]

With commercialization and the need to communicate to clients bearing heavily on the public facing the work of the designer, why is the sketchbook so conducive to the creative endeavour? Surely, the work of a designer has to engage with the process of actualization on all phases of the design process? To some extent, designers engage their creative processing skills during each step of the design process. However, the job-of-work nature of design-employment, by virtue of its status as an applied art and commodity, is a complex process riddled with control measures meted out by clients, users and market forces. It is a process codified and defined by following a strict brief often subjected to a host of complex and rigorous control systems. Consider the intransigence exerted on a designer's imagination through planning regulations, local authority legislature, health and safety requirements, production control measures, manufacturing restraints, material constraints, and so on as an example. These forces assemble to entrap and deploy control over the design in its will to be made. Describing the mundane day-to-day life of the architect, Frichot writes that '…as social actors, often constrained with fixed scripts, susceptible to cliché and opinion, we are happy to brush off the interfering noise of immanence, and just get down to business'.[36] Moreover, design is not a solitary pursuit, since it is normal for it to be a team activity. Consequently, any idea that a designer has undergoes a thorough remoulding, even a complete mutation, often emerging at the end of the process as something quite different from the original intention. By comparison, the sketchbook can open up a set of radical opportunities that are quite *other* than the normative processes associated with the total concerns of the design process. It allows escapism within the mundanity of the design process, offering the designer a kind of 'in-between-ness', a liminal 'otherness', crucially lying between the virtual and the actual, the day-to-day and the imagination, in which they can explore a fuller, richer set of potentialities for their practice. When the sketchbook phenomenon is left to run, it generates an opportunity for a designer to explore the fantastic, the ridiculous, and the absurd; hence, legitimizing the pursuance of unpredictable lines of flight.[38] In this sense it represents a threshold through which transgressing positions and alternative customs of imagining might be realized. Left to run as an experimental interface bridging the virtual and the actual, the sketchbook offers up a wealth of creative opportunities for devising alternative working methodologies, ones quite *other* to the homogenizing tendencies of commercial practice.

The sketchbook presents the designer with a fluid and transient space through which they can explore their own potentiality as creative beings. It is the means whereby a portal opens to the virtual, where the scratches and marks exerted onto the surface of white cartridge sheets folds the virtual into being through willing hands. Creative intention flows across this interface and, as ideas pass into storage, the sketchbook builds a kind of taxonomy of moments where the virtual has entered the actual. Each new blank page presents this interface between the virtual and the actual, for as the hand moves across the page and leaves its mark, so the virtual processes the actual into being. With each fresh page, latent potentialities become new actualities.

The sketchbook offers an alternate mode of practice for the designer, a more immediate, intimate, dynamic, almost visceral engagement with the emergence of ideas, concepts and ways of thinking. Moreover, the sketchbook is a tool, or more poignantly, it is a Deleuzian machine, through which the immanent potentialities at play in the virtual might find their expression in the actual. It offers the designer a special kind of freedom, a freedom to ignite and engage their creativity wherever and with whatever they find themselves working. It offers a freedom of expression quite alien to the normative constraints of a designer's everyday praxis. As each pristine sheet of cartridge paper bestows a new, immanent field of limitless potentiality, the only restriction, it seems, is that of our own frailty.

7.3   Potentialities become actualities. Source: Drawing: Douglas Gittens 2012

BIBLIOGRAPHY

Ballantyne, Andrew. *Deleuze and Guattari for Architects*. Oxon: Routledge, 2007.

Blackburn, Simon. *Oxford Dictionary of Philosophy*. Oxford: Oxford University Press, 1994.

Butterfield, Jeremy, John Daintith, Andrew Holmes, Alan Isaacs, Jonathan Law, Elizabeth Martin and Elspeth Summers, eds. *Collins English Dictionary*. 6th Edition. Glasgow: Harper Collins Publishers, 2003.

Deleuze, Gilles. *Bergsonism*. Translated by Hugh Tomlinson and Barbara Habberjam. New York: Zone Books, 1991.

_____. *Difference and Repetition*. Translated by Paul Patton. New York: Columbia University Press, 1994.

_____. *Francis Bacon*. Translated by Daniel W. Smith. London: Continuum, 2005.

Deleuze, Gilles, and Claire Parnet. *Dialogues II*. Translated by Hugh Tomlinson and Barbara Habberjam. London, Continuum, 1987.

Deleuze, Gilles, and Felix Guattari. *A Thousand Plateaus*. Translated by Brian Massumi. London: Continuum, 1988.

Frichot, Helene. "Stealing into Gilles Deleuze's Baroque House," in *Deleuze and Space*, edited by Ian Buchanan and Gregg Lambert, 61–79. Edinburgh: Edinburgh University Press, 2005.

Massumi, Brian. *A User's Guide to Capitalism and Schizophrenia, Deviations from Deleuze and Guattari*. Massachusetts: MIT, 1992.

_____. "Line Parable for the Virtual (On the Superiority of the Analog)," in *The Virtual Dimension: Architecture, Representation and Crash Culture*. Edited by John Beckmann, 304–321. New York: Princeton Architectural Press, 1998.

May, Todd. *Gilles Deleuze, An Introduction*. Cambridge: Cambridge University Press, 2005.

NOTES

1   I am referring to the '*virtual*' in relation to the '*virtual and the actual*' here, as defined in the theories of Gilles Deleuze. A common mistake concerning the definition of the virtual and the actual is to consider them in the same way as the possible and the real. The virtual is not a possibility, as a possibility is not real, whereas the virtual is real in that it exists, but has yet to be actualized. For Deleuze, the virtual exists, but is not actualized, and is opposed to the actual. Todd May provides an excellent autopsy on these ideas in Chapter 2 of his book '*Gilles Deleuze, An Introduction*'.

2   Andrew Ballantyne, *Deleuze and Guattari for Architects* (Oxon: Routledge, 2007), 26.

3   Gilles Deleuze and Felix Guattari, *A Thousand Plateaus,* trans. Brian Massumi (London: Continuum, 1988), 3.

4   Gilles Deleuze, *Difference and Repetition*, trans. Paul Patton (New York: Columbia University Press, 1994), 208.

5   Ballantyne, *Deleuze and Guattari for Architects*, 26.

6   Deleuze and Guattari, *A Thousand Plateaus*, 18.

7   As discussed in Deleuze and Guattari, *A Thousand Plateaus*, 18.

8   As discussed in Deleuze and Guattari, *A Thousand Plateaus*, 15.

9   Deleuze and Guattari, *A Thousand Plateaus*, 15.

10 Deleuze and Guattari, *A Thousand Plateaus*, 5.

11 Gilles Deleuze, *Francis Bacon*, trans. Daniel W. Smith (London: Continuum, 2005), 57.

12 Helen Frichot, "Stealing into Gilles Deleuze's Baroque House," in *Deleuze and Space*, ed. Ian Buchanan and Gregg Lambert, (Edinburgh: Edinburgh University Press, 2005), 61–79.

13 Frichot, "Stealing into Gilles Deleuze's Baroque House," 61–79.

14 Brian Massumi, *A User's Guide to Capitalism and Schizophrenia, Deviations from Deleuze and Guattari* (Massachusetts: MIT, 1992), 5.

15 Jeremy Butterfield et al., eds, *Collins English Dictionary*, 6th (Glasgow: Harper Collins Publishers, 2003), p. 1795.

16 Butterfield et al., *Collins English Dictionary*, 1795.

17 Butterfield et al., *Collins English Dictionary*, 17.

18 Simon Blackburn, *Oxford Dictionary of Philosophy* (Oxford: Oxford University Press, 1994), 6.

19 Both terms are discussed in: Todd May, *Gilles Deleuze, An Introduction* (Cambridge: Cambridge University Press, 2005).

20 Discussed in Gilles Deleuze, *Bergsonism*, trans. Hugh Tomlinson and Barbara Habberjam (New York: Zone Books, 1991), 59.

21 As discussed in May, *Gilles Deleuze, An Introduction*, 46.

22 May, *Gilles Deleuze, An Introduction*, 52.

23 As discussed in May, *Gilles Deleuze, An Introduction*, 49.

24 Discussed in Frichot, "Stealing into Gilles Deleuze's Baroque House," 61–79.

25 See the references to a 'Body without Organs' (or BoW) in A Thousand Plateaus, 'How do you make yourself a body without organs?', page 154, for an example.

26 Ballantyne, *Deleuze and Guattari for Architects*, 36.

27 Brian Massumi, "Line Parable for the Virtual (On the Superiority of the Analog)," in *The Virtual Dimension: Architecture, Representation and Crash Culture*, ed. John Beckman (New York: Princeton Architectural Press, 1998), 304–321.

28 Frichot, "Stealing into Gilles Deleuze's Baroque House," 61–79.

29 Frichot, "Stealing into Gilles Deleuze's Baroque House," 61–79.

30 Frichot, "Stealing into Gilles Deleuze's Baroque House," 61–79.

31 Ballantyne, *Deleuze and Guattari for Architects*, 31.

32 As discussed in Frichot, "Stealing into Gilles Deleuze's Baroque House," 79.

33 Frichot, "Stealing into Gilles Deleuze's Baroque House," 61–79.

34 Deleuze, *Bergsonism*, 91.

35   Gilles Deleuze and Claire Parnet, *Dialogues II*, trans. Hugh Tomlinson and Babara Habberjam (London: Continuum, 1987), 30.

36   Frichot, "Stealing into Gilles Deleuze's Baroque House," 61–79.

8

Drawn to Each Other: A Love Affair with Sketches

Rachel Hurst

INTRODUCTION

Diaries and journals have often recorded the emergence of love affairs, the pages documenting the first awakenings of interest, the pivotal moments of reciprocation, and then the consolidation of mutual moments and histories into written archives of affection. What if sketchbooks could tell similar stories, through the catalogue of drawings there? What if the compulsion so many artists, illustrators and architects have to record and draw their observations and ideas is motivated by a desire to communicate, not only with themselves but with some 'other' – whether it be an emerging concept, an object of the material world or an object of affection? How might one read parallel passions for drawing, the things drawn, and another person within a companion set of sketchbooks?

According to Pliny, drawing originated in Diboutades' poignant tracing on the wall of her departing lover's silhouette. Robin Evans suggests in his essay 'Translations from Drawing to Building' that the ingredients for drawing are a source of light, a subject, a surface and something to trace with. This chapter revisits that analysis and its implicit connection to visual representation as a projection of desire to consider the significance of *eros* in the sketch, extrapolated to include love of the other, and love of the drawing.

This chapter uses drawing journals from two architects to examine the sketch as a revelatory trace. It tells the story of an inconvenient but ardent affair between them, separated as they are by distance and marital logistics, but united by professional circumstances and synergies. The two lovers come from different far apart cities; she is an architectural academic, he a practising architect; both are married. Brought together in an intense professional jury tour of contemporary architecture, the journals chronicle their liaison between copious lines of architectural depiction. The drawings not only map architectural objects and observations, perceived simultaneously but differently by both authors, but also constitute a form of architectural discourse between them in their complicated, covert situation.

The drawing journals used for this analysis describe a visual conversation that strengthens with repeated shared architectural experiences. The individual sketchbooks, which document monthly assignations for these separated lovers, begin to complement the qualities of the other: hers acquire more contrast and weight, while his demonstrate increased precision and finish. Yet inherent tendencies persist, perhaps related to their different professional preoccupations: she sketches with a focus on surface, light and texture, while he concentrates on structure, proportion and partis. Carefully labeled and date-stamped, each is consciously curated with obvious sentiment, like love letters tenderly wrapped with ribbon. Taken as a collection, these sketchbooks offer an opportunity to examine drawing practices both as an independent, idiosyncratic discipline, and a poetic mode of communication.

Using key comparative illustrations as a conversation between image and text, this chapter uses the motif of a love story to consider the sketch as a recorder of more than the visual. Framed by a (discreet) outline of the nature and circumstance of the lovers' affair, and an overview of the sketchbook material, it then examines how this material supports and illustrates what Albert Pérez Gómez describes in *Built Upon Love* as 'the architectural space of Eros',[1] namely how the conditions that characterize sexual desire and love can be found not only in the sketch, but also extended to the phenomenon of the sketchbook. These parallels go some way to explaining our fascination and fetishizing of sketches as drawings from the

8.1   More than a dozen sketchbooks document not only a love affair between two architects, but a love affair with drawing. Source: Image: Rachel Hurst, 2011

heart. A recurring theme that emerges is the multi-sensorial nature of love and the sketch (i.e. the complex mind – emotion – body engagement negotiations that are evident in both – and that critical expectant and open-ended quality that is evident in the dynamics of both passionate love affairs and proficient sketches). But like a sketch, where the first mark is not always obvious, it doesn't neatly begin at the beginning.

ONE MUST JUMP INTO THE MIDDLE OF THE SHEET OF PAPER[2]

Torn neatly from the one of his preferred plain brown card covered sketchbooks, the drawing is an addition to his love letter to her. In loose graphite lines against bisque paper, it shows bathers at an iconic Australian public swimming pool, famous for its incongruous Italian sign *Aqua Profunda*. If the depicted sign itself inadvertently acquired significance in Australian culture (through contemporary fiction and film), there is nothing that is unintentional about the focus in this drawing on its translated meaning – 'Deep Water'. The sketch is a metaphor for the relationship the letter describes, a visual allusion to the depths of sensory immersion the two lovers are in, and its intense black inscription on smooth cream surface an appropriate extrapolation of the medium of drawing that drew them together.

    This chapter acts as a plunge into deep water too. Sketches by their very nature are manifestations of the content they intend to convey, and inevitably of the

8.2 'Fitzroy Swimming Pool.' A sketch from a love letter shares both an architectural observation and an allusion to the two lovers' illicit situation. Source: Sketch: Peter Malatt, 2011

hand that made them and the place and time of their making. They are essentially fragmentary self-portraits, an idea eloquently expressed by Jorge Luis Borges:

> A man sets himself the task of portraying the world. Over the years he fills a given surface with images of provinces and kingdoms, mountains, bays, ships, islands, fish, rooms, instruments, heavenly bodies, horses and people. Shortly before he dies he discovers that this patient labyrinth of lines is a drawing of his own face.[3]

Discussions of the sketchbook and the trace are bound to deal with these ideas, and as this chapter deals with a prolonged, contemporary lovers' conversation through sketches, it reveals much that is intimate, like some form of visual eavesdropping. And while it aims to connect this story to the broader context of sketching, analogue drawing and architecture, it is, unashamedly or not, an *exposé* of two people's private exchange. Is there any point in trying to conceal identity, to stand apart from the clearly interior understanding of the material of this chapter? Will the choice of anonymous terms 'he/his' and 'she/her' fool anyone? After all, the captions to the figures make clear who the players are. Their anonymity is not important, yet neither are their personas: they act as protagonists, as 'everyman' and 'everywoman' to the analogy. However, as this is *my lived own story*, I have struggled with how to present it objectively, and with decorum. Writing architectural discourse from such a subjective position has been legitimized by recent (mostly female) authors, like Jennifer Bloomer and Jane Rendell, by ficto-critical texts, or the 'writing about affect' approach of those such as Elspyth Probyn. Yet, as Probyn points out, it requires 'a self made of glass'.[4] It is perilous, possibly self-indulgent, and risks the accusation of solipsism, or in this particular case, given the marital circumstances of these 'anonymous' lovers, moral disapproval. The sketchbooks and the affair are one however, an entity, as this discussion aims to show, and just as a good sketch is candid and brave, uncensored and unedited, this story needs to be told with candour if it is to have any significance (for the readers) or authority as an honest account. Nevertheless, a sketch is often at its most evocative when it selectively represents what it records: accordingly, the narrative will concentrate on the essential, rather than salacious details of its personal setting. This is not a soap opera in sketches, however the very intimacy of its subject matter resonates with the deeply personal character of sketchbooks themselves: where size, binding and preferred ground are all deliberate expressions of our idiosyncrasies, before we even put pen to paper. Held close to the body, carried as near constant companions, they are almost extensions of our self, senses and memories.

CONSTRUCTION LINES

Sketching, for all the skill it requires, can be unpredictable, coincidental, and serendipitous. In an early essay 'Drawing', John Berger for example describes the contingency in his drawing process, and 'which spontaneous gestures had evaded a problem, and which had been instinctively right.' He uses the image of the pencil hovering 'rather like the stick of a water-diviner' to marry the act of looking and drawing as a kind of truth'.[5] Similarly, in a mesmerising meditation on drawing, Hélène Cixous asks 'what is this moment called when we suddenly recognize what we have never seen?'[6] She is writing of a chance encounter with Picasso's *Etude pour 'La Repasseuse'* (Study for the woman ironing), and the 'electric current' that passes between her and this very vigorous working sketch. The accident of her viewing, and the visible accidents within the study itself, all give a precarious sensibility to her perceptions and to the drawing, and her words could be hijacked to describe the accident that brought the two lovers together. Selected to serve on a national architectural award panel of five professionals, both individuals were replacements for jurors unable to commit to the lengthy process.[7] It sounds hackneyed to talk of love at first sight, yet at their first daylong-meeting, there was an 'electric current' in a Cixousian sense, the recognition for both of them of something 'never seen'. The sketchbook almost instantaneously assumed a pivotal role in the tentative dialogue of interest between them – admitted only to themselves. He showed her, almost incidentally, his sketchbook from recent journeys in the heart of Australia, a collection of drawings of landscape formations, simple vernacular mission buildings, indigenous rock markings and the odd native animal. The elegant economy of the drawings, the selectivity of subject matter, were an unwitting but instant seduction of her, an immediate bond between two professionals who had individually championed hand-drawing in their respective careers of private practice and academia.

In the weeks between that meeting, and the continuous two weeks of site visits around Australia, the sketch provided the subterfugal subject for emails. She offered images of sketches by C. R. Mackintosh and Enrique Miralles; he shared observations of the way notable Australian architects draw. Yet it was during the site tours that their mutual practices of drawing became a covert declaration of desire. As the pair assiduously documented each of the more than forty projects under review, their individual sketchbooks were the vehicle for endless conversations and comparisons of both architecture and drawing techniques, a way to flatter and flirt in an otherwise public and professional setting. They spontaneously found opportunities to exchange lovers' gifts: tellingly both were aids to the drawing. She happily sacrificed a favourite large lead holder to him when he lost his standard clutch pencil; he gave her the rubber stamp he used to date each page of sketches. Halfway through the tour they were secret lovers, and now drawing each other in the back pages of their books.

The story becomes murkier here, the drawings fewer, as the lovers return to their normal situations – a melancholy portrait from memory, an illustration of a domestic setting the other will never see, a remote landscape to underscore the distance now imposed between them. Ironically, just as the two are most divorced in time and place, their tour sketchbooks unite them publically, as the cover feature, editorial and illustration for the awards issue of the major national architectural journal. These sketchbooks, and those of the succeeding eighteen (when the couple's circumstances alter to allow them frequent assignations), are the primary sources for this chapter. There is one of each prior to their meeting; four of his and one of hers from the tour; one each from a joint visit to the Venice Biennale; two scarlet covered books dedicated to life drawings, and a group of

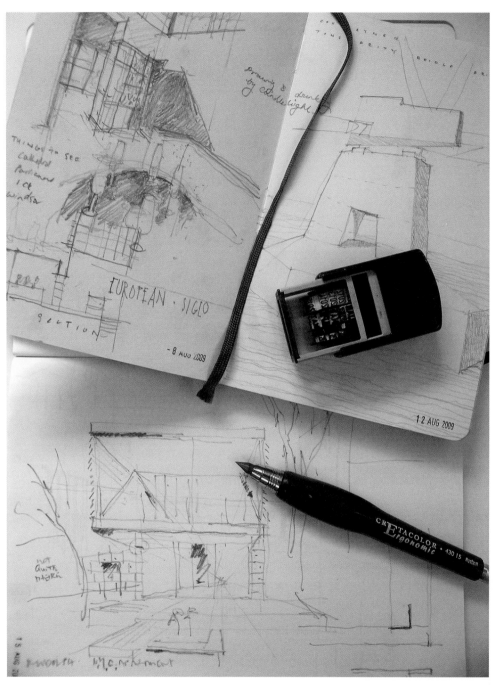

8.3 Through the process of drawing together the lovers establish a professional and personal rapport, and begin an exchange of affection. Source: Image: Peter Malatt and Rachel Hurst, 2010

'everyday' books that chronicle the pattern of their separate architectural lives and the heterotopic interludes where they overlap. It is possible to read in this collection not just the narrative of a romantic collaboration, or different modes of architectural representation, but also the traces of what Frascari would call the facture of the sketch.[8]

BARELY TRACED[9]

Juhanni Pallasmaa begins the chapter 'The Drawing Hand' in his recent book *The Thinking Hand* with the observation that 'Sketching and drawing are spatial and haptic exercises that fuse the external reality of space and matter, and the internal reality of perception, thought and mental imagery into singular and dialectic entities'.[10] He goes on to discuss in detail the tactility and physicality of sketching, however, he concentrates on the connection between mind and body, rather than on the material environment beyond.

If all analogue drawings are fusions of space and matter, the peripatetic sketch more than any other type of drawing bears the trace of where and how it is made, as its immediacy of production places drawer and drawing in a dynamic setting. Examining the sketchbooks reveals the drawings' responses in scale, composition and detail to accommodate the inherent weight of the tools at hand, the page size and constitution of the book itself, the consistency of the graphite, and the size of the lead holder. There is a shift early on, for example, where he borrows her fat Parisian pencil, the pencil she later gives him. His large books flex and distort at the margins, encouraging looseness. Her smaller rigid ones impose invisible margins with not enough room to rest and stabilize the hand: the drawings tighten at the edges. Prolific, skeletal and high contrast drawings emerge from his chunkier tools and flexible books, while more fastidious, layered drawings characterize hers, produced with finer implements and in a single smaller compendium.

Sketchbooks are utilitarian objects to be used and handled. They cannot avoid the *messy* business of making (just as love is a notoriously *messy* affair), and the lovers' books are a rich palimpsest of marks: a few torn edges, a sheen of dried sweat, a dot of lipstick and, for verisimilitude, coffee stains on the edge of a drawing of a café. We can also trace the tempo of their making. There are incomplete drawings, abandoned because of limited time or false starts, and drawings that slip awkwardly off the page. While these blemishes preclude the possibility of a perfect or 'ideal' drawing they are not so much errors, but a history of a drawing's construction and engagement with the material world. As faults they are acceptable ones for, as in love, we learn to love because of, rather than in spite of, imperfections and flaws.

Frascari goes further to suggest that the inevitable physicality of the hand-factured drawing coalesces with the imaginative intent behind it to reveal more:

> Their materiality is dominant; the ink, the paper, the pencil marks, and all the other media used to make them takes over and play a major role in enhancing their power of storytelling. Although they may appear vague and imprecise, they have the exactness of creative thinking impressed in sensual acts of communication.[11]

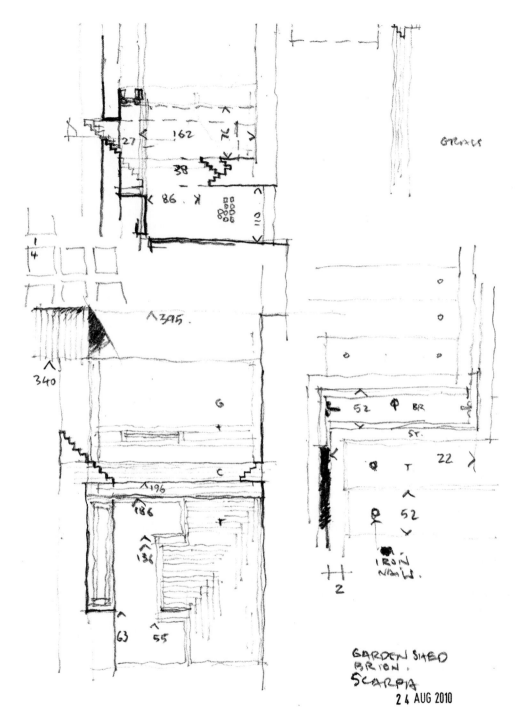

8.4 A comparison of the two hands reveals synchronicities and differences in the way each of the lovers records the same architectural experience. His, on the left, suggest a desire to disassemble the projects. Hers, on the right concentrate on the overall spatial experience. Source: Images: Peter Malatt and Rachel Hurst, 2010

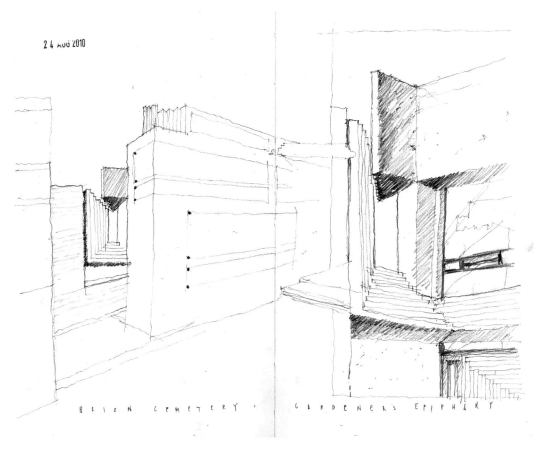

8.5   A comparison of the two hands reveals synchronicities and differences in the way each of the lovers records the same architectural experience. His, on the left, suggest a desire to disassemble the projects. Hers, on the right concentrate on the overall spatial experience. Source: Images: Peter Malatt and Rachel Hurst, 2010

Many of the sketches here are vague and imprecise, yet they allow us to trace two complementary ways of architectural thinking. Commenting on their publication in *Australia Australia*, the editor Justine Clark noted: 'Although quite different, both sets of drawings index the work of coming to a detailed understanding of the projects under consideration. These are drawings made to allow the drawer to see, to understand and remember'.[12] In 'The Drafting Knife and The Pen' Frascari has written of the pen as the dissecting tool of architecture,[13] and the sketches of the architectural practitioner in this love story demonstrate a kind of forensic desire to unravel and disassemble the projects through drawing. His books are full of structural summaries, dimensioned plans, annotated sections and axonometric details. Spread expansively across individual pages, many are practical recordings that compartmentalize and sort the material into discrete ideas or tactics – a compendium for future architectural borrowings or reference. By comparison, hers seem motivated by a desire for comprehensive narrative or didacticism, instinctive to her academic vocation as a teacher of architectural design and drawing. They are scenographic, atmospheric, concentrating on perspective representations, tactile evocations and the entourage and paraphernalia of use and occupation. Generally layered densely on double spread pages, they attempt to collage and evoke the experience of being in a particular place, in order to hand those perceptions on to others. Together the sketchbooks map a commonality of the pair's architectural concerns, as well as delineating the differences that make for intrigue and attraction in any relationship.

I DRAW WITH MY HEART IN MY MOUTH

In the prolific, energetic pages of these sketchbooks two love stories are being played out – that between him and her, and the other a *ménage à trois* with the drawing. We can trace the empathy between the lovers from the first drawings in the recurrent coincidence of the subjects they choose to draw and of the same locality. Later, there are drawings made together, but as deliberate companions to each other. Sometimes there are uncanny synchronicities of drawings done separately, but of identical subjects – for example two versions of airplane wings, as the lovers flew from each other, to different destinations. There are drawings made for each other – studies of architecture, illustrations of shared obsessions of art and food. And drawings of each other's work, built, exhibited or presented academically.[14] Or drawings which attempt to conjure up the absent lover's presence – a hesitant portrait in profile (like some latter day Diboutades); an empty table setting inviting their company; an agitated rendering of the beloved's astrological constellation in the night sky. But it is in the life drawings they make of each other that their love story is expressed most directly: firm sinuous lines, repeated delicate pencil strokes of silhouette and the softest tonal shading act as surrogate caresses, where the pencil replaces the hand, the mouth, in its affectionate embrace of subject. The choice of yielding graphite as preferred medium, as opposed to the indelibility and precision of an ink pen – Frascari's architectural drafting knife – resonates in this context. These *are* architectural drawings, nonetheless, topographical explorations trying to understand not only supporting structure, weight, surface and double curvature, but also the play of light and shade.

They are sketches of love, sketches made in love, with love, and blatantly erotic. Teasingly framed to crop facial features, and with every crevasse and fold of skin tenderly rendered, these images are voyeuristic, not quite pornographic. Yet arguably almost all analogue drawings can be read as a manifestation of erotic desire, characterized as they are by the inherent sensuality of their facture, but more fundamentally, by their optimistic projection towards something ultimately unattainable. 'Desire...' as Alberto Pérez-Gómez points out, '... is experienced as an open horizon ... a phenomenon primary in all things human'.[15] In his extensive discussion of the concept of Eros in architecture he asserts that an underlying aspect of human existence is its essential sense of being that keeps us 'apart' from the world. Besides the obvious parallels of these two lovers separated by some five hundred miles, Pérez-Gómez's identification of Eros as the critical antidote to 'separateness' has wider relevance. The obvious symbolic role of Eros as the spirit that brings male and female together extrapolates to the human desire to unify, or 'be as one', to understand and reconcile separateness in all things, day and night, pleasure and pain, life and death, mind and body. He elaborates:

2 7 JAN 2011

8.6   Life drawings explore not only the topology of space and surface, but the erotic, haptic
quality of hand-drawing drawings. Source: Image: Peter Malatt and Rachel Hurst, 2010

8.7   Life drawings explore not only the topology of space and surface, but the erotic, haptic quality of hand-drawing drawings. Source: Image: Peter Malatt and Rachel Hurst, 2010

Throughout our lives we constantly look for 'something', something that is missing and that might complete us – be it the physical presence of another, the acquisition of knowledge, or the experience of art and architecture.[16]

This lack, however, can also be a gift, as it sets up a dynamic search for fulfilment, for imagination and action.[17] The nature of human space, laden with intention, effort and multi-sensorial experience, is thus the space of desire. The sketch, as the embryonic expression of spatial concepts is then the first visible expression of desire. Its restless incompleteness and economy is the 'open-ended horizon' of potentiality, either initially for a finished drawing, or, beyond that, the projection of a (yet to be) built work (in the manner Robin Evans writes of in *Translations from Drawing to Building*).[18] In gentle graphite explorations and approximations, sketches show the same tender reaching toward knowledge, familiarity and affinity with the subject that a lover's actions to the beloved show. They hover in a delirious position 'midway between wisdom and ignorance'.[19] Falling into sketching, into the absorbed, abandoned mental and physical state it requires, is like falling in love – according to Socrates 'both madness and a revelation of the world as it really is'.[20]

A BIRD CATCHER OF INSTANTS

Like erotic love, sketches are active, often performative and of the instant. While they remain as tangible artifacts, these are merely the traces of an attempt to capture what Hélène Cixous describes as 'the happening of the instant', for [to paraphrase her], 'what is a painter – [sketcher] – but a bird catcher of instants'.[21] In her essay 'The Last Painting or The Portrait Of God' she elucidates on this through analogy with love:

But in life it is "only in the act of love – by the clear, starlike abstraction of what one feels [that] we capture the unknown quality of the instant, which is hard and crystalline and vibrant in the air, and life is that incalculable instant, greater than the event itself."[22]

If the sketch with its insatiable gaze aims to catch Cixous' 'present absolute',[23] the sketchbook paradoxically represents them as history. Pérez-Gómez outlines three structural components of Eros as lack: the lover, the beloved, and the space-time that comes between them, (for the myths of Eros are generally of love deferred or obstructed, just as in this lovers' tale).[24] In the sketch analogy the lover is the artist, the beloved the architectural subject, and the sketchbook is space-time made manifest in the translation from observation of an instant to archival record. Like love, which is both a series of distinct events and a field of sensation, they collect, curate and solidify specific experiences into a whole greater than the sum of its parts.

Sketchbooks by their very form suggest permanence: bound multiple pages that are robustly covered, and often with useful details of end-pockets and bookmarks, they are intended as repositories, albeit informal active ones. Their scale and materiality – hand-sized, often covered with skin or leather (evocative of flesh and carnality?), and able to be held fast with elastic binding – makes them semi-precious, personal possessions to hold dear. Imbued with inherent material 'worth' as objects – books rather than mere paper – most sketchbooks are filled if not self-consciously, then at least with an implicit investment in self-reflection. Their structure compels a narrative, reading by convention from front to back, left to right, and for the most part the sketchbooks here are chronological journals, carefully dated or stamped. The occasional disruption to their chronology is revealing. Tell-tale torn or cut pages indicate not erasure of unsuccessful drawings, but drawings removed as gifts for the other, drawings too personal, too brazen for these otherwise public volumes. She often leaves the first pages blank, to be back filled with a 'significant enough' subject to introduce the collection – like a first kiss that is replayed again and again in lovers' accounts of their meeting. His are more direct. He starts and finishes each book methodically but casually, though keeps the last pages for written material, so as not to dilute the pictorial flow of the book. His practice of dating each book, each page, not with hand written numerals but stamps or labelling tape from his portable kit, gives lie to any sense of the impromptu. She borrows not only the stamp but the ritual also, as a revisiting obsessive tending for the sketchbooks, and an affirmation of the romantic connection.

Other exchanges take place through the course of these books, however, like a true love affair the exchange is not a subjugation of self to the other but a mutual liberation. Is it imaginary or is there a change in each of their work after

8.8   Drawing between the two collaborators becomes an exchange of technique and approach, as well as a communication of ideas and observations. Source: Images: Peter Malatt and Rachel Hurst, 2010

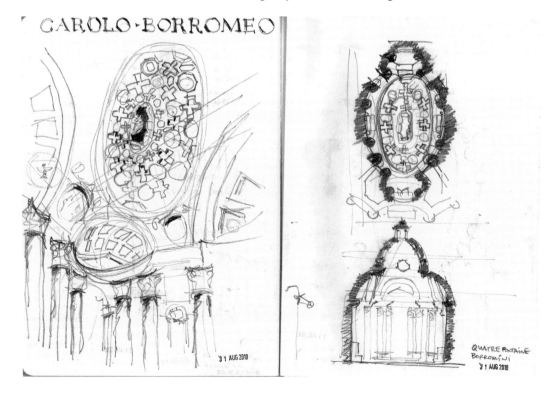

the relationship is consummated? He starts a new book and makes gentle dawn drawings of elegantly proportioned Georgian warehouses: hers become looser, larger and with more contrast. A year, eighteen months later these shifts continue but are more obvious: his drawings show more detail and finish, sometimes layering multiple images on one page, and in life drawings he eschews line in favour of tonal explorations. Hers are stronger, faster, greedier of the page, less fastidious and learning to let go of completion as she learns to let go of a certain future. Yet, these sketchbooks remain intensely of their makers, literally holding the DNA of the drawer fixed in their pages. One cannot consistently disguise one's hand in the spontaneous embodied expression that is sketching, as Chwalisz declares:

> There is no "not getting wet" in this manoeuvre, as there is no escaping the self when sketching ... all things that have passed "through" you, all the horror and delight, pleasure and pain, every word and vision and lovers' touch affects the sketch.[25]

PARTNERS IN LINE

There must be other pairings, more famous, more noteworthy which merit examination more than this one; couples for whom the sketch was a medium for aesthetic, creative as well as erotic, loving exchange? The history of art and architecture is, after all, rife with creative sexual partnerships, especially since women assumed a more visible role in its production. What, for example, of the

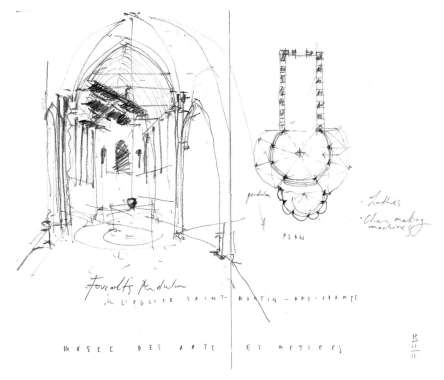

8.9   Drawing between the two collaborators becomes an exchange of technique and approach, as well as a communication of ideas and observations. Source: Images: Peter Malatt and Rachel Hurst, 2010

Mackintoshes, both remarkable artists, or Walter Burley Griffin and his wife Marion Mahoney? What of the liaisons between Ray and Charles Eames, Alvar and Aino Aalto, Louis Kahn and Anne Tyng? But this case study is the one closest to hand, and like a sketch, it benefits from immediacy, immersion and intensity. And like a sketch, it has aimed to explore – sometimes with a brash sweep, sometimes with tentative, delicate probing – the intimacies of how we relate to the world, through the seductively risky act of drawing. How to conclude then, when I want no conclusion, when the horizon is open, no sure sunset to sail into, when I don't know if there's a happy-ever-after? Cixous writes that 'As soon as we draw (as soon as, following the pen, we advance into the unknown, hearts beating , mad with desire) we are little, we do not know, we start out avidly, we're going to lose ourselves'.[26] It is a willing disorientation, both into the beckoning blankness of another new sketchbook and into love. Cixous provides if not the final word, the Mills & Boon asterisks for the end of the chapter: 'Drawing, writing, what expeditions, what wanderings, and at the end, no end, we won't finish, rather time will put an end to it'.[27]

BIBLIOGRAPHY

Barthes, Roland. *Camera Lucida: Reflections on Photography.* London: Flamingo, 1984. Berger, John. "Drawing," in *John Berger: Selected Essays*. Ed. Geoff Dyer. London: Bloomsbury, 2001: 10–14.

_____ "Drawn to that Moment," in *John Berger: Selected Essays:* 419–423.

Borges, Jorge Luis. Epilogue for "The Maker," in *Jorge Luis Borges: Selected Poem*. Ed. Alexander Coleman. New York and London: Penguin, 2000.

Chwalisz, Damien. "12 Letters to the Sketch." Honours dissertation, University of South Australia, 2006.

Cixous, Hélène. "The Last Painting or The Portrait of God," in *Coming to Writing and Other Essays*. Ed. Deborah Jenson. Cambridge, Mass.: Harvard University Press, 1992.

_____. "Without End, No, State Of Drawingness, No, Rather: The Executioner's Taking Off," in *Stigmata*. Edited by Hélène Cixous. Oxford: Routledge, 2005: 25–40.

Clark, Justine. "Drawing out the awards," in *Architecture Australia*. Vol. 98 No. 6 (November / December, 2009): 12.

Evans, Robin. *Translations from Drawing to Building and Other Essays*. London: Architectural Association Publications AA Documents 2, 2003.

Frascari, Marco. "The Drafting Knife and The Pen," in *Implementing Architecture*. Atlanta: Nexus Press, 1988.

_____. "A reflection on paper and its virtues within the material and invisible *factures* of architecture," in *From Models to Drawings: Imagination and representation in architecture,* ed. Marco Frascari, Jonathan Hale, and Bradley Starkey. London: Routledge, 2007: 23–33.

_____. *The Virtue of Architecture: A 2009 Strenna*. United Kingdom: Lulu.com, 2009.

Pallasmaa, Juhani. *The Thinking Hand: Existential and Embodied Wisdom in Architecture.* Chichester U.K.: AD Primers, John Wiley & Sons, 2009.

Pérez-Gómez, Alberto. *Built Upon Love: Architectural Longing after Ethics and Aesthetics.* Cambridge Mass.: MIT Press, 2006.

Probyn, Elspeth. "Glass Selves: Emotions, subjectivity and the research process," in *Oxford Handbook of the Self.* Ed. Shaun Gallagher. Oxford: Oxford Handbooks Online, 2011: 29. Accessed on 27 October 2011: http://www.oxfordhandbooks. com/oso/public/content/oho_philosophy/9780199548019/toc.html. doi:10.1093/ oxfordhb/9780199548019.001.0001.

NOTES

1   Alberto Pérez Gómez, *Built Upon Love: Architectural Longing after Ethics and Aesthetics* (Cambridge Mass.: MIT Press, 2006), 31–68.

2   Hélène Cixous, "Without End, No, State Of Drawingness, No, Rather: The Executioner's Taking Off", in *Stigmata*, ed. Hélène Cixous (Oxford: Routledge, 2005), 36.

3   Jorge Luis Borges, Epilogue for "The Maker", in *Jorge Luis Borges: Selected Poems,* ed. Alexander Coleman (New York and London: Penguin, 2000), 143.

4   Elspeth Probyn, "Glass Selves: Emotions, subjectivity and the research process", in the *Oxford Handbook of the Self,* ed. Shaun Gallagher. (Oxford: Oxford Handbooks Online, 2011), accessed 27 October 2011: http://www.oxfordhandbooks.com/ oso/public/content/oho_philosophy/9780199548019/toc.html. doi:10.1093/ oxfordhb/9780199548019.001.0001

5   John Berger, "Drawing", in *John Berger: Selected Essays,* ed. Geoff Dyer (London: Bloomsbury, 2001), 14.

6   Cixous, "Without End", 32.

7   The panel refereed to was the Australian Institute of Architects National Awards 2009 jury. In this annual process, five distinguished members of the architectural profession are invited to judge approximately 500 awarded state and international entries for recognition at a national level. This is done through a process of preliminary shortlisting and intensive site visits around the country, where the jury effectively 'goes on the road' for a fortnight.

8   Marco Frascari, "A reflection on paper and its virtues within the material and invisible *factures* of architecture", in *From Models to Drawings: Imagination and representation in architecture,* ed. Marco Frascari et al, (London: Routledge, 2007), 23.

9   Cixous, "Without End," 28.

10   Juhani Pallasmaa, *The Thinking Hand: Existential and Embodied Wisdom in Architecture* (Chichester U.K.: AD Primers, John Wiley & Sons, 2009), 89.

11   Marco Frascari, *The Virtue of Architecture: A 2009 Strenna,* (United Kingdom: Lulu.com, 2009), 63.

12   Justine Clark, "Drawing out the awards", *Architecture Australia*, Vol. 98 No. 6 (Nov/Dec 2009): 12.

13   Marco Frascari, "The Drafting Knife and The Pen", in *Implementing Architecture* (Atlanta: Nexus Press, 1988), un-paginated.

14   In addition to site visits to some of his built works under construction or recently completed, the pair collaborated on a numerous public architectural events, lectures,

symposia and presentations. They would characteristically record and illustrate these events in their sketchbooks.

15   Pérez-Gómez, *Built Upon Love*, 7.

16   Pérez-Gómez, *Built Upon Love*, 6.

17   It could be argued that persistent and prolonged lack can also wither desire, and lead to eventual extinguishing of action, replacement or morbidity. The spontaneous 'lived' sketch may become transformed in this case to a tangible trace of loss – a *memento mori* – in the manner that Barthes discusses the photograph as a 'death mask' in Roland Barthes, *Camera Lucida: Reflections on Photography* (London: Flamingo, 1984). For another perspective on the notion of life, and death in drawing see John Berger, "Drawn to that Moment", in *John Berger: Selected Essays,* 419–423.

18   Robin Evans, "Translations from Drawing to Building", in *Translations from Drawing to Building and Other Essays* (London: Architectural Association Publications, AA Documents 2, 2003), 153–93.

19   Pérez-Gómez, *Built Upon Love*, 69.

20   Pérez-Gómez, *Built Upon Love*.

21   Hélène Cixous, "The Last Painting or The Portrait of God", in *Coming to Writing and Other Essays*, ed. Deborah Jenson (Cambridge, Mass.: Harvard University Press, 1992), 104–5.

22   Cixous, "The Last Painting", 104–5.

23   Cixous, "The Last Painting", 104–5.

24   Pérez-Gómez, *Built Upon Love*, 32.

25   Damien Chwalisz, "12 Letters to the Sketch" (Honours dissertation, University of South Australia, 2006), 35.

26   Cixous, "Without End," 26.

27   Cixous, "Without End," 26.

9

One Wound, Two Wounds: The Body as the Site for Writing

Catalina Mejia Moreno

PREAMBLE

The sketchbook is a written/drawn artefact that performs unvaryingly with a site, more precisely two sites, two lines, two traces and two threads. It monitors, documents, and becomes the site of a 'site-writing' project I staged called *One Wound, Two Wounds* to be discussed in this text.

As a means of exploring textual and material possibilities (the patterning of words on a page, the design of the page itself, its edges, boundaries, thresholds, surfaces, the relation of one page to another), the sketchbook becomes the (personal) place for destabilizing an innate signified and signifier,[1] that of a wound and pain. These point to the space where possible new meanings were constructed out from deconstructive processes of drawing, writing, cutting, and pasting. They also offer the material evidence of new critical explorations and possibilities, both autobiographical and performative.

The *One Wound, Two Wounds* site-writing project, 'writes', rather than 'writes about'a(two) site(s), allowing it(them) to intervene and reinterpret itself(themselves) by remaking it(them) on my own terms.

> [A wound] My first visit to London and my first visit to Tate Modern. In the
> concrete slab of the Turbine hall, there was a remembrance, Doris Salcedo's
> 'Shibboleth.' Sliding from the entrance all the way down to the hall's boundaries,
> it opens, closes, thickens, and darkens. It is not open anymore. It is closed and
> sealed, present as a still and timeless reminder. Six floors above, a window is
> facing London's skyline. Sitting there, I see a reflection – the scar on my chest.
> Closed and sealed and also still there present and timeless. [Two wounds]

INTRODUCTION

One Wound, Two Wounds is synonymous with a red sketchbook that lives inside a transparent case, and probably in the mind of some that have seen it and heard its story. As a site-writing project it proposes to look at the question of the body and the building as sites for writing. It is an exploration of the body, in relation to building and to a sculptorical trace whose place of encounter is a red sketchbook. Through a combination of texts, photographs, photo-montages, collages and through the use of traditional and material tools of architectural investigation (scale, form, material, site) the project offers a re-interpretation of 'site', 'self' and 'space' as they relate with one another. Thus it aims to suggest new and unexpected relationships between them.

Acting as a third site, the sketchbook acts as the space where possible new meanings are built from deconstructive processes[2] of drawing, writing, cutting and pasting. It is the result of a process that has been through different stages. A process of understanding London-Colombia, past-present and illness-health, the parts of my present and past that I have not been able to uncover. What you are about to read relates above all to an ongoing healing process.

> *September 30, 2009 – London, Rainy Sunday afternoon, Tate Modern:[3] Walking into the Tate Modern for the first time, the first place visited when arriving to London. The Turbine Hall was cold, silent and empty. It generated an uncanny, but peaceful feeling. I searched for the Shibboleth, a meaningful inscription left by a Colombian artist in the concrete slabs of the Turbine Hall. There I saw a line, I saw a surface, I felt its trace, I felt home. That this trace would become a site of memory, I could not imagine then, and even less that it would become '…the site of struggle of memory against forgetting.'[4]*

> *January 24, 2010 – London, Cold Tuesday morning, Bartlett School of Architecture (Room 101):[5] 'Theorising Practices/Practicing Theories' seminar at the Bartlett.[6] My first task and my first challenge is to choose a site. The aim is to develop a site-writing project that as a kind of criticism operates as a mode of practice that '…should aim to perform – through writing – a new kind of criticism, one which draws out the spatial qualities of the critic's engagement with a work, and the reader's interaction with the page. These include the sites – material, emotional, political and conceptual – of the work's construction, exhibition and documentation, as well as those remembered, dreamed and imagined'.[7]*

> *'Site: v1. Intr: To grieve. v2. Trans: To locate, to place. n2. The place or position occupied by some specified thing. Freq. implying original or fixed position.'[8]*

> *'The site is a place where a piece should be but isn't.'[9]*

THE TRACE OF DORIS SALCEDO'S *SHIBBOLETH*

Doris Salcedo, a Colombian artist, is part of the group of international artists selected to site work in the Tate's Modern Turbine Hall in London. In 2007 she spoke in favour of subtleness and soreness. Instead of occupying the space vertically and massively, she opted for the construction of a negative sculpture,[10] *Shibboleth*.

As an open crack running throughout the concrete slabs of the entire floor surface, *Shibboleth* '…refers to the danger at crossing borders or to being rejected in the moment of crossing borders. (...) It is a piece about people who have been exposed to extreme experiences of racial hatred and subjected to human conditions in the first world.'[11] By introducing the Turbine Hall to another perspective, the idea is that '…all look down and maybe try to encounter the experience of these people … it is a piece that is both the epicentre of catastrophe and the same time outside catastrophe. As you look in you can see, you can get the feeling of catastrophe but nonetheless outside is quite subtle. I wanted to make a piece that intrudes the space, that is unwelcome, like an immigrant, that just intrudes without permission, slowly, and all of the sudden is there, and it is a big presence.'[12]

As a temporary installation it was sited for only a short period of time. Afterwards it would disappear by being closed and sealed without leaving any trace. The space would return to its previous complete state for the next artist. Today the sculpture remains as a line scratched in a piece of paper, as a permanent inscription in the building and as a compelling scar. The trace is barely visible, but it is there. It lives within the building. Intended to disappear its trace is now permanent.

> *February 18, 2010 – London, Sunny Wednesday afternoon. Tate Turbine Hall.[13] The site chosen was not only talking about my relation to the space and the place through the artwork of Doris Salcedo, but through the feelings that the artwork evoked for me. As a Colombian arriving in London for the first time, she was considered suspicious and held in immigration at the airport for two hours. Even with a student visa given by the UK Border Agency in Bogotá one month prior to travel, she had in her hand a police paper with a box ticked 'retained.' Being observed and questioned reminded me of my status as an immigrant. My chest hurt.*

> *'Trace, n: 1. A mark or line left by something that has passed. 2. A vestige of some past thing 3. Something traced or drawn. Trace, vt: 1. To delineate, sketch. 2. To write painstakingly. 3. To copy by following the lines or letters as seen through a semitransparent superimposed sheet.'[14]*

DORIS SALCEDO'S CONSTRUCTED SURFACE FOR *SHIBBOLETH*

As a starting point my project was based on Doris Salcedo being Colombian, and that she gave expressions in her artwork of notions of difference as well as the context of immigrant struggles and realities. The artist's work was a place in space, a place in history and from then onwards a place in my own history.

My sketchbook pages began to be filled with drawings, words and collages. The interest in *Shibboleth* slowly began to shift, hence unveiling my attraction for the intriguing installation's superficial appearance, to its materiality, its permanence, and to how it was and to how it is, and to what it was and what it is. When opened, it appeared as a crack, as an accidental cut. According to the artist's intention, it was a constructed cut, a thoughtful inscription, a line full of meaning, a reminder, 'a question mark, a disruption, not only in the space but also in time, what is it before and what is going to happen after'.[15]

Shibboleth is a story of overlapping and hidden meanings, materials, and of construction methods. Today it is a trace that is nothing more than the memory of itself, nothing other than the representation of a past memory and in which surface acts as the representation of a construction made in time that remains under and over the concrete slabs of the Tate's Turbine Hall floor, with its last layer as its visible surface. This surface reverberated inside me. I felt a poetic drive rising as I began to experience resonances, sentimental repercussions and reminders of my past.[16]

> *April 01, 2003 – Bogotá. Santafé Hospital. Waiting, staring silently at the neon lights:*[17] *A surgery room is always an uneasy place, marked by anxiety, nervousness, and uneasiness. Waiting for a surgeon to come while being left in a hospital bed. Light after light above me. Bright white light and the awkward smell of cleanliness. I kept staring insistently at the huge intervention tools over a table. The surgeon's words echoing in my mind: 'You are a beautiful woman with a beautiful torso. I will draw a line. The cut will be smooth. I will take care of you. I promise it will be a beautiful scar.'*

> *'Cut n1: The drawing or casting of lots: †with or by cut, by lot. Obs. Cut adj: a. Gashed or wounded with a sharp-edged instrument; having an incision made in it.'*[18]

DECONSTRUCTING THE TRACE CONSTRUCTED BY DORIS SALCEDO'S *SHIBBOLETH*

Facing the intervened concrete slabs, my question was how to proceed. The first step was to deconstruct graphically and pictorially the *Shibboleth's* trace. The place to do this would be a sketchbook. The space was its white paper. My intention was to destabilize its innate relationship between signified and signifier[19] as I looked to construct from this deconstructive process. I hoped to isolate it from its political and cultural significance wanting to transform its inherent signification that somehow affected me. As a chosen site, the encounter forced me to reflect upon myself. I began rubbing, measuring and redrawing, cutting, pasting and translating a response to the artwork in a sketchbook, by trying to describe its layers and understanding it means of construction. That was, to quote de Certau, 'my way of operating.'[20]

> *February 18, 2010 – London, Cloudy Saturday evening. Tate Modern, 7th floor.*[21] *One day, after working over the Shibboleth's trace and while staring at the Thames, a reflection, and another trace came into prominence – the scar on my chest. I kept staring at it realizing that every time I see myself reflected I look for my scar. In that moment and almost unconsciously, I was looking for it in the reflection. Observing and thinking about it, its reflection in the window gained more importance than the silhouette of St Paul's Cathedral behind.*

> *'Scar, n: The trace of a healed wound, sore, or burn. Scar, n: A crack, chink; a cut, incision. Obs.'*[22]

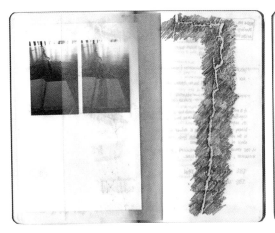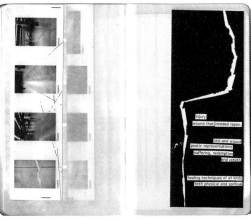

The scar, its trace, as an inscription in my body, brought with it parts of my past which I had not healed entirely and which in that moment, I did not want to think about. *[One wound]* Instead, seven floors down and on my way out, a trace in the Turbine's hall floor: Doris Salcedo's *Shibboleth*. An inscription, that as the scar in my chest, I unconsciously looked for every time I visited Tate Modern. *[Two wounds]*

> 'Wound, n: A hurt caused by the laceration or separation of the tissues of the body by a hard or sharp instrument, a bullet, etc.; an external injury.'[23]

9.1   Sketchbook pages. (De)construction work in progress. First contact with Shibboleth. First thoughts brought up by Shibboleth. Source: Image: Catalina Mejia Moreno 18 February 2010

EVADED AND REAL SITE OF INTERVENTION: MY SCAR

Into the pages of the sketchbook, anatomical representations began to appear subtly as an allegory of the engineering work done by Salcedo in Tate Modern as an attempt to propose a dialogue between anatomical and architectural representations in drawings and texts. The deconstruction of *Shibboleth* was slowly becoming a process of deconstruction of the scar on my chest[24]. I confronted the picture before me and within me. What began as cultural history and artistic representations became a search for my intimate geography. Rather than situating my body, I was trying to defamiliarize it through drawings that reflected my bodily scar.

Evidencing my approach to the representations of the trace left in the concrete slabs and the trace left on my skin, the sketchbook became the space for analyzing and reflecting upon their common language, which resembled Kathy's Prendergast artwork.[25] 'Her maps and objects chart the territory of the unconscious making apparent a fluid, volatile world that ebbs and flows beneath the surface of everyday life'.[26] 'The verbal unit (word, sentence) is reconceived as a material unit, the page. But the whole page in turn must now be reconceived as capable, beyond its own material fragility, of somehow bearing the record of the material world.'[27] My drawings, photographs and montages timidly constructed page after page of the sketchbook, evoking a series of associations beyond any rational interpretation,

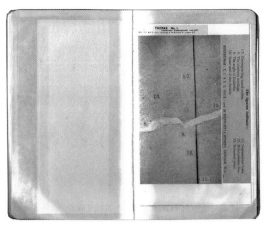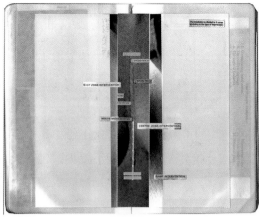

9.2 Sketchbook pages. (De) construction work in progress. First anatomical and architectural dialogue. On the left Shibboleth, on the right, my scar. Source: Image: Catalina Mejia Moreno 15 March 2010

and seeming to spring from a personal coded impulse. Rather than describe the site as a given topology or geometry, they seemed to recall a particular kind of perceptual encounter relating to exposure.

Through a 'free-association' process,[28] *Shibboleth's* trace evoked Salcedo's thoughts to make it and the object inseparable from one another. It started to evoke and act as what Christopher Bollas referred to as an 'evocative object' in that '…those objects leave an imprint in our unconscious that is partly the property of the thing-itself and mostly the result of its meaning within our individual self. If any of these experiences is usually evocative it will, according to Freud's model at least, "drive a shaft" down into the self's unconscious, where it will join existent and moving lines of thought'.[29]

I wondered about the process of the project and how it had been easier to deconstruct the trace in the floor than to deconstruct the trace on my skin. As Dennis Cosgrove noted in relation to trust in the European 'discoverers' of the new world, '…measuring and mapping, imagining the landscape in the mind or inscribing it onto paper are more rapid, less dangerous and more secure ways of coping with unknown space than penetrating the Appalachian forests with axe or trekking the featureless grasslands.'[30] I continued working in the same way and with the same method of deconstructing technical drawings, photographs and descriptive texts to construct new meaning. I saw this process as deconstructing to reconstruct. Unconsciously I was following the allegorical procedure as referred to by Benjamin's terms.[31] Every page of the sketchbook evidenced the intention of transforming items and objects into signs, and of transforming signs into new signs in appearance and context.

Initially, the word 'trace' as signifier, meant pain to me, both physical and emotional. By destabilizing this through a deconstruction of the original plans and descriptive texts, which depicted both the construction of *Shibboleth* and the surgical intervention in my body, I was looking to be able to replace the notion of pain. A transformation of 'pain' to 'heal' would take place. The words 'wound' and 'scar' as signifiers that relate to pain also began to change and the pain slowly began to heal. 'These forms of intercourse are spiritual moments if we understand by this that each embodiment carries with it the spirit of the signifier....,'[32] and this was happening. *Shibboleth* became the mirror of my personal, intimate experience, considered as a bodily sensory trace or an 'undigested experience.'[33] The sketchbook became the place for these traces to live.

> *March 23, 2010 – London, rainy Wednesday evening. Jeremy Bentham's Pub:*[34]
> *Talking about the project, everyone seemed relaxed. I kept silent. Then the question, what did I think about mine. Confused, I started crying. They said 'you can not see it because you are scared. It is there, it is your sketchbook, what else are you looking for?' Evidently, I was evading the real site I was working with. I was scared of opening a wound I thought I had closed years ago, but which had not healed. I was scared of being hurt. There were memories embedded in 'the object' I was dealing with that I did not know if I was prepared to work upon.*

> *'Pain, n: Physical or bodily suffering; a continuous, strongly unpleasant or agonizing sensation in the body (usually in a particular part), such as arises from illness, injury, harmful physical contact, etc.'*

THE RED SKETCHBOOK: ONE WOUND, TWO WOUNDS

Gradually my project shifted from the architectural building to that of the human body. In enacting the body as the site of writing, it assumed and addressed the unforeseen connection between the building's scar and the construction of my own experience. In line with the projections of Wodiczko's the work attempted '...to provoke a bodily confrontation with architecture. You can really match part of the body with part of the building, something that is hard to imagine without seeing it.'[35] It presented an unexpected mourning, through which it was possible 'to see projected images as though they were projected from inside the body out, onto the building'[36] and its' reverse.

As a dialogue working over the disjunction between body and building as text, sketch and as lived experience, the process was questioning the limits of the artwork to reflect the body as site, and bodily association to a building in order to reveal their reflected construction. It presents an encounter in which architecture and place address the individual's experience through their placement within it. The site-writing project '...defined in these relationships between spaces and spatial practices, [how] this site-specific work tests the stability and limits of the very places it *acts out*, at once relying on the other of the sites it is so frequently seeks to question or disrupt. In this sense, site-specific art is defined precisely in these ellipses, drifts, and leaks of meaning, through which the artwork and its place may be momentarily, articulated one in the other.'[37] Memory, history, site, home, self and place collapse. The body became the primary site of memory and expression and the primary site of the experience of pain. The place for deconstruction was the sketchbook; the space for reconstruction was its white paper. The sketchbook here was capable of providing an external image of internal events.

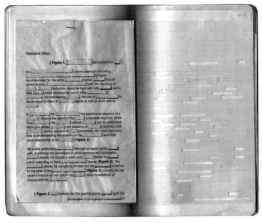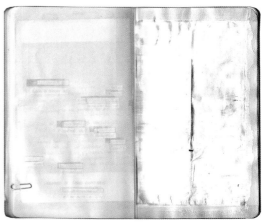

9.3   Sketchbook pages. Sketchbook. (Re)construction process. Manipulated description of a *Thoracotomy* (surgery). A cut that starts to heal. Source: Image: Catalina Mejia Moreno 10 April 2010

April 27, 2010 – Room 101, Bartlett School of Architecture. Project submission: I opened a transparent case. Inside it was a much travelled and manipulated sketchbook. Page by page I began to narrate its story, page by page I began to explain its construction, I turned page after page as all my classmates, the tutor and the invited critics gathered around the table. Page by page I shared my project of mourning.[38]

'Heal, n: Sound bodily condition; freedom from sickness; health. b. Recovery, a cure. Heal, v: To recover.'[39]

BIBLIOGRAPHY

Blunt, Gillian and Gillian Rose, eds. *Writing Women and Space. Colonial and Postcolonial Geographies*. New York: The Guilford Press, 1994.

Bollas, Christopher. *The Evocative Object World*. New York: Routledge, 2009.

Corner, James. & Alex McLean, eds. *Taking Measures Across the American Landscape*. New Haven: Yale University Press, 1996.

Cowan, Bainard. "Walter Benjamin's Theory of Allegory," in *New German Critique* No. 22 Special Issue on Modernism Winter 1981: 109–122.

de Certau, Michel. *The Practice of Everyday Life*. Berkeley: University of California Press, 1984.

Derrida, Jacques. *Dissemination*. London: The Athlone Press, 1981.

Elam, Diane. *Feminism and Deconstruction: Ms en Abyme*. London: Routledge, 1994.

Flam, Jack, ed. *Robert Smithson: The Collected Writing*. Berkeley: University of Californa Press, 1996.

Hooks, Bell. *Yearning: Race, Gender and Cultural Politics*. New York: Turnaround Press, 1991.

Jones, Amelia and Andrew Stephenson. *Performing the Body / Performing the Text*. London: Routledge, 1999.

Kaye, Nick. *Site-Specific Art: Performance, Place and Documentation*. London: Routledge, London, 2000.

McKee, Francis. *Kathy Prendergast: The End and the Beginning*. Dublin: Merrel Publishers in association with the Irish Museum of Modern Art, 1999.

Muntadas, Antoni. *On Translation: Paper BP/MVDR. Intervention in the Mies Van der Rohe Pavilion*: Barcelona: Fundació Mies Van der Rohe, 2010.

Rendell, Jane. *Art and Architecture A Place Between*. London: I.B. Tauris, 2008.

_____. *Site-Writing: Architecture of Art Criticism*. London: I.B. Tauris, 2011.

Scarry, Elaine. *Literature and the Body. Essays on Populations and Persons*. Baltimore: The Johns Hopkins University Press, 1988.

_____. *The Body in Pain: The Making and Unmaking of the World*. Oxford: Oxford University Press, 1985.

Symington, Joan and Neville Symington. *The Clinical Thinking of Wilfred Bion*. London: Routledge, 1996.

Wodiczko, Krzysztof. *Krzysztof Wodiczko: Instruments, Projeccions, Vehicles*. Barcelona: Fundacio Antoni Tapies, 1992.

NOTES

1   As discussed in Jacques Derrida, *Dissemination* (London: The Athlone Press, 1981), vii–xxxii.

2   Broadly speaking, my approach in this project takes up certain precepts of deconstructivism as a way of interacting with objects and writings. It aims to destabilize binary assumptions, as Jane Rendell has proposed in her book *Art and Architecture: A Place in Between* (London: Tauris, 2006), as well as to open spaces for 'undecidability' and 'determinate oscillation between possibilities' as Diane Elam has argued in *Feminism and Deconstruction: Ms en abyme* (London: Routledge, 1994). By questioning established and unified methodologies of thinking, the deconstructive process attempts to understand and re-constitute 'self', 'site' and 'space' without resorting to linear, hierarchical, holistic or binary ways of being.

3   Diary entry recorded in sketchbook. 30 September 2009.

4   Bell Hooks, *Yearning: Race, Gender and Cultural Politics* (New York: Turnaround Press, 1991), 148.

5   Diary entry recorded in sketchbook. 24 January 2010.

6   Discussed by Rendell in 'Course Introduction: Theorising Practices/Practicing Theories,' 2010.

7   Jane Rendell, *Site-Writing: Architecture of Art Criticism* (London: I.B. Tauris, 2011).

8   *"Oxford English Dictionary,"* accessed 26 April 2013 (http://www.oed.com).

9   Jack Flam, *Robert Smithson: The Collected Writing*, ed. (Berkeley, Cal.: University of Californa Press, 1996), 249–50.

10 As discussed in Mieke Bal, '*Montage in the Turbine Hall: Doris Salcedo's Political Aesthetics,*' Bartlett International Lecture Series. 12 December 2007.

11 Doris Salcedo, 'Shibboleth'. *The Unilever Series: Doris Salcedo*, http://channel.tate.org.uk/tateshots-blog/2007/10/05/issue-8/.

12   Salcedo, 'Shibboleth'. *The Unilever Series: Doris Salcedo*, http://channel.tate.org.uk/tateshots-blog/2007/10/05/issue-8/.

13   Diary entry recorded in sketchbook. 18 February 2010.

14   *"Oxford English Dictionary."*

15   Salcedo, 'Shibboleth'. *The Unilever Series: Doris Salcedo*, http://channel.tate.org.uk/tateshots-blog/2007/10/05/issue-8/.

16   Christopher Bollas, *The Evocative Object World* (New York: Routledge, 2009), 53.

17   Diary entry recorded in sketchbook. 26 February 2010.

18   *"Oxford English Dictionary."*

19   Derrida, *Dissemination,* vii–xxxii.

20   Ways of operating, as De Certau states, 'are styles of action that intervene in a field which regulates them at a first level (...), but they introduce into it a way of turning it to their advantage that obeys other rules and constitutes something like a second level interwoven into the first.' Discussed in Michel de Certau, *The Practice of Everyday Life* (Berkeley: University of California Press, 1984), 30.

21   Diary entry recorded in sketchbook, 18 February 2010.

22   *"Oxford English Dictionary."*

23   *"Oxford English Dictionary."*

24   'The philosophy of deconstruction developed by Jacques Derrida has allowed us to critique binary thinking and understand how the hierarchical relationship often assigned to two terms in a pair is not natural or pre given but a social construction that can change according to how we are positioned. In a binary model, everything that one is, the other cannot be, thus limiting the possibility of thinking of two terms together'. Jane Rendell, *Art and Architecture A Place Between* (London and New York: I.B. Tauris, 2008), 9.

25   Her images 'problematize both the discourse on geography and the representation of women and their reciprocal use. Both share this process of making the unknown known, through exploration, investigation and inscription. Though Kathy Prendergast presents a naked female body, her drawings unsettle the customary erotic potential of images of the female body by using codes of cartography. (...) Her images draw us in as explorers, navigators, engineers, in search of fullness, wholeness, and simplicity of meaning, only to disrupt the process of reasoning and understanding by their ambiguity. This search, and its frustration by ambiguity, provokes recognition of complicity in forms of knowledge acquisition and the power relation claims to know, to speak for, and to represent. (...) Kathy Prendergast draws on traditions of representation of women in order to deconstruct their supposed neutrality'. See: Catherine Nash, 'Remapping the Body/Land: New cartographies of Identity, Gender and Landscape in Ireland', in *Writing Women and Space. Colonial and Postcolonial Geographies*, eds. Alison Blunt and Gillian Rose (New York: The Guilford Press, 1994), 234.

26   Francis McKee, *Kathy Prendergast: The End and the Beginning* (Dublin: Merrel Publishers, in association with the Irish Museum of Modern Art, December 1999), 18.

27   Elaine Scarry, *Literature and the Body. Essays on Populations and Persons*, (Baltimore: The Johns Hopkins University Press, 1988), 76.

28   'Free association is always a 'compromise formation' between psychic truths and the self's effort to avoid the pain of such truths'. See Bollas, *The Evocative Object World*, 9.

29   Bollas, *The Evocative Object World*, 83.

30   Discussed by Dennis Cosgrove in 'The Measures of America', in *Taking Measures Across the American Landscape*, eds. J. Corner & A. McLean (New Haven: Yale University Press, 1996).

31   'Allegory is pre-eminently a kind of experience. A paraphrase of his exposition might begin by stating that allegory arises from an apprehension of the world as no longer permanent, as passing out of being: a sense of its 'transitoriness', an intimation of mortality, or a conviction, as in Dickinson, that "this world is not conclusion." Allegory would then be the expression of this sudden intuition. However, allegory is more than an outward form of expression; it is also the intuition, the inner experience itself. The form such an experience of the world takes is fragmentary and enigmatic; here the world ceases to be purely physical and becomes an aggregation of signs'. See Bainard Cowan, 'Walter Benjamin's Theory of Allegory', *New German Critique*, No. 22, Special Issue on Modernism (Winter, 1981), 110.

32   Bollas, *The Evocative Object World*, 72.

33   Discussed by Joan and Neville Symington in *The Clinical Thinking of Wilfred Bion* (London: Routledge, 1996).

34   Diary entry recorded in sketchbook. 23 March 2010.

35   Krzysztof Wodiczko, *Krzysztof Wodiczko: Instruments, Projeccions, Vehicles*. (Barcelona: Fundacio Antoni Tapies, 1992), 202

36   Wodiczko, *Krzysztof Wodiczko: Instruments, Projeccions, Vehicles*, 202.

37   Nick Kaye. *Site-Specific Art. Performance, Place and Documentation* (London: Routledge, London, 2000), 57.

38   Diary entry recorded in sketchbook. 27 April 2010.

39   "*Oxford English Dictionary*."

10

Let's Draw the Line: The Hidden Pages of Pakistani Artists

Roohi Shafiq Ahmed and Abdullah Muhammad Iyhab Syed

INTRODUCTION

In February 2008 we curated a show entitled: 'Let's Draw the Line' at the Chawkandi Art gallery in Karachi, Pakistan. The show exhibited an introductory survey of drawing practices by twenty-two Pakistani artists (thirteen males, nine females), who either use drawing as their primary means of expression or as a source of gathering knowledge and their own artistic vocabulary. The premise of the exhibition was 'to project a polarity of ideas', viewing drawing as a linear activity, and to connect drawing to 'its maker and viewer…public or private.'[1] The exhibition was the first in Pakistan to examine drawing as both a finished artwork and as a process of study.

Besides finished drawings, a selection of studies and pages from sketchbooks were shown that otherwise may never have been viewed. The inclusion of such sketches stemmed from a necessity to offer insight into the development of each artist's practice. The process of collecting these specimens for exhibition was met with enthusiasm from some artists, while others saw their sketches as a private activity, having either no critical or commercial worth, or being of unimaginable personal value. After offering our assurances of research and critical value, the artists provided sketches that they felt comfortable in sharing. Some even invited us to be actively involved in the selection process. We passionately and critically analysed their 'hidden' collection of sketches, recommending possible inclusions. The examples ranged from the messy and torn to neatly bound and organized Moleskine sketchbooks. Loose sketches drawn on a wide variety of found paper, from invitation cards to newspapers, magazine covers to electric bills and calendar diaries. The experience of sifting through these examples pushed us to closely investigate the nuances of these collections, including the self-censorship of these hidden pages. This chapter is a result of this experience and identifies the role of drawing and sketching among the artists and the degree of self-imposed censorship in their art practice and where they 'draw a line' in terms of sharing and articulating their ideas, specifically on a sketchbook. Furthermore, the present chapter goes beyond the scope of the original exhibition to include evidence from a fresh group of artists.

Pakistan has a strong historical connection with the idea of a 'drawn line', both in public and private spaces. The first such *line* drawn on 14 August 1947, occurred when the geography of the Indian subcontinent was altered to bring Pakistan into being. Since its inception, the nation has been in a continuous process of drawing, erasing and redrawing lines to sketch a separate identity for Pakistan. As a new nation, Pakistan was an amalgam of a number of ethnicities, regional languages and religions dominated by the state religion, Islam. Muhammad Ali Jinnah (1876–1948), the founding father of Pakistan and the unifying factor of its diverse identities, passed away within a year of Pakistan's founding. A decade without strong leadership then ensued, followed by a series of military rulers, effectively blurring the line between democracy and dictatorship. Furthermore, struggles between the political parties, religious groups and the military created an entanglement of ideological lines that permeated every strata of society, while the border lines with Afghanistan, Iran, China, and the newly-created and disputed border of Kashmir with India, produced an on-going political game of power and blame that further impacted on the nation's mind-set. Today, these physical and psychological boundaries are constantly challenged due to a lack of stable infrastructure and the thrust of globalization, the distinction between the private and the public is becoming less pronounced in Pakistan, forcing individuals to protect their wellbeing and retain the identity. Such are the challenges faced by Pakistani artists. They form their public identity through these issues, which go deeper to inform their private lives; the crossover from the public to the private generates varying degrees of self-imposed boundaries based on beliefs, opinions or prejudices. The situation is aptly summarized by renowned artist, curator, and Dean of School of Visual Art – Beaconhouse University, Salima Hashmi that the Pakistani nation live in an environment too volatile for anybody else to make sense of it, '[W]e barely make sense of it ourselves, but we live it and that is sense enough'.[2]

DRAWING AND SKETCHES IN PAKISTAN

Art making in Pakistan is still rooted in tradition, and the role of the sketchbook has been revered to the point that the act of sketching is regarded as an intimate activity that remains obscure. Despite this construct, in the short history of contemporary Pakistani art, sketchbooks have been a fertile ground for artistic exploration. Contemporary Pakistani Masters such as Sadequain, Ali Imam, Gulgee, Bashir Mirza, Jamil Naqsh and Zahoor ul Akhlaq, have all had explored drawing and kept sketchbooks. Sadequain and Gulgee flaunted their drawing and calligraphic skills in public, however, the sketchbooks of such masters were seldom exhibited. Riffat Alvi, prominent artist and the art director of V.M. Art Gallery, when asked if the sketches have been part of the Pakistani exhibition scene, responded: 'No, never!'[3] Furthermore, she can only recall Bashir Mirza exhibiting his drawings in his own gallery in 1975 and the exhibition of Tassaduq Sohail's few drawings upon his return from the UK during the 1980s. The eminent Pakistani art historian and critic Marjorie Husain added to this short list with the exhibition of Jamil Naqsh's sketches at the Momart gallery in 1995 in Karachi, and of Sadequain's drawing and sketches in Sadequain: The Holy Sinner 1954–1987, a retrospective exhibition held in 2006 at the Mohatta Palace Museum, Karachi. Other than that, she cannot recall any gallery showing sketches as a focused investigation of drawing and sketches until our curatorial project, 'Let's Draw the Line' in 2008.

The 'Let's Draw the Line' participating artists' views on what sketching and drawing is were recorded. Some did not differentiate sketching from drawing, using them as interchangeable concepts, though others identified distinct characteristics for each. In 'Let's Draw the Line' exhibition catalogue (2008), Durriya Kazi sees a drawing as approximating 'an idea [or] the thinking process.'[4] For Meher Afroz, 'drawing is a living obsession', and sketches are 'just records of my surroundings, a type of memory or reverberation of my thoughts.'[5] Miniature painter, Waseem Ahmed uses drawing as preparatory work.[6] For Nahid Raza, drawing is a methodology of gathering thoughts and symbols.[7] Muhammad Ali Talpur[8] and Rabia Zuberi[9] see drawing as a record of their everyday lives. For Tassaduq Sohail, drawing is a way to preserve 'haunting memories.'[10] In her review of 'Let's Draw the Line', art critic Salwat Ali noted that 'the show attests to the unique properties of drawing and its standing as the most intimate, immediate and versatile art medium' and the sketches 'provide clues but still [solicit] inquiry'. She further positions drawing as 'completely subjective of all visual art activities' but 'no longer enjoys the spotlight it once had… prompt[ing] conjecture on its status and importance in current art practice.'[11] After observing Anwar Jalal Shemza's sketches, artist and art historian Iftikhar Dadi concludes that an artist's experiment with ideas in a sketchbook that '… consequently merit detailed study with reference to [the artist's] evolving praxis and in tracing how the [artists] realized [their] ideas in finished works.'[12] Such views, subsequently, highlighted the fact that sketches remain a subtext, and sketchbooks stay hidden, demanding a focused investigation to reveal a clear picture of their importance in Pakistani art.

SKETCHBOOK PAGES OF PAKISTANI ARTISTS: CASE STUDIES

For this research, besides reviewing the statements provided by the artists of the 'Let's Draw The Line' exhibition, interviews were conducted to collect data. The participants comprised of eleven males and eight females, ranging in age from 21–65. Participants were both emerging and established artists, along with an art critic, a curator, and a gallery director. These one-on-one interviews were conducted in accordance with a pre-set questionnaire that was designed to extricate responses on the following topics: 1) the definition and differences between a sketch and a drawing; 2) the intrinsic physical and emotional value of an artist's sketchbook; 3) perception of a sketchbook either as public or private enquiry and ownership, and; 4) whether sketchbooks are censored in the

Pakistani art milieu, either through censorship (self-imposed or otherwise) or issues related with exhibition, ranging from display to sale. Furthermore, a wide variety of sketchbooks were observed, presenting diverse styles, subject matter, and artistic skill (Ranging from those that are dirty, messy, full of writing, poetry, scribbles, songs, political slogans, wishes and prayers, to those that are clean, organized and well-articulated). These sketchbooks oscillate between notions of hidden meaning and the revelation of what has been imagined and what is finally presented. The data yields nine major themes.

Theme One, 'Kaccha Pakka' (Immature): Underdeveloped Ideas and Lack of Skills

Since the Pakistani art scene is strongly rooted in traditions such as Persian and Mughal miniature painting, or the Bengal school, there is a tendency to judge artists by their command over drawing skills vis-à-vis realistic rendition, specifically the human body, portraiture and still life. Out of nineteen participants, twelve believed that if the artists' sketchbook provides evidence of such skills then the artist is 'genuine' regardless of whether he or she needs such skills in a more 'abstract' contemporary art practice. Artists who do not keep a traditional sketchbook and fail to produce such an evidence of skills, are perceived as either 'immature' or 'incompetent'. Ather Jamal, a leading water-colourist, prolific draftsman and associate professor at the Indus Valley School of Art and Architecture (IVS) highlights this perspective that 'people escape sketchbooks at times because they do not have very strong drawing skills.'[13] Jamil Baloch, another avid drawer and assistant professor at the National College of Arts (NCA) also declares, 'I think you can know about your skills well enough when you go through sketchbooks.'[14] Similarly Riffat Alvi confident in her drawing and sketch practice declares, 'I know my line quality.'[15]

In both academic and professional environments, such strong attitudes towards defining drawing as a skills-based process as opposed to a 'conceptual' approach, makes artists hesitant to share their 'unpolished' sketchbooks. R. M. Naeem, who has an exceptional command over figurative drawing and is an assistant professor at NCA, highlights the value of this process by reflecting on his own training, '[as a student] I was scolded by my seniors when I used to look at their sketchbooks. They thought that their work is *kaccha pakka* and not worth sharing but I find that original.'[16]

Theme Two, Naqal (Copying): Fear of Plagiarism

Almost half of the participants expressed the opinion that sharing sketchbooks can lead to the copying or plagiarizing of ideas. These participants shared examples on condition of anonymity. This 'hijacking' of ideas, so to speak, leaves artists with a fear of being copied. Gulgee, a renowned Pakistani painter who had demonstrated drawing skills in public during the 1970s, later feared of being copied and eventually became extremely private. Marjorie Husain reflects on Gulgee's example and elaborates, '[T]here used to be a freeness before, where artists would go to each other's studios and share, but now it does not happen anymore as there is a fear of being copied.'[17]

Husain's observation of artists working in isolation was further confirmed during the course of this research where the majority of interviewed artists demonstrated considerable interest in going through each other's sketchbooks and sharing ideas, where they had hardly expressed this desire beforehand.

Theme Three, Mashq (Exercise): Preliminary Activity or a Mediating Practice?

Almost all participants regard their sketchbooks as a preliminary process to art making, as a kind of mediation. Leading contemporary drawing artist, curator and writer, Naiza H. Khan very succinctly stated: 'I think everybody finds a mediating space between the initial thought of something, [its] expansion… the simmering of that thought and then its next manifestation into a more public exhibition… I think this mediating space is very important.'[18]

Because of the preliminary nature of sketchbooks, more than half of the participants believed a sketchbook is not something to be shared or displayed in public. For them, the sketches are collections of disjointed ramblings, a means to do *mashq* (exercise), and cannot be classified as finished product to be viewed. Some view sketches akin to experimental specimens in a lab leading them to a discovery, and hence it would not make sense for them to be shared. Participants also hinted at the vulnerability they feel towards their privacy, indicating that they could share a selection of their sketches if they saw critical and commercial value assured by either the curator or the gallery. Moeen Faruqi sees sketches as 'unfinished… more like rough drawings of paintings.'[19] Ironically, when he was approached by us to participate in 'Let's Draw the Line', Faruqi agreed to exhibit a 'self-portraiture study (1989)' (see Figure 10.1) that was executed in the style of a scribbling exercise on a found paper that differed distinctively from his usual style of mark making. The sketch received both critical and commercial success, fuelling the artist's desire to create and exhibit more drawings, including self-portrait. Quoting one of the master painters of Pakistan, Abdur Rahman Chughtai, Marjorie Husain summarizes this desire by agreeing with Chughtai completely where he says 'you must keep your hand flexible,

10.1 Moeen Faruqi, *Self-Portrait Study*, 17.5 × 23 cm, ball point on paper, 1989. Source: Image: Roohi Shafiq Ahmed and Abdullah Muhammad Iyhab Syed

you must keep your line, you must keep on doing this [sketching]… it's like exercise to keep you fit as an artist'.

Theme Four, Zati (Private): Not Wanting to Reveal the Personal

Almost all the participating established artists, who are considered highly skilled and prolific, have shown a certain type of satisfaction in their accomplishments. However, when it comes to sharing their sketchbooks they seem to be uncomfortable and withdrawn. Similar uneasiness is recorded among a cross-section of emerging artists. R. M. Naeem illustrates this inhibition while showing a cupboard full of sketchbooks and loose papers, 'whatever content it has, I call them sketches. If anyone asks me to display it, it will scare the hell out of me.'[20] For 'Let's Draw The Line', despite reservations, Naeem conceded to exhibit a very personal drawing of his wife while she was pregnant, and two sketches of his toddler son from a stack in his cupboard with scribbles of how much milk he had consumed in a day recording the date, time and quantity. He revealed a desire to exhibit some of these private records following the passing of a certain period of time. However, an extremely private collection of sketches will remain hidden never to be shared. Afshar Malik, printmaker and associate professor at NCA, has similarly been drawing and using sketchbooks religiously over the years. He considers sketching as 'romantic' and 'personal'. In his opinion, 'it is a personal portfolio not to be exhibited.'[21] Such views are consistent with the other participating artists, who categorize sketches as 'intimate', which should remain 'private', and which can only be revealed under certain circumstances after a certain time. Munawar Ali Syed brings his private life in this discourse and said that he even keeps such sketchbooks hidden from his family members, alluding to the possible shame and embarrassment that it may cause him or his family. Salima Hashmi sees her sketchbooks as 'very private' and yet, after a while, she feels comfortable in sharing some of them. Nevertheless she declares, 'there are still some that I would not like to share with anybody.'[22] Adeela Suleman, artist and the Coordinator of Fine Arts Department at IVS, asserts that leafing through another artist's sketchbook is synonymous with an 'invasion of privacy'; emphasizing that 'it is like you are prying into someone's drawer.' She continues: '[it's] like looking into someone else's mind and it will corrupt your own thought process.'[23]

Theme Five, Badtameezi (Naughtiness): Transgressions, Censorship and Backlash

The strong discretion governed by the notion of propriety and societal and religious values both in public and private space in Pakistan, can take precedence in the participating artist's art display and sketchbook sharing choices. Munawar Ali Syed illustrates an example that if 'I have drawn nude sketches and if I don't want to show them publicly I won't display them.'[24] Whereas others were of the opinion that art gives the freedom to express oneself, in ways that one may not normally do in everyday life. For artists such as Anwar Saeed, the hidden sketchbook pages are sites of transgression that allow him to be 'free' from social and religious backlash and political correctness. Saeed, a well-established painter and printmaker who has recently gained considerable international attention for his 'queer' art and discourse, welcomes such freedom and remarks that 'you have the freedom to doodle in it [sketchbook] and do a little badtameezi (naughtiness).'[25] Adeela Suleman shares Saeed's thoughts that in a sketchbook one 'can be as cynical, as critical, as badtameez (naughty) as you want without using words'. Although Saeed did not give examples of the resulting consequences, both internal and external, of sharing such 'naughty' thoughts on a sketchbook page, Suleman provides insight to this claim that 'a sketchbook is like reading a diary…words are direct and have the potential to hurt more.'[26]

The possibility that a sketchbook page can inflict harm, either on the viewer, the artist, gallery or the institution, is further argued under the notion of self-censorship by Salima Hashmi, who exhibited Anwar Saeed's sketches on a found book 'I, Pierre Seel, Deported Homosexual: A Memoir of Nazi Terror' (see Figure 10.2) in 'Hanging Fire', an exhibition curated by her at Asia House Museum, New York in 2010. When questioned about self-censorship among artists, she reflects:

> Anwar Saeed's book…was never meant to be public. It was very much a private document. He had to be really persuaded to share it, and even then we did not exhibit some pages and we did not print certain pages and that was a very conscious choice or option. Though, mind you, there was an electronic accompaniment to that where each single page was shown. So I think, there are certain things that an artist makes a decision about and one respects that decision.[27]

10.2 Anwar Saeed, *I Pierre Seel, Deported Homosexual: A Memoir of Nazi Terror* (detail). Source: Image: Roohi Shafiq Ahmed and Abdullah Muhammad Iyhab Syed

THEME SIX, MUGHALTA (FALLACY): MISINTERPRETATION OF WRITTEN WORDS, SENTENCES AND ARTWORKS

With the present multiple interpretations of art, according to Rashid Rana, sketchbooks are 'often misinterpreted and may even be misleading' when read out of context. He gave an example where he shared some pages of his diary style sketchbook with an art researcher to show 'what goes on in the life of an artist' and then later regretted not having edited the sentence 'I am a traditionalist'. The author conducting the interview took the sentence out of context and used it to construct a misleading interpretation of the artist's art practice. Rana further emphasized that although he wrote the text and avoided self-censorship, he should have been asked to explain in 'what context [he] had written, and what [he] actually meant by it.'[28] Similarly, Anwar Saeed feels vulnerable, hinting at the possibility of increasingly being misinterpreted and targeted specifically after the exhibition of his openly homoerotic themed sketchbook. He remarks that 'one arrives at a stage where one feels that one can share it with others, but before that it is better not to reveal it as others start discussing or something happens.'[29] Such views indicate that the personal notes, words, reflections and even doodles in the sketchbook can be taken out of context and can be detrimental to an artist, personally and professionally.

Theme Seven, Mukhafaf and Isteara (Abbreviation and Metaphor)

Some participants described their sketchbooks as a domain where a type of code, or shorthand, is used to record highly personal thoughts. These encryptions not only act as a safety net, a camouflage, but also a time saving tool. Rashid Rana explains that sketchbooks are 'innocent' containing things that are not for publication, for example, 'sometimes I write two words and they are references to recall something, it maybe extremely hard for people to decode them.'[30]

For Niaza Khan, a sketchbook 'abbreviates thought process a…bit like a footnote to something'. Some participants have further described this abbreviated nature of sketchbook as metaphors of their physical being. For R. M. Naeem, the sketchbook is 'like oxygen'. Whereas for Naiza Khan, 'it as a second skin' (see Figure 10.3). Khan explains this physical manifestation of a sketchbook:

> I say second skin very spontaneously…For me it is not only physically carrying it with me everywhere but also the fact that it soaks up all your emotions…
> and sometimes I think it becomes a kind of a neutral space between your very personal ideas and a public space.[31]

Theme Eight, Roznamcha (Record of Everyday Life): A Chronicle

All participants saw their sketchbooks doubling as a diary, their everyday life finding its way in. Uniquely, artist Mansur Saleem uses calendar diaries themselves as sketchbooks, delineating between the public and private, art and life. For him, these diaries are 'a means to record his flashes'[32], providing blueprints for his

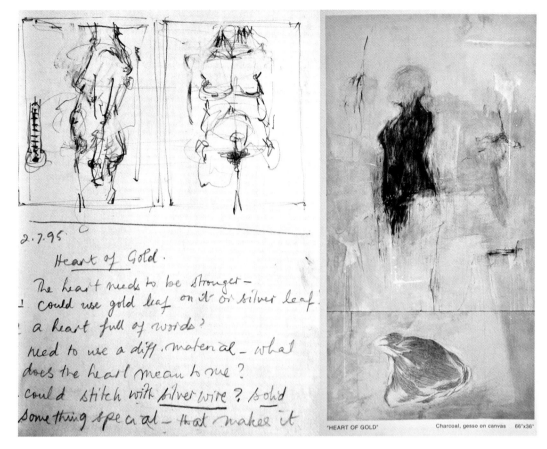

2.7.95

Heart of Gold.

The heart needs to be stronger –
I could use gold leaf on it or silver leaf.
a heart full of words?
need to use a diff. material – what
does the heart mean to me?
could stitch with silver wire? solid
Something special – that makes it

"HEART OF GOLD"   Charcoal, gesso on canvas   66"x36"

artwork. For Naiza Khan sketchbooks are 'records of a time and place…chart(ing) physical and emotional journey.'[33] Rashid Rana talks about his sketchbook as an everyday diary, a travelogue he carries with him. He explained that one can find a to do list, such as 'collect my laundry', and 'drawings or sketches or note[s]…that they are just for yourself.'[34] Aisha Khalid remarks similarly that when she travels, she usually has 'a small diary…[to] write certain things in it. Predominantly they are private thoughts but being an introvert, I don't write in them, maybe a few words for my own reference.'[35]

Theme Nine, Elania (Uncensored Public Display): Rejection or Call for Redefinition

Only a handful of the artists noticeably remarked that sketchbooks are, in fact, not private at all, and can be shared with others without any hesitation, or that the physical sketchbook is not necessary for their art practice. Ather Jamal sees no issues in sharing his sketchbook and sees it as 'an integral part of any visual profession.'[36] Jamil Baloch enthusiastically shares sketches both in private and in public spaces and finds this sharing experience as an 'art form' unto itself.

10.3   Naiza H. Khan, *Sketch of 'Heart of Gold'* (left), 1995 Finished charcoal and gesso drawing on canvas (right), 1995, Artists postcard. Source: Image: Roohi Shafiq Ahmed and Abdullah Muhammad Iyhab Syed

For Imran Qureshi, a leading contemporary miniature painter and associate professor at NCA, there is nothing private about the sketchbook, which is there for everyone to see. In fact, he obliterates the distinction between sketchbook and artwork and proudly remarks that, 'what people do in their sketchbooks I do that directly on my work with paint.'[37] Similarly, Adeel-uz-Zafar, Munawar Ali Syed, Roohi S. Ahmed and Abdullah M. I. Syed also see drawing as 'experimental' and occasionally take advantage of what technology has to offer. Despite training in traditional modes of academic drawing practices, they all consider digital documentations, photographs and performative actions as unconventional sketches (see Figure 10.4) and calls for updating the current perceived notions of sketchbooks and drawing practices.

POST LET'S DRAW THE LINE APPEARANCES OF SKETCHBOOK PAGES

10.4   Abdullah M. I. Syed, *Digital notes and sketch of 'Blooming' installation* (left), 2011. Digitally coloured circles sketch (right), 2011. Source: Image: Abdullah Muhammad Iyhab Syed

In recent years, there has been increased interest in exhibiting drawings and sketches of Pakistani artists both internationally and in Pakistan. Projects such as Anwar Jalal Shemza's 'Take 1' and 'Take 2' (2009–2010) and 'The Drawn from Life' (2008–2010) in London, organized by the UK-based organization Green Cardamom, and 'Hanging Fire: Contemporary Art from Pakistan' (2009–2010) in New York, highlight this resurging interest. The critical and/or commercial success of exhibitions in Pakistan (such as Muhammad Zeeshan's 'Recent Drawings' 2010, Adeel-uz-Zafar and Ayaz Jokhio's 'Two Person Show' at Canvas Gallery, Karachi, 2011, 'Whitewash' at Gandhra Art, Karachi, 2011, and Saeed Akhtar's 'Sketchbook' at Ejaz Gallery, Lahore, 2011) provides evidence that artists, curators and collectors find value in the ritual of drawing and sketching. Marjorie Husain considers this

as 'a revival of interest in drawings in local galleries' and further cites 'many group exhibitions of graphite, ink and charcoal artworks…[as] immensely successful'. She further reasons that the 'art dealers opined that serious collectors of classic art often search for drawings of the Masters as they are considered to be better investments, easier to authenticate and harder to fake.'[38] Furthermore, the public display of sketches and drawings is changing the perception of what is private and what is public in terms of art making and exhibiting. Saira Ansari, who exhibited her 'experimental' drawings and sketches titled 'The Work That Will Probably Never End' at the Grey Noise gallery Lahore in 2010, recalls her experience, 'what was surprising for me was that a lot of people were stopping and reading and that was the first time private and public space did break for me.'[39]

CONCLUSION

In Pakistan, art making is still rooted in tradition and the role of the sketchbook has been revered, yet it remained obscure and without a serious investigation. During the research, asking artists to show their studies and speak about their drawing process and sketchbooks was far more daunting than anticipated. Although a few artists enthusiastically shared their sketches with us, most were not comfortable with the idea of displaying their 'private' work. In Pakistani art milieu, the perceptions of sketchbook pages vary from imaginary spaces to the collective shared space and from free, uncensored image making to records of 'embarrassing truth' about the artists drawing ability. A sketchbook can also hold dangerous ideas and private and intimate thoughts. As a result, many artists feel the need to self-censor. Furthermore, the call for redefining the meaning of the term 'sketch' is eminent. Young Pakistani artists who are exploring technology are sidestepping the paper sketchbooks, defining their digital files as sketches and digital memory storage devices as sketchbooks. Similarly for those pursuing a sculptural practice, a collection of objects and maquettes are akin to sketches. For them the traditional sketchbook can constrain their creativity or slow them down. Such emergent views on the nature of sketching require further research. It is observed that, although many artists see the value in keeping a sketchbook, they rarely see their peers' sketchbooks, despite being very curious about this material. Finally, the paradoxical anatomy of sketchbook as being in some way 'free' and 'hidden' is driven by prevailing religious and social values, as well as the stereotypical view of art per se, where contemporary Western art practice is considered the antithesis of such values. Until artists set aside their personal and professional reservations in sharing their sketches with peers in private, their sketchbooks and sketches will remain hidden from the public arena.

BIBLIOGRAPHY

Alvi, Riffat, interview by Abdullah Syed Muhammad Iyhab and Ahmed Roohi. *Voice Recorded Interview* (December 6, 2010).

Iftikkar, Dadi. *www.greencardamom.net*. October 9, 2009. http://www.greencardamom.net/exhibitions/exhibitions_page.php?id=39 (accessed July 15, 2011).

Syed Muhammad Iyhab, Abdullah, and Ahmed Roohi. *Let's Draw the Line*. Karachi: Chawkandi Art Publications, 2008.

Salwart, Ali. *Archives/45223*. March 8, 2008. http://archives.dawn.com/archives/45223 (accessed June 30, 2011).

AUTHORS' OWN INTERVIEWS

Ansari, Saira, interview by Syed Muhammad Iyhab Abdullah and Roohi Ahmed. *Voice Recorded Interview* (November 12, 2010).

Baloch, Jamil, interview by Syed Muhammad Iyhab Abdullah and Roohi Ahmed. *Voice Recorded Interview* (November 20, 2010).

Faruqi, Moeen, interview by Syed Muhammad Iyhab Abdullah and Roohi Ahmed. *Voice Recorded Interview* (November 20, 2010).

Hashmi, Salima, interview by Abdullah Syed Muhammad Iyhab and Ahmed Roohi. *Voice Recorded Interview* (November 12, 2010).

Husain, Marjorie, interview by Syed Muhammad Iyhab Abdullah and Roohi Ahmed. *Voice Recorded Interview* (December 2010).

Jamal, Ather, interview by Syed Muhammad Iyhab Abdullah and Roohi Ahmed. *Voice Recorded Interview* (December 14, 2010).

Khalid, Aisha, interview by Syed Muhammad Iyhab Abdullah and Roohi Ahmed. *Voice Recorded Interview* (November 12, 2010).

Khan, Naiza, interview by Syed Muhammad Iyhab Abdullah and Roohi Ahmed. *Voice Redcorded Interview* (November 28, 2010).

Malik, Afshar, interview by Syed Muhammad Iyhab Abdullah and Roohi Ahmed. *Voice Recorded Interview* (November 13, 2010).

Naeem, R. M., interview by Syed Muhammad Iyhab Abdullah and Roohi Ahmed. *Voice Recorded Interview* (November 13, 2010).

Qureshi, Imran, interview by Syed Muhammad Iyhab Abdullah and Roohi Ahmed. *Voice Recorded Interview* (November 12, 2010).

Rana, Rashid, interview by Syed Muhammad Iyhab Abdullah and Roohi Ahmed. *Voice Recorded Interview* (November 12, 2010).

Saeed, Anwer, interview by Syed Muhammad Iyhab Abdullah and Roohi Ahmed. *Voice Recorded Interview* (December 14, 2010).

Saleem, Mansur, interview by Syed Muhammad Iyhab Abdullah and Roohi Ahmed. *Voice recorded Interview* (October 19, 2010).

Suleman, Adeela, interview by Syed Muhammad Iyhab Abdullah and Roohi Ahmed. *Voice Recorded Interview* (December 14, 2010).

Syed, Munawar Ali, interview by Syed Muhammad Iyhab Abdullah and Roohi Ahmed. *Voice Recorded Interview* (November 8, 2010).

NOTES

1   Abdullah Syed Muhammad Iyhab and Ahmed Roohi, *Let's Draw the Line* (Karachi: Chawkandi Art Publications, 2008).

2   Salima Hashmi, interview by Abdullah Syed Muhammad Iyhab and Ahmed Roohi, *Voice Recorded Interview*, (12 November 2010).

3   Riffat Alvi, interview by Abdullah Syed Muhammad Iyhab and Ahmed Roohi, *Voice Recorded Interview*, (6 December 2010).

4   Iyhab and Roohi, *Let's Draw the Line*, 26.

5   Iyhab and Roohi, *Let's Draw the Line*, 4.

6   Iyhab and Roohi, *Let's Draw the Line*, 8.

7   Iyhab and Roohi, *Let's Draw the Line*, 34.

8   Iyhab and Roohi, *Let's Draw the Line*, 42.

9   Iyhab and Roohi, *Let's Draw the Line*, 46.

10   Iyhab and Roohi, *Let's Draw the Line*, 36.

11   Iyhab and Roohi, *Let's Draw the Line*.

12   Dadi Iftikkar, *www.greencardamom.net*, 9 October 2009: www.greencardamom.net/exhibitions/exhibitions_page.php?id=39 (accessed July 15, 2011), 3.

13   Ather Jamal, interview by Syed Muhammad Iyhab Abdullah and Roohi Ahmed, *Voice Recorded Interview*, (14 December 2010).

14   Jamil Baloch, interview by Syed Muhammad Iyhab Abdullah and Roohi Ahmed, *Voice Recorded Interview*, (undated November 2010).

15   Riffat Alvi, interview by Abdullah Syed Muhammad Iyhab and Ahmed Roohi, *Voice Recorded Interview*, (6 December 2010).

16   R. M. Naeem, interview by Syed Muhammad Iyhab Abdullah and Roohi Ahmed, *Voice Recorded Interview*, (13 November 2010).

17   Marjorie Husain, interview by Syed Muhammad Iyhab Abdullah and Roohi Ahmed, *Voice Recorded Interview*, (undated December 2010).

18   Naiza Khan, interview by Syed Muhammad Iyhab Abdullah and Roohi Ahmed, *Voice Redcorded Interview*, (28 November 2010).

19   Moeen Faruqi, interview by Syed Muhammad Iyhab Abdullah and Roohi Ahmed, *Voice Recorded Interview*, (20 November 2010).

20   R. M. Naeem, interview by Syed Muhammad Iyhab Abdullah and Roohi Ahmed, *Voice Recorded Interview*, (13 November 2010).

21   Afshar Malik, interview by Syed Muhammad Iyhab Abdullah and Roohi Ahmed, *Voice Recorded Interview*, (13 November 2010).

22   Salima Hashmi, interview by Abdullah Syed Muhammad Iyhab and Ahmed Roohi, *Voice Recorded Interview*, (12 November 2010).

23   Adeela Suleman, interview by Syed Muhammad Iyhab Abdullah and Roohi Ahmed, *Voice Recorded Interview*, (14 December 2010).

24   Munawar Ali Syed, interview by Syed Muhammad Iyhab Abdullah and Roohi Ahmed, *Voice Recorded Interview*, (8 November 2010).

25   Anwer Saeed, interview by Syed Muhammad Iyhab Abdullah and Roohi Ahmed, *Voice Recorded Interview*, (14 December 2010).

26   Adeela Suleman, interview by Syed Muhammad Iyhab Abdullah and Roohi Ahmed, *Voice Recorded Interview*, (14 December 2010).

27   Salima Hashmi, interview by Abdullah Syed Muhammad Iyhab and Ahmed Roohi, *Voice Recorded Interview*, (12 November 2010).

28   Rashid Rana, interview by Syed Muhammad Iyhab Abdullah and Roohi Ahmed, *Voice Recorded Interview*, (12 November 2010).

29   Anwer Saeed, interview by Syed Muhammad Iyhab Abdullah and Roohi Ahmed, *Voice Recorded Interview*, (14 December 2010).

30   Rashid Rana, interview by Syed Muhammad Iyhab Abdullah and Roohi Ahmed, *Voice Recorded Interview*, (12 November 2010).

31   Naiza Khan, interview by Syed Muhammad Iyhab Abdullah and Roohi Ahmed, *Voice Redcorded Interview*, (28 November 2010).

32   Mansur Saleem, interview by Syed Muhammad Iyhab Abdullah and Roohi Ahmed, *Voice recorded Interview*, (19 October 2010).

33   Naiza Khan, interview by Syed Muhammad Iyhab Abdullah and Roohi Ahmed, *Voice Redcorded Interview*, (28 November 2010).

34   Rashid Rana, interview by Syed Muhammad Iyhab Abdullah and Roohi Ahmed, *Voice Recorded Interview*, (12 November 2010).

35   Aisha Khalid, interview by Syed Muhammad Iyhab Abdullah and Roohi Ahmed, *Voice Recorded Interview*, (12 November 2010).

36   Ather Jamal, interview by Syed Muhammad Iyhab Abdullah and Roohi Ahmed, *Voice Recorded Interview*, (14 December 2010).

37   Imran Qureshi, interview by Syed Muhammad Iyhab Abdullah and Roohi Ahmed, *Voice Recorded Interview*, (12 November 2010).

38   Marjorie Husain, interview by Syed Muhammad Iyhab Abdullah and Roohi Ahmed, *Voice Recorded Interview*, (undated December 2010).

39   Saira Ansari, interview by Syed Muhammad Iyhab Abdullah and Roohi Ahmed, *Voice Recorded Interview*, (12 November 2010).

11

The Destruction of Ideas: Disregarding and Discarding Sketchbooks and Avoiding Prying Eyes

Angela Bartram

I

When a sketchbook is complete, I throw it in the waste bin. For me its use is done, its purpose is over. No longer will it serve as an accessory carried as a constant companion in a back pocket or bag. For '*in*-process' the sketchbook exists as the place where reflections and conceptual mappings and suggestions for my work as an artist reside, and as such it necessitates being placed in close proximity to day-to-day activities. I work predominantly, although not exclusively, in live art, sculpture, and video and ideas for works may occur for example on trains, buses, observing a happening or walking in the park. Current and *in* use the now defunct and redundant object functioned as a much needed and well-thumbed pocket storage vessel that captures my creative thoughts, ideas, workings out, tests, trials, measurements, formulae, 'what if's', shopping lists, who to ring, what to pack and top ten 'to do's'. A vital and precious object held physically and psychologically close and with care. The bonded and intense connectivity established with this intimate and cherished personal accessory from its first blank page until the last, was both captivating and crucial to my working artistic process. The sketchbook must therefore be constantly about my person in order to be '*in*-process' and to record ideas, musings and meanderings as they occur. Without this proximity, ideas may otherwise be frustratingly forgotten and lost. Yet, at the removal of the pen from the final blank page, and at the shutting of its cover for the last time of its use, this intimacy becomes irrelevant. Our relationship is spent. Once the last page is crammed with the final batch of unrestrained and untamed developmental marks and notes, the object in its entirety is cast aside. The intensity previously established with the sketchbook, where I consider it an aid in the creative process, undergoes a transformation. Almost immediately, it becomes a historical relic *of* process regarded with the same indifference as when purchased. The vitality once bestowed upon it as the co-conversant in the dialogue of making becomes redundant. It is severed from the active and current process. Here, it was a partner in two-way creative debate, and its role was so important in this dialogue to afford it a status of near personification to be regarded as a best friend, a buddy. Indeed, the hardback pocket sized volume with which I have been indulgently conversing has my allegiance and my trust when in use. But, like a relationship that has served it's purpose it is tossed away and replaced when I can no longer devote my thoughts to its pages due to lack of space. The affection withers and dies. Stripped of the attributes of significance and its 'personable' value, which is invalid in its full condition, the sketchbook returns to its beginnings as an object of little importance in the process of production. The beginnings of ideas and anticipated outcomes on its pages, exciting in the possible potential they hold in the moment when the works are being formulated, infuse the creative process but become less significant to me as it unfolds.

Other artists may be reminiscent about their sketches as the beginnings of a work when their function is complete, but this is not the case for me. An enhanced affection may occur upon revisiting the sketchbook's pages for others, but this sentimentality does not exist in my working process. I become indifferent to their existence and move on, seeking other pages to draw over and inscribe. For me the sketchbook, packed with emergent scribbles and details is now an outmoded research relic, once treasured in the practice of formulating ideas, a mere ghost and distant memory of the course of action in which it was engaged. With a shiny new and fresh one to take its place the old is confined to the recycling bin.

To discard the fully utilized and obsolete sketchbook is reasonable and sensible practice for my work as an artist, as it only has personal value when it is central to the purposes of developing and documenting conceptual progression. There is no sentiment for the object's historical significance to the evolution of ideas; its usefulness is located firmly and reservedly in the moment of conceptual development and its role in the process. There is no reverence for it as a treasured object in this situation, as this only exists when it is an active and valid agent in the situating of my practice. In fact, this methodology of disregarding to progress on from the defunct and historical is so entrenched in my practice that with each sketchbook page turned the one that precedes it becomes discounted. Its status changes from being a significant and valued artistic accompaniment to being that of a waste bi-product of the creative journey. With this transformation, the document becomes an awkward and obsolete volume that records the evolution of past process and production. This discarding of the sketchbook is integral to how I work, how I process and manipulate thought into method and material. Yet, while this approach to sketchbooks may be suitable for the methods and structures that define and shape my practice, their eventual disregard can seem bizarre for others who value them. The person who invests in its pages, the author of its lifeblood, has the right to cherish or banish their creative material, as they deem appropriate. They have rendered the pages of the sketchbook, dedicated time to its existence and allowed intimacy to co-exist between this object and their own art practice and self.

II

The attachments to a sketchbook that are established by its author are formulated through an entrusting of the value of ideas to document, and a dependency on the sketchbook that it will be available as needed to serve that purpose. The author, who relies on the sketchbook to securely contain their research, as it effectively progresses, would generate this attachment to the sketchbook. Creative practitioners often produce their initial research as a series of condensed and controlled experiments in communicating meaning to others within the confines of a sketchbook. They need a vehicle of containment for their creative art-in-progress ideas for effective management. The crucial role the sketchbook has in the development and housing of such trials and discoveries can make its eventual discarding appear rather bizarre. This may even appear as a self-imposed abusive violation of the creative trajectory of the individual's artwork. Beyond the primary user, others who happen to look upon such sketching-documents anticipate that the cover once opened will reveal insight and knowledge about the author. The interest and fascination of the creative mind of the author becomes invigorated for the audience by the promise of an insight into the process of creating making. The sketchbook folios bring the hope that understanding and meaning will evolve about how a creative mind operates upon their reading. The belief that they will allow for a discovery of the thought processes that inform and detail an individual's creative position are expected through the exploration of their content.

The core developmental role of the sketchbook in individual practices, and the insight found through it by artists and observers who are other than its author, results in it being predominantly considered as a precious object that ought not be disregarded. Perhaps this is because the owner's investment in its pages are considered so intimate and open (in that the owner feels at liberty to use it with no, or little restraint) as to make the 'treasured' object an archive of his or her own creative, cognitive and personal development. For this makes it a critically insightful tool to understand how the specific individual creative mind of an artist operates. It promises an understanding of the cultural cultivation of the individual artist who sketched the image, shaped the object, and set the design; since one is directly linked to source-inspirations in looking at initial sketchbook-drafts. The initial indentations, marks, and notes reveal the beginnings of the artwork, design, or crafted object in its rendered and carefully considered entirety. They are the possessors of its secrets, and the crucial developmental twists and turns of the artwork it serves. Subsequent formalization elucidates, fabricates, realizes, and externalizes the initial moment's appeal and substance, but it never can be a true record of it as it occurred. Even if the covers of the sketchbook intend to remain closed to outsiders, the desire to look inside and discover the contents may feel irresistible. Consequently, the sketchbook has acquired a respected position in creative practices that see its regard given heightened value. This is what gives the sketchbook its intrigue and potency. Here it is cherished in the same respect as a favourite or culturally respected book, heirloom, or artifact of personal significance.

III

To destroy is to devalue and cancel out any previous worth. With this in mind, the significance given to safekeeping to posterity of creative sketchbooks, diaries, and archival systems is perhaps the correct and acceptable legacy for the role they played in the process of visual production. Regarded as a notable artifact of both the manipulation of thought into being and of the mind responsible of its fashioning, it may seem abhorrent to destroy or throw away such a device, a safe-keeper, a journal of ideas and creative endeavour. To do so appears unfathomable. Yet, artists have a history of destroying their work in the method of making an exhibition, and this is an acknowledged and established process. As an example of the ways in which artists destroy their work in culturally specific places, the artist Michael Landy produced 'Break Down' in the former C & A store on Oxford Street, a work created by through crushing everything he owned in February 2001. Items on an inventory list produced by Landy, which needed three years to complete, included over seven thousand objects. During 'Break Down' a large grinding machine and overall clad operators reduced the items to dust over two weeks in a performative installation reminiscent of a factory production line. This work points to a nihilism, and to the allusion of ascribing value to artworks. This is specifically significant as 'Break Down' occurred in the financial boom period that began in the 1980s for some artists, including Landy, as Charles Saatchi began acquiring artworks for his private collection. The work also operated beyond the gallery space and brought its attention to an audience who may not be gallery visitors, therefore offering a critique of the value of art beyond this tradition. Additionally, Gustav Metzger produced his first public demonstration of 'auto-destructive' at London's Temple Gallery in June 1960. The performance, which saw Metzger appear from behind a sheet of white fabric as it rotted through his application of hydrochloric acid with a modified paintbrush, was the first work produced from a manifesto written on the subject. The manifesto written by Metzger in November 1969 emphasized how mechanically produced objects are bestowed with dangerous levels of faith in society, even though they eventually degrade and breakdown. This, for Metzger, demonstrated the obsession society has with destruction and the effect it has on items of importance. The object in Metzger's manifesto is akin to the sketchbook here: albeit, even though the sketchbook is not mechanically produced, it is rather subjected to the same potential for being an object of cultural obsession and faith. Although concerned with its contents the reception of the sketchbook in culture, as creative and desirable object, anticipates the same levels of fascination. Cornelia Parker is an artist who also demonstrates the concept of 'destroying to make' in her practice. In 1991 Parker exploded a garden shed and reassembled its disparate elements for the installation 'Cold Dark Matter: An Exploded View' at London's Chisenhale Gallery. The reconfigured 'shed' (installed as an artwork for the first time at Chisenhale Gallery) constituted an assemblage of its suspended, blown up parts. The installation referenced the shed's former self through the delicate and fragile representation of its devastation, and this provoked reconsideration of this otherwise overlooked garden furniture.

Even if the understanding and need of the destruction on display is limited and questionable to audiences, the placement within a gallery or museum context gives it significance. In *Being and Nothingness: An Essay on Phenomenological Ontology*, Jean-Paul Sartre stated that objects '…occupy a determined place…',[1] which I am using in this instance to describe the exhibition space. Galleries and museums were designed specifically to show cultural artifacts. Any object from whatever discipline that is placed within their walls is to be understood this way. The determination of these spaces of making-culture-public ensures that viewers can expect to value exhibits on display. Distressed artifacts, performance relics, obsolete objects, and destroyed paintings for example can be better understood for their value as cultural artifacts if placed within a gallery or a museum. The location of their display situates them as 'cultural' objects. This effect also occurs in 'alternative' venues that label their contents as culturally specific, such as temporary sites. By having the information that a given display is an *artwork*, there is the perception that it *is* 'art' because the information informs of this status.

IV

The sketchbook, as a part of the process and methodology that brings the work into existence, is as vulnerable to destruction as the exhibition piece. The entirety of the work is in the unity of its integral components, of which the sketchbook is pivotal and integral. The mapping and shaping of a cultural product does not merely contain the item on display, but rather the full range of the effects that have brought it into being. If the exhibition object can be destroyed as part of its conceptual meaning, so too can its formative elements.

As the home of the unformulated and ad-hoc means of construction, the sketchbook has qualities that make it a visitor-enticing exhibition-document if placed on display. The knowledge of how creative objects come into being allows for intimacy with the thought-processes that have governed and directed their making, and this generates a fascination that goes beyond the viewing of the final object alone. As a consequence there are an increasing amount of exhibitions dedicated to the sketchbook, the draught, and the working drawings of the creative. From sculptors' drawings, to architects' plans, to designers' prototypes, to painters' diaries, exposures to processes have become increasingly embedded in the cultural landscape of curating and judging art, architecture and design. The 'Diary Drawings' exhibition by Bobby Baker (at London's Wellcome Collection in 2009) and 'The Moment of Privacy Has Past at Lincoln's Usher Gallery in 2010–2011,[2] are two examples of this occurrence. With this in mind it is possible to see why it may be deemed unreasonable and unwarranted to destroy a sketchbook or commit artworks to waste. Such items of art could go on display and allow others to understand the mechanisms that are employed in producing dexterous and accomplished works. For the various stages of an artwork's development can tell a more complete story of how it has come into being.

The intimate relationship between author and authored informs the need in others to view the content as it evolved, and as a way to understand the dialogues inherent in the artwork and the manifestations that are produced therefore. In citing Freud in her essay *Visual Pleasure and Narrative Cinema*, Laura Mulvey named the desire to look 'scopophilia'[3], and using her suggestion of '...looking itself is a source of pleasure...'[4], this interest may be explainable. There is satisfaction to be had in what Luce Irigaray termed the '...omnipotence of the gaze...'[5] that informs the scopophilic dynamic. In some respects this can be likened to delving into the psychological machinations of the mind directly, as through a conversation or an interview. This suggests that the sketchbook, as the possessor of thoughts made physical, may act as the visual substitute for verbal dialogue in communicating intent and idea to others. The sense of discovery through its pages is similar to that of knowing how an artist's mind operates.

The exhibition of the life 'diaries' by Dieter Roth at London's Camden Arts Centre ('Diaries', 17 May – 14 July 2013) contained multiscreen video-footage taken by Roth of his daily routines in the last year of his life. This comprised his ordered archive of found trash from his travels, works on the wall, and a collection of his existing diaries *cum* sketchbooks produced between 1965 and 1998. The video-screens and archive acted as open and accessible material through which to understand and take a position of the working machinations of Roth as artist and man, providing a framework to establish knowledge of his daily endeavours. The video-footage shot in various cities, being of his wanders around the studio, reading in bed, and sitting at his desk sketching amongst other activities, presented a non-textual diary account of the un-sensational everyday life of this artist. Shown on a wall of multiple stacked monitors, the footage was repetitious and lacking in dynamism, yet despite the monotonous overture of this collection of visual material, this communicated a sense of Roth the artist and man. The attribute of a figure recorded and presented allows this to happen more profoundly, as the viewer finds it easier to attach an anchor onto the subject that one recognizes in relation to the self. Knowing what it is to live and exist inside a human body generates a connection (by empathy) to another we resemble.

Coupled with the archive of trash, the discarded items of what Roth termed the 'vagaries of life', the diary video-footage provided the opportunity to unpick, unravel, and geographically locate Roth's practice and life. A more complete and substantial understanding of Roth the artist was attainable through these works. However the 'diaries' (which act as intimate sketchbooks for Roth despite the terminology) containing drawings, to do lists, agendas, notes, thoughts and records, offered the promise and the denial of cognitive understanding of who he was. Placed waist height on a large white plinth, the diaries took chronological order for their surviving years (as not all were salvaged) to account for the entire period on display. No diary conformed to type or style, and an array of covers was in evidence at approximately A5 size. Theses items were the most intriguing and potent within the exhibition, yet they presented the promise of uncovering the daily mind to paper exercises of Roth whilst also denying this. To touch an object of interest is to be close to any potential mysteries, clues, and insights held within its mass, yet this was not possible at this exhibition. The closed well-thumbed, stained, and threadbare covers entreated a fascination, an urge to be opened so the content could be devoured, yet the display mechanism made this impossible. A Perspex lid that held any fondling by prying eyes at bay sealed the plinth. Cheated and bereft by this sealed offering of Roth's artistic thought process, the visitor was potentially left feeling confounded and wanting more. This assault on the viewer had pathos. Whilst attending the exhibition in June 2013, I observed a sense of disquiet in the audience at having their nosiness held at bay, and this was both sad and engaging. For the curator's of this show (which originated in Fruitmarket Gallery, Edinburgh in 2012) had opened up the realm to 'know' Roth's working strategies without giving away its secrets, and this mechanism teased the audience with the promise of getting close to the ideas of Roth without delivering. That the diaries were *closed* made fingers itch to peel open the covers, yet the plinth, the second seal surrounding his drafted ideas, prevented that from happening. The most important and insightful artifacts on exhibition, the diaries were ultimately kept hidden and out of reach. The intimacy between Roth and these objects remained intimate to him alone through the inability of others to read or touch them. As Roth died in 1998, and long before the curation of the exhibition, this was perhaps the most fitting result. For his privacy was only exposed when he could no longer experience the inevitable sense of subjectivity, or the invasion of his privacy, which would surround the exhibition of his 'diaries'. He was saved the blushes and afforded the kindness of having his most private 'diaries' contained in a Perspex box. Even if Roth intended that some of his sketchbooks are displayed, his permission and input in curatorial decisions was not to be gained.

V

With the promise of a cultural experience that the closed covers and cases of specific objects provide, a sketchbook's binding can seem to act, in some respects, like the case for a musical instrument. For the promise and the resonance of the instrument inside and its musical capacity permeates its secure case and resonates on its surface. This creates a desire to unlock the holding clasps and delve inside so that the item's potential can be discovered and understood. With a musical instrument that promise relies on the right user. The instrument promises that, played by a knowledgeable and musically dexterous and accomplished individual, its full capabilities will be unleashed. This potential is engrained in the fabric of the object and its case, for the case suggests it contains the impending musical splendour. The sketchbook acts similarly. The sketchbook's resonance is in the capabilities of its users and its function as a portal to understanding their methods. The musical instrument and the sketchbook-page contain the foundation of the notes of their user, and their casings wear their potential promise on their surface. For Jean-Luc Nancy in *Corpus* the notion of interior resonance and its promise is discussed in alignment with the human body,[6] and this is included here as a 'case' of another kind. Nancy sees the body as a phenomenological resonant chamber that contains sound, vibration, and the creative moment, and this notion allows an analysis of the resonant body with the sketchbook and the musical instrument. All possess exteriors which house the potential for creativity to be felt, imagined and experienced within. The inner resonance of each communicates an experience of immersion, of being consumed by a private engagement within the moment. To the outsider this demonstrates what it is to be absorbed by the immediate and personal. In applying Nancy's idea of the resonant corpus to the sketchbook, it is possible to offer a suggestion for its interest as an artifact of curiosity. By imagining the sketchbook as the modus operandi through which the artist, designer or architect experiences their creative subject, it is possible to align it to the inner body that functions as the experiential vehicle of sound resonance.

The body and the sketchbook both function as repositories of private, emotional and subjective experience. They are places where creativity can be manifested, worked through and developed. The relationships between the body-resonant and sketchbook to the author, although appearing divergent, are somewhat similar. The creativity of the artist is bestowed upon the blank inner pages of the possessive object to be (certainly at first) read and understood by them alone. The body as habitat for resonant sound infuses an immediate and visceral sensation through cognitive realization. The guttural and consuming experience of vibrations through the body enacts a private experience for it alone. Played for one by one. The sketchbook, as the archive of creative indulgence, functions in a similar way for its bound covers protest against entry by the prying eyes of others. This singular indulgence is restrictive and defensive when the threat of sharing the experience is made apparent. Vulnerability grows in the self when the '...membrane separating self from self and self from world becomes permeable...',[7] as Robert Stam suggested in *Subversive Pleasures: Bakhtin, Cultural Criticism, and Film*. Although Stam was directing this to the grotesquery as described in the medieval literature of Mikhail Bakhtin, the complexities of viewing and of being viewed, of spectacle and of being spectator this also has significance here. The closed covers of a sketchbook seek not to allow others in. The closed covers constitute a membrane between the creative practitioner and their public work. To make the sketches visible is to puncture the permeable membrane between these two positions, and this creates a sense of vulnerability through subjectivity. It inevitably may appear intrusive and sneaky to attempt to view the workings of another's mind when uninvited, to peruse and contemplate their unashamed and untamed scribbles, draughts and notes when this is considered. This, however, is the allure, for it is tempting and exciting to pour over the pages and experiences, which were intended as private. The experience intended for one made by one have become an intrigue as a consequence. Much like desiring an understanding of feeling as another does, the need to understand creativity in its development has produced an interest in the sketchbook as modus operandi for the maturity and growing dexterity of ideas.

VI

Touching and a sense of being touched is important in intimacy, and an act akin to sharing the intimacies of another can be gathered through touching what they have once touched. So to touch the drawings and inscriptions of another presents an opportunity to share the experience, to get close to the act and moment of touch and, in this case, creativity. It allows a consumption to happen in the moment of precision, a heightened and insightful experience of what transpired. The touch, and acknowledgement of that exchange, can see the spectator in their mind enter the core of the relational dynamic. Their involvement becomes potent: their presence necessary. For Antonin Artaud this means a '…direct communication will be established between the spectator and the spectacle…'[8] through a process of unwanted interpolation. The encounter sees the viewer enter the relationship between 'maker' and 'made', even if this result is only for a moment. Yet, however ungainly and unconsidered the etched pages appear, these private musings are the beginnings of something more substantial, more precise, developed and public. Privacy and intrusion of private thought are central to how creative artists negotiate sketchbooks, and why they contain dynamic and evocative content as a result. To believe a document is private is to allow an unreserved and carefree approach to be unleashed. It provides the opportunity for freethinking and spontaneous adventure, where anything is possible, and nothing is open to eradication.

Maurice Merleau-Ponty suggested in *The Primacy of Perception* that I '…consider my perceptions as simple sensations, they are private.'[9] This proposition puts forward the idea that there is good reason for creative experiences to be solitary and self-contained and this informs the position of keeping one's sketchbooks private. The intimacy established in their pages through working from idea to artifact is engrained in the fabric of the sketchbook and this renders it a private space for contemplation. The act of privacy for the author is integral to how sketchbooks function in the creative process, as this allows for the occurrence of mistakes and errors without the threat of their exposure. There is safety within it's covers that allows creative development to be unhindered and freed of the constraints of looking correct, finalized and with rough edges polished.

Central to privacy in terms of the use of a sketchbook is trust. When working in a sketchbook the author expects and trusts that their work will remain private and safe unless otherwise agreed. Personal worth and value is ascribed to the sketchbook as an object in itself through this relationship, making it precious to its owner, as it frees the author from potential shame as that which for Sartre '…realizes an intimate relation of myself to myself…'[10] and which informs the pressures within subjectivity and vulnerability. A cover is an exterior binding and a public cloak on which representation and understanding are worn. It is the non-private exterior shield for the private and personal within. *In Skin: On the Cultural Border between Self and the World* Claudia Benthien defined 'shame' as an Indo-Germanic word '…which means to cover.'[11] In emphasizing the association between emotional anxiety and public prominence, Benthien equates the permeation of an outer cloak directly with how the individual may come to experience distress. Although

Benthien references the body in this text, it is possible to apply her notion of shame to exterior receptacles created by and for the self. Covers and bindings, whether of the body, a diary, a personal repository, or a sketchbook, are places where unease, and its transformation to become vulnerability and shame, can proliferate if the contents are available without warning or consent. This can make anxiety a consequence. Anxiety, as defined by Stanley Rachman as '…the apprehensiveness that people feel when entering novel or troublesome social situations…'[12] is aggravated in the creative at the possibility of exposure and invasion into their private thoughts and ideas. The exterior cover of the sketchbook and the act of covering are crucial herein, for they keep individual creative secrets private. This is important for the creative artists who need to maintain their relationship of workable trust with the receptacle of their ideas. Keeping the sketchbook firmly shut means anxiety, vulnerably, and shame at having ones thoughts explored and made public.

Considering shame and anxiety allows for understanding the violation that an intrusion into a sketchbook without the author's consent can provoke. The author may not wish to allow others to ponder their untamed and undeveloped ideas, preferring to keep them safe and enclosed. On a personal level, it produces a sense of horror that my sketchbooks could be subject to plundering against my will. The thought is too abusive and barbaric. It is important that my ideas in their flimsy and tentative state remain untouched and unread by others to keep their potency alive. At the sketchbook stage, ideas are for my eyes only. When the contents of a sketchbook are safe and secure from prying eyes, the object is free of the burden of subjectivity and, by association, so is the author. The experience of subjectivity challenges an artist's self-confidence, particularly when done without concern for inarticulate scribbles, clumsy edges, and carefree annotations. For others wishing to unpick and unpack the creative mind however, subjectivity is brought to these objects and their maker. The same sense of ideas being open to scrutiny occurs when their reading is possible, and the freedom and non-subjective regard with which they are made is lost. Privacy is key. For the ultimate act of privacy is to destroy a sketchbook to stop an unwanted invasion by the prying eyes of the uninvited. Destruction ensures the private act remains just that. Without this in my creative practice I would feel vulnerable and aggrieved that my desire to keep sketches and sketchbooks personal could be betrayed. Destroying sketchbooks ultimately keeps their contents safe from the possibility of public display without consent.

BIBLIOGRAPHY

Artaud, Antonin. *The Theater and Its Double*. Translated by M. C. Richards. New York: Grove Press, 1958.

Benthien, Claudia. *Skin: On the Cultural Border between Self and the World*. Translated by T. Dunlap. New York: Columbia University Press, 2002.

Chatzichristodoulou, Maria and Zerihan, Rachel, eds. *Intimacy Across Visceral and Digital Performance*. Basingstoke: Palgrave MacMillan, 2012.

Derrida, Jacques. *On Touching – Jean-Luc Nancy*. Translated by C. Irizarry. Stanford: Stanford University Press, 2005.

Irigaray, Luce. *Speculum of the Other Woman*. Translated by G. C. Gill. New York: Cornell University Press, 1985.

Merleau-Ponty, Maurice. *The Primacy of Perception*. Evanston: Northwestern University Press, 1964.

Mulvey, Laura. *Visual and Other Pleasures*. Basingstoke: Macmillan, 1989.

Nancy, Jean-Luc. *Corpus*. Translated by R. A. Rand. New York: Fordham University Press, 2008.

Rachman, Stanley. *Anxiety*. Hove: Psychology Press Ltd, 2004.

Sartre, Jean-Paul. *Being and Nothingness: An Essay on Phenomenological Ontology*. Translated by H. E. Barnes. London: Methuen, 1958.

Stam, Robert. *Subversive Pleasures: Bakhtin, Cultural Criticism, and Film*. London: The John Hopkins University Press, 1989.

NOTES

1   Jean-Paul Sartre, *Being and Nothingness: An Essay on Phenomenological Ontology*, trans. H. E. Barnes (London: Methuen, 1958), 231.

2   This exhibition preceded the international colloquium in February 2011, held at The Collection (the art and archaeology gallery in Lincoln, UK) in association with the Faculty of Art, Architecture and Design at the University of Lincoln, which formulated this publication.

3   Scopophilia means a 'love of watching', which Freud associated with the anal stage of development. The term is in alignment with voyeurism and this aspect Mulvey relates to narrative and cinema.

4   Laura Mulvey, *Visual and Other Pleasures* (Basingstoke: Macmillan, 1989), 8.

5   Luce Irigaray, *Speculum of the Other Woman*, trans .G. C. Gill (New York: Cornell University Press, 1985), 47.

6   Discussed in Jean-Luc Nancy, *Corpus*, trans. R. A. Rand (New York: Fordham University Press, 2008).

7   Robert Stam, *Subversive Pleasures: Bakhtin, Cultural Criticism, and Film* (London: The John Hopkins University Press, 1989), 157.

8   Antonin Artaud, *The Theater and Its Double*, trans. M. C. Richards (New York: Grove Press, 1958), 96.

9   Maurice Merleau-Ponty, *The Primacy of Perception* (Evanston: Northwestern University Press, 1964), 17.

10   Sartre, *Being and Nothingness,* 221.

11   Claudia Benthien, *Skin: On the Cultural Border between Self and the World*, trans. T. Dunlap (New York: Columbia University Press, 2002), 100.

12   Stanley Rachman, *Anxiety* (Hove: Psychology Press Ltd, 2004), 147.

Curating Sketchbooks: Interpretation, Preservation, Display

Miriam Stewart

In 2006 I organized the exhibition *Under Cover: Artist's Sketchbooks*, in which I set out to investigate the many implications of sketchbook practice and its physical manifestations between the eighteenth century and the present.[1] Along the way, many observations about the study, preservation, and display of sketchbooks came to the fore (Fig. 12.1). The exhibition of sketchbooks mobilizes technical issues that are arguably different from those at play when installing a gallery of oil paintings or marble sculpture. The special qualities of the sketchbook, its' informality and intimacy, as well as its active quality, are lost when it is displayed.[2] How does one animate the sketchbook and provide the experience of something whose essential nature is not fixed? One of the hallmark experiences of the sketch, and one that is inherent to its very definition, is the summary, ephemeral, or diminished presence it holds as a result of its always assumed relation to something more finished, something larger, something more museum friendly. The curator finds themselves often choosing the most visually compelling opening at the expense of what might be the true character of the sketchbook's overall and even passing contents. The viewer may be frustrated by the intractable and perhaps seemingly arbitrary choice of the unturned page. The visitor is further removed from the sketchbook by the angle of the mount and the glazing of the case. Only a hint can be offered of its myriad immediacies. It can seem that the exhibition of sketchbooks, by necessity, is as devoted to producing the opposite of the object's original intent.

The sketchbook's implied intention is constantly qualified by the conditions of observation made necessary by the environment in which it is encountered. Thus, a large part of the ambition of the exhibition was to still convey something rich of the actual historical practice of sketchbook-production amidst the limitations of display. It seemed best and most capaciously deferential to the essence of sketchbook-work to organize the exhibition into two broad sections: 'Observation' and 'Invention.' The former encompassed itinerant sketchbooks, copies after the old masters, and architectural, figure and nature studies. Invention comprised studies for works in other media, doodles, visual exercises, and products of the imagination. A closer reading of the materials makes plain the emergent issues.

12.1   Selection of sketchbooks in the collection of the Harvard Art Museums. Source: Photograph: Katya Kallsen 2011

John Ruskin prescribed keeping '…a small memorandum-book in the breast-pocket, with its well-cut sheathed pencil, ready for notes on passing opportunities: but never being without this.'[3] I note briefly the vividness of Ruskin's advice here, but it is worth stopping for a moment on the typically rich and variegated implications of the critic's words, for he does, even in passing reference to just one model of a sketchbook, surface a host of issues.

It is arguably one of the leitmotifs of sketchbook materiality that the object is both an extension of the artist as well as her/his faithful companion. It is small, stored close to the body, and redolent even of the body's curve and heat. It is also deeply conceptual – a memorandum book noting opportunities: ideas that might result in later fruition. What I came to perceive is the familial nature of the many sheets in the sketchbook, each page rubbing shoulders with its siblings, so to speak, the family contained in the embrace of the parent cover. Each sibling informs the other and yet is individuated. Concomitantly, I came to see pages no longer a part of their familial or parental setting as orphans (a designation that will be revisited below). The bodily analogy then is both always pertinent and highly contingent. It is entirely possible that one never considers anything having to do with any part of the sketchbook experience without always already taking into consideration how it relates to any and all other parts.

Consideration of some particular examples of sketchbook traits is pertinent. I want to be sure to draw the distinction between two terms that can be used a little carelessly: 'sketchbooks' and 'albums.' A 'sketchbook' is a sheaf of pages bound into a book, by the artist or commercially prepared. An 'album' is an assemblage of objects that are pasted onto the pages of a book. The active sketchbook is in motion, so to speak – the artist is in the process of filling it, whereas the album is in the process of being assembled. The sketchbook suggests the future, and the album suggests the past.

The sketchbook as a whole may be conceived as a work of art in itself. It should not be confused with what we refer to as an 'artist's book' although the boundaries can be blurred. By its nature, the sketchbook in action is in the process of 'becoming,' while the artist's book may begin as a concept and end as an integrated whole, its project completed. The sketchbook may provide a collated view of the artist's process, a way to see ideas in proximity, of one leading to the next. One can trace the germination of an idea through the artist's exploratory studies in what Martin Kemp has referred to as 'brainstorming' when describing Leonardo's sketches.[4]

Although as Ruskin noted, sketchbooks are often pocket-sized, they can be as large as portfolios and as small as a pack of cards.[5] Thickness can also vary dramatically, from biblical proportions to just a few leaves. Many of Turner's sketchbooks include over hundred pages.[6] A now dismantled sketchbook by Jan van Goyen was reportedly one hundred and seventy nine leaves and approxiamtely an inch and a half thick,[7] while a sketchbook by Sanford Gifford in our collection is only ten pages.[8] The traditional view of sketchbooks is aligned with the capacities of a pocket on a person's article of clothing. A sketchbook may also be part of an artist's toolkit – at least in the nineteenth century along with a white umbrella, camp stool and paint-box – and thus by extension might seem to be part of a much larger and potentially unwieldy machinery of *plein air* work. To this extent, the sketchbook assumes a telescopic character, pulling in and out in terms of size implications depending upon its relation to the rest of the artist's materials, setting of work, and intentions in a given situation.

In use, or at rest, the sketchbook can be held in one hand, propped up, or flattened on a table, addressed from on high, at an angle or straight on. As well, issues of left-handedness versus right-handedness must always be in play when confronted with the mechanics of an open book. Moreover, the bodily relation of artist to sketchbook now confronts issues of angle and orientation as a result of manual definition. The visual character of a given page might very well owe much to the artist's physical relation to the book. While we most often read left to right in horizontal bands, in sketchbook practice it can seem as if such protocols are not reliable indicators. The sketchbook can be picked up at any time, the pages are not necessarily drawn in sequentially, the orientation can vary from horizontal to vertical, from left to right, or a sketchbook can be turned upside down, back to front. Let us not forget that the terms 'recto' and 'verso', so casually invoked in describing drawings, derive from descriptions of books and manuscripts: 'folio recto' or 'right leaf' and 'folio verso' or 'turned leaf'.

The format and structure of a sketchbook cannot help but call up issues of start and finish, and indeed many artists proceed systematically throughout a given book in congruence with the notion that the sketchbook has an endpoint. However, the issue of finish may very well be a chimera. An artist might use only three pages of a sketchbook and never pick it up again. Edward Burne-Jones used only the first half of a sketchbook now at the Harvard Art Museums, leaving the remainder in a

12.2   Jacques-Louis David, *Napoleon Crowning Josephine*, from Sketchbook No. 20: Studies for 'The Coronation of Napoleon', 1805–24. Graphite and black crayon on off-white antique laid paper, each page: 21 × 16.4 cm (8 1/4 × 6 7/16 inches). Harvard Art Museums / Fogg Museum, Bequest of Grenville L. Winthrop, 1943.1815.13 pages 55 *verso* and 54 *recto*. Source: Photograph: Allan Macintyre © President and Fellows of Harvard College

still uncut block.[9] Other artists fill every page, including the endpapers. Even more radically, one artist I know faithfully carries her two favourite sketchbooks with her on every trip, but has never put a mark down in either as of yet. The real question is whether finish is at all an operative word here.

The format of a sketchbook, while at once seemingly straightforward and even perhaps mono-directional, is always also potentially at issue. Take, for instance, the issue of the gutter, that space where two pages join. As the pages ease into the binding they often curve and the artist must adjust his marks accordingly. Frequently the constraints of an individual page are transgressed and the artist draws across the gutter expansively (Fig. 12.2). In either case the media must be manipulated so that the ink or watercolour does not run and the charcoal does not smear. Constant consideration of borders and spaces, both specific and less defined, is necessary. The gutter as well plays an essential part in the maintenance of the family and its separation.

Even before such a component makes itself felt, an experience of a space somehow beyond or outside of the enclosing interior is called into question by the frequent inclusion of a pencil sleeve on one or another of the outer edges of the sketchbook. So often, what in its origins was a significant material appendage to the sketchbook now is most commonly experienced as an empty void that once held the artist's instrument (not one of the sketchbooks at the Harvard Art Museums retains the pencil that came with it). Replete with drawing implement, the sleeve truly rendered the sketchbook self-contained, ready to go, and at the same time telegraphed upon approach to the book itself, that the artist's hand would as much define the book as any preordained properties. The convenient offering of the

special sketchbook pencil however, was often subverted by the artist who could, of course, use any number of materials. One sketchbook might include drawings in ink, graphite, chalk, crayon, watercolour, pastel or metal-point.

Bindings can be leather, cloth, or plain or decorated paper. Frequently the pages are held together by clasps or some kind of tie. Ties also keep the book open and can prevent a page from flopping over while working on its opposite. Often these are lost, leaving only ghostly remnants. In the present day, an elastic band might perform the same function. These fasteners keep the pages together and prevent or protect the insertion of foreign materials. Frequently, however, the sketchbook serves as a repository, storing pressed flowers, ticket stubs, errant drawings, and other ephemera. In such cases, the sketchbook is in effect a scrapbook as well as an album.[10]

In a given sketchbook, the pages themselves are usually uniform, white or cream, of wove or laid paper. Sketchbooks could also be composed of a variety of different coloured papers – usually tan, blue, green, and grey in addition to the usual white or cream – so that artists could choose an appropriate ground for their studies. Whatever the book contains, the snug proximity of the closed pages tends to protect them from light, and the colours of media and pages may remain surprisingly vibrant. Conversely, that closeness allows friable materials to rub against each other, to smudge, to offset, to leave traces, compromising the original sketched page. Frequent rifling discolours and erodes the edges of the pages, further contributing to their homely appearance. A sketchbook carelessly left in the artist's studio can be a magnet for wayward oil or paint splotches.

A tiny book used by Frederic Leighton included a 'prepared pencil' (a metal-point stylus) that was inserted into the sheath attached to the book's cover.[11] A label inside the book promised that it would be 'a great advantage to Travellers and all persons who wish to preserve their Writing', a response to complaints about the smudgy offset caused by pencilled notes or drawings on adjoining pages in regular sketchbooks or notebooks. The pages were prepared with a rough, opaque coating that shaved off minute bits of the metallic stylus, leaving a thin, un-gradated line that did not smear. Although it is clear that the manufacturer intended the book to be used for written, rather than drawn, notations, Leighton filled it with diminutive sketches as well as notes.

The sketchbook often functions as a notebook, with hasty reminders of addresses, laundry lists, train schedules, movies to see, recipes for plaster or the fabrication of a sculpture.[12] To this end, the interiority of a sketchbook can be considerable, seeming at times even an extension of the artist's consciousness. Perhaps the most representative of these are the frequently seen doodles wherein the only thing separating such marks from the mind of the artist is their visibility.[13] A large number of sketchbooks in the Harvard Art Museums collection contain these kinds of practical notations. We know, for example, that Sargent ordered a frame for his portrait of Lady Playfair, and visited with Lawrence Alma-Tadema on 'Tuesday' and 'Thursday', and that he went to Rouen on 9 April and Dijon on 11 April, where he purchased frames and faience.[14] In two renowned sketchbooks in our collection, Jacques-Louis David recorded the heights of the guests at the Coronation of Napoleon, as well as details of their garments, hats, and shoes.[15]

Many people appreciate drawings for their intimacy, for the sense of closeness to the artist's creative process. However, leafing through a sketchbook and seeing the notes and drawings can result in a disconcerting sense of having invaded the artist's privacy. Such impressions are heightened by the book format of a sketchbook – its formal similarity to a journal or diary. The book is private, as when at rest its pages are closed, often bound together and held close to the heart in a pocket. One might speak of the artist confiding his drawings to his sketchbook. Unlike a journal, the order is not preordained, although many artists start at the front and progress forward, page by page. The drawings are records of fleeting thoughts, of things seen and absorbed, of projects yet to come. They may be revisited at a later date, amended in pencil or worked up in watercolour; the journal turning back in on itself, its' temporality and even its sequence being disturbed.

In the nineteenth century, the privacy of a sketchbook was in marked contrast to the staged presentation of the artist's studio. The sketchbook is, so to speak, the man behind the curtain, the invisible foundation of the grand production. It represents the artist at work. It is enclosed, perhaps secretive, or even confessional; a reference book. Nevertheless, the sketchbook can also be performative, like a journal or studio, as the artist wilfully shapes his reputation. The self-conscious presentation of the sketchbook can be signalled by heightened awareness of the margins, signed pages, or the use of fixative to protect friable materials. Artists may also 'curate' the sketchbook by removing unsatisfactory drawings.

Fully intact sketchbooks can be hard to find. Over time, bindings yield, and pages give way, succumbing to wear from curious thumbs and fingers as the pages are turned, becoming lost in the welter of an artist's studio. Artists may also have dismantled their sketchbooks. Burne-Jones frequently extracted pages from his sketchbooks for exhibition, and Ruskin broke up many of Turner's sketchbooks so that individual drawings could be exhibited. Sketchbooks are most often taken apart by dealers who find willing clients for single sheets.

Sometimes deteriorating sketchbooks are disassembled in order to preserve them. Individually mounting or matting the sheets allows for both preservation and for exhibition. Inevitably, some of the special quality of the sketchbook is lost. One must take care to record the original position of the pages in the sketchbook so that the proper context is understood. Other sketchbooks are rebound over time. We know that some of Turner's sketchbooks underwent this procedure, and sometimes the pages were not rebound in the original order.

Failure to recognize drawings as sketchbook pages can limit our understanding and interpretation of their meaning, allowing only an incomplete picture of the artist's process.[16] Those who work closely with drawings will come across what I call 'orphans', pages that have been separated from their original sketchbook family. Their physical makeup may reveal hints of their origins. The edges provide the most obvious clue. The pages may have been wrenched from their binding, leaving a scarred edge. The stitching of the binding may have been severed, leaving injured holes. Fringed perforations from a spiral binding suggest mutilation. We casually refer to 'broken up' or 'dismembered' sketchbooks.

'Orphans' may often be identified by their small size, rounded corners, soiled edges, and the offset from a previous neighbour. Sometimes the pages bear a number, the lone indicator of a now incomplete sequence numbered by the artist or a previous owner (Fig. 12.3).[17] The orientation of the recto of an orphan in relation to the verso may vary. One may be horizontal and the other vertical. Anyone who has to catalogue (and indeed mount) a double-sided sheet faces the dilemma of which is the *recto* and which is the *verso*?[18] How does one privilege one side over the other? Without the confines of the sketchbook, the context is lost. It is not always possible to tell whether an orphan was executed before or after its removal from the sketchbook. A ragged edge is an indication that a page could have been torn from either a sketchbook or bound pad of paper. The artist could have worked her way through a sketchpad, removing each drawn page as it was executed, or she could have drawn on a page that had been removed. In this case, each drawing may not truly be seen as an orphan.

Jacques-Louis David was present, sketchbook in hand, at the coronation of Napoleon in 1804, and at the emperor's bidding he produced an enormous painting of the elaborate ceremony, which he finished in 1807. The two sketchbooks in the Harvard Art Museums contain studies for the painting, which includes a cast of nearly two hundred participants. The composition had already been established when these drawings were made, as the figures are generally in the poses they would assume in the final work. Most of the studies are squared for transfer to the canvas, and some of the figures are nude (the artist worked from models to fix the poses). Although David tended to work systematically in his sketchbooks, in one of

12.3   Jan van Goyen, *Three Studies of a Cow*, c. 1650. Black chalk and grey wash on cream antique laid paper, 9.7 × 15.6 cm (3 13/16 × 6 1/8 inches). Harvard Art Museums/ Fogg Museum, Bequest of Marian H. Phinney, 1962.39. Source: Photograph: Allan Macintyre © President and Fellows of Harvard College

the books, he worked from both ends, so that the figures meet somewhere in the middle of the sketchbook upside down in relation to each other. The numbering of the pages, probably done by one of David's heirs, becomes necessarily confused here, as the versos become rectos.[19] Close examination of the signatures in David's sketchbooks reveals that some of the pages were removed before they were numbered.

The Harvard Art Museums own an example of a reconstituted, or revivified, early sketchbook by Fragonard, one of only two known sketchbooks by the artist.[20] It was acquired from Fragonard's great grandson in the early twentieth century by a collector who discovered that the sketchbook, with its original binding, had been preserved because it had been used as an album, with drawings of Old Testament subjects from the circle of François Verdier pasted onto the original pages. When the Verdier drawings were removed, Fragonard's exceptionally loose and dynamic sketches – some virtually indecipherable – were revealed. It is likely that Fragonard himself pasted the drawings into the book, having no further use for a youthful project. The sketchbook, which originally contained about fifty pages, was sold in the 1950s and subsequently broken up, the pages dispersed. In 1968, the Harvard Art Museums were able to purchase a clutch of thirty pages, and the sketchbook was reassembled by matching offsets and edges. The modern binding of marbled paper was chosen because it was similar to the remains of the original covers. Since then, a few other pages from the sketchbook have appeared on the market. This sketchbook, then, is only a fragment of the original, and while some of the relationships between the pages are preserved, the whole can only remain incomplete and imagined.

The estate sale of Fragonard's fellow artist Hubert Robert in 1809 included fifty sketchbooks, described in the catalogue as '…most clever and useful for compositions.'[21] By 1989, only two sketchbooks survived intact – one in the Morgan Library, and the other from a private collection, consigned for sale at Sotheby's Monaco.[22] Composed of ninety-seven pages, this sketchbook was a record of Robert's travels through Italy in the 1760s. Although the pages are relatively small, measuring approximately 7 × 9 inches, they encompassed enough room for expansive views of churches, villas, gardens, and ruins, executed in chalk or sparkling brown wash. Before it was offered for sale, Sotheby's advised the owner that the individual leaves would fetch higher prices than the sketchbook itself, and the book was dismantled. The destruction of the book created a controversy, prompting articles in the *New York Times* and elsewhere with quotations from scholars and dealers that included words like 'scandal', 'grotesque', and 'vandalism.'[23] Eunice Williams, an authority on French drawings and a consultant to Sotheby's, resigned in protest, referring to sketchbooks as an 'endangered species.'[24] The auction house defended its actions, pointing out that it was obligated to seek the highest price for its clients, and that there was no guarantee that a subsequent owner would respect the integrity of the sketchbook. In response to the criticism, however, Sotheby's took the unusual step of offering to sell the sketchbook, intact, to anyone who was willing to meet or exceed the total value of the individual pages on the day of the sale. No single buyer emerged, and the pages were dispersed. Tellingly, pages with more summary drawings were not reproduced in the catalogue, and were sold as parts of lots with more finished sheets. Drawings on the versos were also not illustrated. The variety and rhythm of the sketchbook were sublimated to suit the market.

Even when the integrity of the sketchbook is maintained, there is something in its character that suggests that its purpose is in part to be taken from the protective confines of a studio setting into the outside world. At base, sketchbooks transcend the studio and move beyond it by virtue of their portability. In this case, the sketchbook becomes a sort of travel diary. By attending to inscribed dates and recognizable landmarks, it is possible to trace the artist's movements.[25]

With the ascendance of *plein air* painting, the sketchbook's pages welcomed the outdoor sketch. In his novel *Roderick Hudson* Henry James described the itinerant artist Sam Singleton, who with 'patient industry' was able to improve the quality of his 'daubs.'[26] The sunburnt Singleton, carrying a meagre knapsack, makes occasional appearances in the novel, his modesty and limited ambition a corrective to the intensity of the sculptor Roderick Hudson. James writes that Singleton had been 'pedestrianizing' for six weeks.[27] The word 'pedestrian' in this context resonates with its doubled meaning – referring to perambulation as well as to the humble, seemingly prosaic habit of sketching.

James also alludes to the 'artist-as-squirrel.' Many artists embarked on sketching tours in the summer, returning to their studios with enough material to sustain them for a productive winter of painting. Singleton appears again as the character Rowland Mallet passed '…across the long shadow of a ruined tower, [where] he perceived a small figure at a short distance, bent over a sketch-book…He was making a careful and charming little sketch.'[28] Singleton:

> '…gave an account of his wanderings [over the summer], …he had not been out of Italy, but he had been delving deep into the picturesque heart of the lovely land, and gathering a wonderful store of subjects. He had rambled about among the unvisited villages of the Apennines, pencil in hand and knapsack on back, sleeping on straw and eating black bread and beans, but feasting on local colour, rioting, as it were, on chiaroscuro, and laying up a treasure of pictorial observations.'[29]

The Hudson River School artist Sanford Gifford accumulated sketches for future use, referring to his 'pedestrian tours' in the Catskill Mountains.[30] His friend, the artist Worthington Whittredge, described Gifford's sketching method as:

> …when sketching he preferred to look about for the fleeting effects of nature. He would frequently stop in his tracks to make slight sketches in pencil in a small book which he always carried in his pocket and then pass on, always suspicious that if he stopped too long to look in one direction the most beautiful thing of all might pass him by at his back.'[31]

The artist's sketchbook archive also frequently includes records of cherished artworks. Joshua Reynolds used one of the two sketchbooks in the Harvard Art Museums' collection to record works that he had seen at Blenheim Palace, including a tapestry of the Duke of Marlborough and Time Clipping Cupid's Wings by Anthony van Dyck.[32] Edward Burne-Jones' sketchbook studies after Michelangelo in purple chalk were probably made from small-scale replicas of the Medici tomb figures.[33] Starting in his youth, John Singer Sargent avidly sketched painting and sculpture in every European gallery visited by his intrepid family. This kind of what might be called 'acquisitional' drawing was a lifelong habit for Sargent; as a mature artist he was still drawing cathedral sculpture, and drafting letters to the Italian authorities asking for admission to local museums.[34]

The Harvard Art Museums exhibition *Under Cover*, revealed, among other things, that sketchbooks do not readily divulge their secrets in an exhibition environment. Nevertheless, the show drew a curious and engaged audience, eager to see something rare and unusual. As one might expect, artists were particularly inspired, finding unexpected parallels between their own sketchbook practice and the 'masters'. We tried to enliven the installation by mounting the books on the wall as well as in cases, and interspersing plenty of orphans. The page openings were displayed for the duration of the exhibition; for various reasons, we were not able to change the openings. Financial constraints did not allow us to mount a computer kiosk in the gallery so that visitors could virtually leaf through the pages, something that has since become customary. Instead, we produced true-to-scale facsimiles of four of the sketchbooks that visitors could handle, thus truly gaining a sense of the sketchbook in all its dimensions. We did mount a website that focused on ten of the sketchbooks.[35] On the site, it was possible to 'page through' the sketchbook in a virtual sense, as well as to see every page next to each other in a grid view. Although this kind of lightbox view is enlightening, I still feel that it somehow compromises the integrity of the sketchbook and its unfolding, cinematic nature.

Finally, what I want to emphasize is the physicality, the bodily status, and the concomitant consciousness of sketchbooks, their intrinsic three-dimensional, active quality, and the familial nature of the encompassing parent and its offspring. At Harvard, we are lucky enough to have a study room where visitors may consult works on paper. Students, scholars, and even the general public are welcome. Some of the hardier sketchbooks may be examined and enjoyed. However, many are too fragile to be handled, and we have had to limit access to them. Spines are cracked, covers are fraying, and many pages are suffering from the deteriorative properties of wood pulp paper. We may soon be forced to offer them only as digital surrogates in order to preserve them. Although the sketchbook is very much a living and on-going entity in both practice and theory, it may be that many of its historical manifestations are on the verge of extinction.

BIBLIOGRAPHY

Baur, John, I. H., ed. *The Autobiography of Worthington Whittredge 1820–1910*. New York: Arno Press, 1969.

Harper, James. *Recto-Verso: The Flip Side of Master Drawings*. Cambridge: Harvard Art Museums, 2001.

James, Henry. *Roderick Hudson*. Boston: Houghton Mifflin, 1917.

_____. *Roderick Hudson*. Boston: James R. Osgood, 1876.

Kemp, Martin. *Leonardo da Vinci: the Marvellous Works of Nature and Man*. Oxford: Oxford University Press, 2006.

Khandekar, Narayan, Gianfranco Pocobene and Kate Smith Stewart, eds. *John Singer Sargents 'Triumph of Religion' at the Boston Public Library: Creation and Restoration*. Cambridge: Harvard Art Museums, 2009.

Kimmelman, Michael. "Robert Unbound," in *Art & Auction*, 12 (1989): 24.

Paillet et Olivier. *Catalogue des Tableaux, Dessins, Gouaches, Estampes…Composant le Cabinet et les Etudes de feu Hubert Robert*. Paris: Paillet et Olivier, 1809.

Reid, Callum. "*Annibale Carracci's Holy Family at the National Gallery of Victoria*." Honours thesis, University of Melbourne, 2010.

Ruskin, John. *The Elements of Drawing, in Three Letters to Beginners*. London: Smith Elder and Co, 1857.

Sievers, Ann. H. *Master Drawings from the Smith College Museum of Art*. New York: Hudson Hills Press, 2000.

Willliams, Eunice. *Drawings by Fragonard in North American Collections*. Washington DC: National Gallery of Art, 1978.

NOTES

1   1 August – 22 October 2006, Harvard Art Museums / Fogg Museum (no catalogue). The Harvard Art Museums own an extraordinary collection of drawings ranging from the fourteenth century to the present that has long had an eager audience of students, scholars, and the general public. Among the treasures in the collection is a large group of artists' sketchbooks. I am grateful to Linda Bond, Anne Driesse, Katya Kallsen, Penley Knipe, and Stephan Wolohojian for their observations, expertize, and support. This chapter is dedicated to Eric Rosenberg, with love.

2   The organizers of the exhibition *The Moment of Privacy Has Passed: Sketchbooks by Contemporary Artists, Architects and Designers* at the Usher Gallery, Lincoln (11 December 2010 – 6 March 2011) are to be commended for their innovative display of contemporary artists' sketchbooks in an open bookcase, where visitors were allowed to handle the sketchbooks themselves.

3   John Ruskin, *The Elements of Drawing, in Three Letters to Beginners* (London: Smith Elder and Co, 1857), 148.

4   Martin Kemp, *Leonardo da Vinci: the Marvellous Works of Nature and Man* (Oxford: Oxford University Press, 2006), 35.

5   Sketchbooks were manufactured by artists' colour-men in a variety of sizes and advertised in their catalogues. For example, the 1903 catalogue of the American company Frost & Adams lists traditional sketchbooks in addition to special watercolour sketchbooks bound with rings. In 1926 George Rowney & Co. offered sketchbooks ranging in size from 3 × 5 to 10 × 14 inches. Many of the sketchbooks in the Harvard Art Museums collection bear the labels of their purveyors, which include Emil Geller, Dresden; Georg Stuffler, Munich; Coiffier, Paris; Roberson, London; and Rowney & Co., London.

6   Three examples: *Eclipse Sketchbook, Hastings Sketchbook, Scotch Figures* (Tate Britain, Finberg LXXXV, CXI, and LIX).

7   Ann H. Sievers, *Master Drawings from the Smith College Museum of Art* (New York: Hudson Hills Press, 2000), 67.

8   Sanford Gifford, *Sketchbook 1860–63* (Cambridge: Harvard Art Museums/Fogg Museum, 2001), 165.

9   Edward Burne-Jones, *Sketchbook 1870s-80s* (Cambridge: Harvard Art Museums/Fogg Museum, 1943).

10   A sketchbook by Walter Crane from 1865 includes exhibitor passes for the Crystal Palace, a pass to Zoological Society of America, a British Museum reading room call slip and the artist's list of requirements for a sketching trip, including a pocket sketchbook and a tinted sketchbook (Cambridge: Houghton Library, Harvard University, Typ 8300), 65.

11   Frederic Leighton, *Sketchbook c. 1872–73* (Cambridge: Harvard Art Museums/Fogg Museum, 1946), 35.

12   J.M.W. Turner's *Dolbadarn Sketchbook 1799–1800* (London: Tate Britain, Finberg XLVI) lists cotton stockings, boots, shoes, and shirts, along with other clothing. Frederic Leighton's sketchbook in the Harvard Art Museums includes a recipe for plaster (1946). The sculptor Christopher Wilmarth noted kiln temperatures (Cambridge: Harvard Art Museums/Fogg Museum, 2001), 813.

13   John Singer Sargent, *Sketchbook 1869* (Cambridge: Harvard Art Museums/Fogg Museum, 1937).

14   John Singer Sargent, *Sketchbook c. 1902–05* (Cambridge: Harvard Art Museums/Fogg Museum, 1937).

15   Jacques-Louis David, *Sketchbook No. 14: Studies for "The Coronation of Napoleon I"* *1805–06* (Cambridge: Harvard Art Museums/Fogg Museum, 1943), 1815.12.14 verso and 19 verso.

16   Several drawings for *The Sermon on the Mount*, Sargent's never-executed panel for the Boston Public Library, are orphans from the same sketchbook.

17   This drawing is from a sketchbook used by Jan van Goyen on a journey throughout the Netherlands in 1650–1651. Many of the individual pages were later numbered.

18   Discussed in James Harper, *Recto-Verso: The Flip Side of Master Drawings* (Cambridge: Harvard Art Museums, 2001).

19   Jacques-Louis David, *Sketchbook No. 20: Studies for "The Coronation of Napoleon"* *1805–24*, (Cambridge: Harvard Art Museums/Fogg Museum, 1943), 1815.13.

20   Discussed in Eunice Willliams, *Drawings by Fragonard in North American Collection* (Washington DC: National Gallery of Art, 1978). Also Jean-Honoré Fragonard, *Sketchbook c. 1759–61* (Cambridge: Harvard Art Museums/Fogg Museum, 1967), 42. The other, dated ca. 1765–75, is in the Rijksmuseum, Amsterdam (RP-T-1959-538).

21   Paillet et Olivier. *Catalogue des Tableaux, Dessins, Gouaches, Estampes…Composant le Cabinet et les Etudes de feu Hubert Robert* (Paris: Paillet et Olivier, 1809), lot 353.

22   Hubert Robert, *Roman Sketchbook 1760* (New York: The Morgan Library and Museum) B3025A20; Sotheby's, Monaco, 1 December 1989, *passim*.

23   Discussed in Michael Kimmelman, "Robert Unbound," *Art & Auction*, 12 (1989): 24.

24   Eunice Williams in conversation February 2011.

25   A sketchbook by Sanford Gifford records the artist's journey through the Adirondack Mountains in New York State during the summer and fall of 1851 (Cambridge: Harvard Art Museums/Fogg Museum, 2001), 158.

26   Henry James, *Roderick Hudson* (Boston: Houghton Mifflin, 1917), 108.

27   Discussed in James, *Roderick Hudson* (1917), 484.

28   Henry James, *Roderick Hudson* (Boston: James R. Osgood, 1876), 130.

29   James, *Roderick Hudson* (1876), 130.

30   Gifford's sketches of the Shawangunk mountains, in a sketchbook from 1860 (Cambridge: Harvard Art Museums/Fogg Museum, 2001), 162 pages 25 verso and 26 recto, were used as the basis for the painting Shawangunk Mountains 1864 (private collection).

31   John, I. H. Baur, ed., *The Autobiography of Worthington Whittredge 1820–1910* (New York: Arno Press, 1969), 59.

32   Callum Reid, "*Annibale Carracci's Holy Family at the National Gallery of Victoria*" (Honours thesis, University of Melbourne, 2010), 39–40.

33   Edward Burne-Jones, *Sketchbook "Banners"* (Cambridge: Harvard Art Museums/Fogg Museum, 1943) 1815.16.3-8.

34   John Singer Sargent, *Sketchbook c1910* (Cambridge: Harvard Art Museums/Fogg Museum, 1937), 7.16 back pastedown.

35   Unfortunately, the website is no longer live.

13

My Arguments with the World

Mario Minichiello

OVERVIEW

This chapter explores how sketchbooks can aid development of a personalized approach to drawing and to visual thinking. In particular, it considers how original sketches and ideas, which are regarded in this case as the 'retro' (the first initial pages), are developed to provide the final image, the 'verso' (end page). So others can access it, the final image is placed in a public space that, in the examples used in this chapter, happens to be an international newspaper. While the 'retro' and 'verso' are inherently linked (as opposite sides of the same plane), in most cases the 'retro' (the sketched image), having served its purpose, is discarded or left unseen by the public, often remaining hidden in the folds of a sketchbook.

For the artist and designer, the sketchbook remains a private and convenient place to engage with drawing as a means of contemplating the world. As a process, this is key in developing visual memory, researching ideas and of securing a personal point of view. In this way, drawing has been an important part of knowledge generation and helped focus the development of an individual's critical processes. In my view, it is drawing that informs, inspires and elevates imagery as a form of visual communication. Sketchbooks have allowed me to document news and current affairs in ways that are distinctly different from those available to a lens-media or text-based journalism. They have allowed me to use drawings in place of words or photographic media.

Presented in this chapter is a discussion of the application of this approach to contemporary visual communication problem solving, through using drawing as reportage or as a record of enquiry. In particular, through the examples of reportage drawing of the 2007 APEC International World Leaders Conference published in *The Sydney Morning Herald*, 2007. This is a two-fold record: the first book is from direct observation recorded through line work in a small sketchbook; the second drawing book is a combination of memory and visualization. This is where a narrative or argument is developed and ideas and experiences communicated.

The official view of the Asia-Pacific Economic Cooperation,[1] as the official website stipulates, is that it is a collection of 21 'Member Economies' encompassing the premier Asia-Pacific economic forum whose primary goal is to support sustainable economic growth and prosperity in the Asia-Pacific region. Their joint aim is to promote free trade and cooperation between themselves and other parts of the world. My particular view is that APEC performs as a 'club' that seeks to advantage the exclusive interests of already powerful nations. It is this socio-political position that informed my visual authorship of the drawings. In addition, the APEC event in Sydney 2007 had the added dimension of marking the end of two famous political careers, that of the Australian First Minister, John Howard, and the President of the United States of America, George Bush Jnr. This provided a particularly rich narrative about privilege and power, which in turn resulted in protests and demonstrations.

The presence of such important leaders meant that security was a major concern for the police authorities. A large number of Police officers were drafted into the city of Sydney to ensure the safety of international visitors. Large sections of the city were fenced off and the movement of citizens was restricted as reported in ABC news on 30th August 2007:

> Security barriers will be installed in parts of central Sydney during the APEC leaders visit next month, to help police control protesters and protect businesses and VIPs. A spokesman for the New South Wales Police Force has refused to confirm whether the barriers will form a concrete wall around the city centre, stretching from Circular Quay for several blocks towards the Sydney Town Hall.[2]

There were also a number of controls placed on the reporting media in order to prevent the circulation of offensive material and to ensure that the event reflected positively on the Howard government. In my experience there are few non-combat situations where there existed such profound efforts to control the distribution and publishing of photographic material and the prevention of individuals free movement. These restrictions applied to lens media with examples of aggressive enforcement. For example, a female photographer was knocked to the ground and arrested. As Paul Bibby reported in the The Sydney Morning Herald on 11th September 2007:

> Paula Bronstein's camera lens was smashed and she suffered minor bruising to her neck and jaw when police pushed her onto a footpath in a scuffle after the main protest march in the city on Saturday. The clash, captured by hovering camera crews, was splashed across nightly news bulletins around the country and has become one of the defining images of the police response to the protests.[3]

On the other hand *sketching*, at first, seemed to fall outside of the interest (or experience) of the authorities, for I was not subjected to the same level of control and censorship whilst drawing. This, I sensed from my encounters with the police, was due to the act of sketching lacking authority as a mediated form of communication, regarded as a casual, even childlike activity. Furthermore, drawing in newspapers been viewed largely as the '…political cartoon…'[4] or increasingly, as a form of 'decoration' to illustrate articles, rather than an authored critique in itself to be read on the same terms and conditions as the accompanying 'text'. The latter definition of drawing concerns my work in the mass media, which I will discuss in this chapter.

As a visual artist, I use drawing to formulate 'action' research methodology. I draw as it enables me to develop the connection between thinking, reflecting, taking 'action' by making a drawing, and then reflecting on the results before refining the final artwork. This approach enables me to think about and develop my visual language as ongoing and unresolved process. In this way, thinking through drawing takes shape at an intuitive level, as well as at a more consciously determinate one. 'Action' research fits the nature of my work because, as described by McNiff, it is '….a form of inquiry that enables practitioners in every profession to investigate and critically evaluate their work by producing accounts of their practice.'[5] In the APEC investigation, the first stage of drawn investigation was conducted through rapidly drawn line images (the retro) made in the small sketchbook (see Figure 13.1). The second set of detailed drawings (the Verso, see Figure 13.2 and 13.3), were sketched at a slower, more considered pace after reviewing and reflecting on the outcomes of the first batch. Taking action in this way, following further reflection and planning, leads to a number of refinements in the content, composition (placement), and a refined visual narrative (character and story development) within the final drawing.[6]

The ability to engage with the world through drawing requires a special and particular cognitive capacity in addition to a set of acquired technical skills. At root, the purpose of making drawings is to mediate between perception, cognition, and the physical world, and it is important to understand that this process is not primarily mechanical. In creating a drawing, artists utilize a way of incorporating the observed world into intuitive processes in addition to engaging with systematic intellectual problem solving.

One of the most important characteristics of drawing embedded within these approaches and processes is the way in which it facilitates thinking about narrative and encourages the visualization of ideas and concepts.[7] For me, as a practitioner and academic, drawing is the visualized equivalent of my thought processes and key to the development of thinking and memory. This particular approach has enabled me to question how I use drawing as a code to represent or symbolize various aspects of the world around me. Over time, this approach has developed into a form of visual communication where messages are read and understood by others in the context of mass communication, such as in broadcast media or publishing. The rationale given by art directors for the majority of my commissioned drawings is that they represent that which can not be provided by other visual media. In publishing terms, the work has had to develop a series of codes and techniques that form connections between the image and the written word.

In developing these ideas, my sketchbook has become a place of research and development, an integral part of a strategy for adapting and evolving imagery to be more engaging and widely understood. This self-reflective model serves as an example of the role of drawing as a mediator of personal and social concerns. There is still recognition of the place of sketchbooks in reportage, and particularly as used by war artists during the World Wars and subsequent conflicts, yet this process is open to replacement by photography. Indeed the power of lens-based media is such that some artists have sought to rely on the photograph as the original record from which to draw.

An example of ways in which lens and sketchbook may be integrated is visible in the Gulf War work of John Keane. Keane develops paintings from observational photographic images and video footage and, before he left for the Gulf, Keane made no secret of the fact that he intended to use a camera rather than a sketchbook for recording purposes.[8] This seems to be an interesting method; however, from my perspective, this would alter my relationship to the sketchbook as part of the drawing process.

The approach I have taken to reportage drawing is in contrast to that available to lens media artists and journalists, for even a quick sketch may take longer than the opening and closing of a shutter. However, sketching is more efficient in the long term as the selection and compositional decisions become integrated during the cognitive decision making processes associated with the activity itself. Drawing as a process naturally integrates narrative and opinion, as images are formed through observation and by the use of memory and the mark making integral to the artists' visual language. This is part of the process of selection and critical thinking, a process that often includes the use of memory or ideas evoked by the observational and drawing procedure itself. The desire is to make meaningful and informative images and for the sketchbook to become a document where ideas are developed and evolved, rather than merely archived.

In the case of the APEC sketchbooks, I provided an account, adopting the role of the witness and visual author, developing my ideas through the direct observation of events as they unfolded. It is important to stress the role of observation as integral to both art cultures and the sciences. The process of observation has provided a means of discovery and dissemination while remaining dispassionate and analytical in both the arts and the sciences (social and positivist research setting). Historically this is evident in the investigations of Giotto di Bondone and his studies of perspective. There is further historical evidence in the famous observational drawings undertaken by Leonardo da Vinci, which explored and meticulously documented the construction of the human body using cadavers. In a similar way, artistic observation of social and political events allows us to better understand human behaviour and to start a heightening of our relationship to the natural world and society.

THE NATURE OF REPORTAGE DRAWING

It is possible to contrast my work at the 2007 APEC conference with that of the photojournalists and journalists working alongside me. As already highlighted in this chapter, media-tension caused the Australian Government to cage off most of the city, limiting the population's movements with extra police and members of the armed forces. The state resourced rarely used powers to restrict reports, which included the use and deployment of 'photographic' images. To circumvent this decision *The Sydney Morning Herald* newspaper used my drawings instead.

My approach for these drawings involved using line only in the first small sketchbook and each work took twenty to forty seconds to complete via a process of 'on the spot drawing.' In my view, using this process is faster than some digital photography in that there are no wasted 'shots' or 'missed stills' due to focus lag. When my memory was fresh and after I had time for reflection, I developed some of the more detailed line drawings. Drawing is not a passive activity for me – it is physical and can be very energising and exciting. This often provides the draftsman working in this way with the creative momentum and courage to continue. The larger, more detailed drawings took a day or more of work and treated as on-going reflective statements, or visual essays.

The use of reportage drawing was new in this context for the newspaper as its readers were used to drawings that were satirical in their nature. Documentary rather than satirical, my drawings were draughted under different terms and conditions. I am not interested in the snapshot moment and, while my work develops from a political point of view in common with cartoonists such as Steve Bell, it is not satirical in its content. It is, in graphic terms, expressionist in its critical depiction of society. This reportage work, produced as a direct response to eye-witnessed events, visualizes a range of experiences. I wish to suggest that the immediacy and directness, which can emerge from the overt 'authorship' in the direction and representation of an argument to secure a 'point of view' in drawing, is one of its most significant qualities. This approach places my drawn work as visual communication, as a 'language and strategy for social representation and provocation. It is a means of providing alternative forms of narrative and communication to disrupt the accepted order of things. These perspectives are addressed through the concept of '…remediation.'[9] Bolter and Grusin argue:

> Remediation did not begin with the introduction of digital media. We can identify the same process throughout the last several hundred years of Western visual representation. A painting by the seventeenth century artist Pieter Saenredam, a photograph by Edward Weston, and a computer system for virtual reality are different in many important ways but, they are all attempts to achieve immediacy by ignoring or denying the presence of the medium and the act of mediation.[10]

This view suggests that mediated forms simultaneously borrow from previous models of visualization, but innovate through applications and new technologies. It is my contention, however, that photorealism has naturalized how 'reality' is perceived, and it is the primal directness of expression through drawing that revitalizes an intimacy with what we see. The resulting intimacy between object and viewer is such that it can allow the viewer to ignore or even forget the medium. Audiences are not mere spectators, they are participants in a game of the senses, they are not hapless victims that experience a compulsion to look. Berger confirms:

The child looks and recognises before it can speak. But there is also another sense
in which seeing comes before words. It is seeing which establishes our place in the
surrounding world; we explain that world with words, but words can undo the
fact that we are surrounded by it. The relation between what we see and what we
know is never settled.[11]

SKETCHBOOK DRAWING IN THE CONTEXT OF JOURNALISM

'Seeing' establishes a sense of place in our surroundings, but it also develops
a desire to make expression in relation to the world. For many, words are not a
preferred means of expression and may not, as a language, communicate what
the visual world suggests, nor help to express a sense of ourselves within it. My
narrative drawings situate me, and hopefully the viewer, in a particular context
and while politicized, they work differently from the political cartoon, in that it is
not derived from or sustained by satiric intent. This is a significant aspect of the
reception of drawing. I am not engaging here with issues of aesthetics, however, but
the ways in which this facilitates narrative. My first suggestion is that sketchbook
drawings in journalistic contexts operate as the 'recto,' as they present a means to
unobtrusively re-observe that which may not be captured by photography, or if
captured photographically, they somehow remain 'unseen' through their everyday
familiarity. This may suggest why sketch-artists are often employed by news media,
in courtrooms or as war artists, as it is sometimes more appropriate to demonstrate
a situation through drawing rather than photography. In the case of a restricted
environment such as APEC, the sketchbook became a more effective vehicle
for reportage, and consequently, the publication of the drawings enabled the
pedagogies of visual communication, as the audience gains an understanding of
the 'how' of what is drawn, but is directed implicitly to the 'why' of its achievement.

   This brief analysis of this autobiographical intervention is important in
identifying the nature of my work and the claims I wish to make for sketchbook
drawing in a mass-mediated context. I have already suggested some of the ways in
which drawings of this nature have special and specific characteristics. The critical
and theoretical perspectives presented by John Berger address these difficulties
in that:

We know that it is the right hemisphere of the human brain, which 'reads' and
stores our visual experience. This is significant because the areas and centres
where this takes place are strictly identical with those in the left hemisphere,
which process our experience of word. The apparatus with which we deal with
appearances is identical with that with which we deal with verbal language.
Furthermore, appearances in their unmediated state – that is to say, before they
have been interpreted or perceived – lend themselves to reference systems (so
that they may be stored at a certain level in the memory) which are comparable
to those used for words. And this again prompts one to conclude that
appearances possess some of the qualities of a code.[12]

This recognition is a fundamental part of my thinking in combining approaches to narrative drawing within the context of mediated forms. Though I am aware that considerable work has been produced in relation to cognition and the perception of visual stimuli, this is not the foremost preoccupation of my discussion. I wish to prioritize the contexts in which the work functions. For example, reportage drawing often occurs in different situations and in changing social or political contents, yet the physical environment also changes the way a drawing becomes to exist. The reportage draughtsman becomes aware of the effects of nature, the weather, the movement of light and the effects of wind and rain. Drawing on a public street turns the artist into an entertainer with passersby able to view your work and express an opinion. Drawing in legal courtrooms makes a journalist of the artist, or a possible criminal as they experience the perspective of the person accused through observing the effect of standing in the dock. Drawing in a conflict zone forces the artist to be allied with 'a side' and this turns makes for being a potential political target. In the end and in this way, the process of drawing in a sketchbook at times for me has been a way of experiencing pure adrenaline. It is an addictive activity, which forces clear minded approaches about your objectives as a visual communicator.

The APEC drawings 'lead' pictorial content for *The Sydney Morning Herald*, and this editorial decision was in itself provocative, stimulating much reader interest. As a result, Sydney University staged an exhibition and lecture at the college of the arts which allowed me to explain my, and the papers position. I explained that in contrast to the views of the Government and police authorities, I viewed the notion of 'provocative' as adopting a 'questioning' attitude to events. That drawing is a transparent process in which a reader can retrace the decisions that an artist has made. Drawings reveal the process of their own making, their own looking in more clear ways.[13]

THE AIM OF SKETCHBOOK DRAWINGS

Sketchbooks or 'drawing books' fulfil many different roles. The aim is to develop sketchbooks as observational research documents for my artwork, as a means of intensively considering the things and events I am witnessing and experiencing. There are times when I may want to draw something to better understand its purpose or construction. Sometimes, when I do not have a pencil and paper and I need to remember something that I have seen or need to understand better, I draw it into my memory using my finger on the palm of my hand. At other times, I use drawing sketchbooks to develop a visual conversation about the thing that I am looking at and its' meaning.

Good drawing is an organic act, a process by which the artist's repertoire of gestures tracks with, and across, the multitudinous actions and events of the world. Bad drawing is mechanistic, rigid, and fanatic in its attempt to fixate life in surface illusion; it is a hollow shell containing little blood and breath. Drawings are made with '…energy, flow, exaggeration, distortion, subtlety, omission, suggestion, emphasis, changing and moving line, varying speeds and rhythms produces animated forms and scenes which pulsate with vigor.[14] The aim of the APEC drawings was to provide tangible and vital visual experience of the event for the audience, but also communicate my ideas and experience:

> Because the faculty of sight is continuous, because visual categories (red, yellow, dark, thick, thin) remain constant, and because so many things appear to remain in place, one tends to forget that the visual is always the result off the unrepeatable, momentary encounter.[15]

13.1   Police and the rest of us speaking about drawn lines, through lines drawn as Bush drives by. Published in *The Sydney Morning Herald*, 6 × 12 inches, 2007. Source: Drawing: Mario Minichiello, 2007

This approach helped to develop the drawings as part of the agenda for *The Sydney Morning Herald*, which was further encouraged by the reaction to my drawings by its readers. The public's concerns and growing anger had begun to manifest itself on the Internet; the publication of the drawings helped lead authorities to finally relax their stance on the use of images in reporting APEC.

Figure 13.1 is from double page spread drawings made in the smaller (verso) sketchbook. The drawings were made while moving around the city during APEC. They include images of everyday life or observed with very little time to start and complete the drawings. I had to adapt a way of working which placed greater emphasis on my memory and uses the initial simple drawings as base line for information

13.2 *'The Pigs Will Fly.'* APEC: in response to the leader of world's richest nations arriving. Published in *The Sydney Morning Herald* 2007, 2nd–9th September 2007, weekend edition, removed from news web by government request, 17 × 12.5 inches. Source: Drawing: Mario Minichiello, 2007

13.3 *'Police
protect the rich and
property'.* Outside
the Conference
building, in
response to the
leaders staged
'photo-shoots'.
Policing APEC:
here the police
line facing out
with the city's
richest business
community who
are protected
behind the lines.
Published 2nd–9th
September
2007, weekend
edition, 12.5 × 17
inches. Source:
Drawing: Mario
Minichiello, 2007

THE DRAWING PROCESS

The finished illustrations are my visualized opinions, which contrast to photographic still images. They are not exclusively about or reliant on one incident or moment. They are the deliberate layering of different forms of information both observation and the spoken word. This process facilitates a more considered response in contrast to the immediacy of the line drawings in the smaller sketchbooks. For '…to draw is to look, examining the structure of appearances. A drawing of a tree shows, not a tree, but a tree being looked at.'[16]

The drawing process is built from looking at, and transposing what the essence of the observed phenomena is. I make attempts at ways of understanding this phenomena and explaining it through drawing materials and their reaction to a surface. This is how the act of drawing refuses the process of disappearances and proposes the simultaneity of a multitude of moments '…from each glance a drawing assembles a little evidence, but it consists of the evidence of many glances which can be seen together.'[17]

This means of exploring should be considered as different from writing and speaking, as it is produced from different parts of the brain. In her book *Drawing on the Right Side of the Brain,* Betty Edwards described an important aspect of the mind's internal relationships with the image and with seeing. Edwards suggests that '…drawing a perceived form is largely a right-hemisphere function. This has now been empirically tested and documented.'[18] This demonstrates that, for the artist and designer, it is a helpful to shift the minds' priority from left-brain to right brain hemisphere. This gives an advantage to the right-hand side of the brain and to the minds' ability to concentrate more of its resources on absorbing information through seeing and then processing the imagery into drawings. Edwards now also provides a range of drawing exercises (the workbook) as part of her 'drawing on the right-hand side of the brain' publication. This enables the reader to experience the process of shifting the mind's priority from left to right side of the brain. It is accepted that this shift in concentration, as Edwards has cited, is desirable when making drawings in order to ensure that you are using the best cognitive processes for seeing. Edwards' own 'workbook' steers to a more clearly way of considering compositional aspects of images, as well as forms, positive and negative spaces. While these are the building blocks of drawing, as an intellectual process it remains difficult to explain. Professor Horton suggests:

> Drawing does not come out of philosophy, mathematics, linguistics, or scientific method. It is measurable neither by language nor numbers. Thus, in a world, which places such a high value on the word and accountability, it appears an imprecise and vaguely defined method. Yet, this is also its strength. Drawing – the drawn image – remains resistant to other forms of analysis and its singularity forces the viewer to engage with it on its own terms.[19]

I contend that there are advantages in compelling the viewer and the maker to engage with drawing on its own terms and that this is particularly evident in mass-mediated contexts. Indeed, it seems that successful practitioners have developed sophisticated approaches to engaging with mass media. The ways in which their work engages with a reader or viewer necessitates that they find ways for them to enter the drawing and its construction of visual narrative. For example, an illustrator understands a subject through its duality of meaning, how it appears visually and how its description in words. I ensure that an idea, whether read, heard, or observed, is explored through words and images (often a series of sketches and word prompts as in Figure 13.1). This helps to imprint a 'recto' and a 'verso' of its meaning. In these inner exchanges, the idea itself is a 'recto-verso' as it exists on both sides of the brain. The sketchbook is the perfect form in which to house this notion, as there is no obvious primary side, no set rules or order, and it is a space to ramble through thought and process. Sketchbooks are changeable and temporal, a conversation with both sides of the brain of which, at times, it is not totally in control.

CONCLUSION

The sketchbook, as presented here, provides a unique environment to develop visual thinking. While there is no equivalent to a sketchbook in photography, there are comparisons to a diary for writing as a form of notation and reflection. Sketchbooks blur the lines between formal academic approaches to drawing. The process can be difficult to decode because they are private spaces and not generally intended to be 'viewed "or" displayed' to the public. These spaces allow for more freethinking research and experimentation. In this chapter I have argued that drawn narratives enable artists to move the audience beyond representation alone, allowing a sense of intimacy, and providing an emotional and intellectual experience for the viewer of an event or idea. It seeks to combine the immediacy of the moment in what is arguably the journalistic 'instant', with the knowledge prompted by memory and experience, which is part of the 'action' of the drawing process.

The chapter has exposed how such drawing works as a means of communication. Drawing, like writing, enables the viewer to internalize the experience contained in its visual narrative. However, it is not only through a drawing's formal grammar of replicating or remaking reality through observation, and the use of formal systems, such as perspective, mark making, tone and texture, that communication occurs.

> *Communication starts with the act of drawing and that is our point of entry too. The sketchbooks carry the raw material, upon which he later works to produce the more formal illustrative expression of the exhibition pieces. In these his social reflections are aired and his anxieties become more visible, and so they belong with the strong socio-political themes of his commissions for the press; a body of powerful, stylized commentaries, which serve to illuminate and shock us into response. Given such saturation, what role, purpose or integrity lies in illustrative documentation of the sort found in Mario Minichiello's personal journals?*[20]

BIBLIOGRAPHY

ABC. 'Security wall to protect APEC leaders'. *www.abc.net.au/news*. 2007. http://www.abc.net.au/news/2007-08-02/security-wall-to-protect-apec-leaders/2520194 (accessed 8 22, 2011).

APEC. 'Mission Statement'. *www.apec.org*. 2011. http://www.apec.org/About-Us/About-APEC/Mission-Statement.aspx (accessed 8 22, 2011).

Bell, Steve. *Apes of Wrath*. London: Methuen, 2004.

Berger, John. *Berger on Drawing*. Cork: Occasional Press, 2005.

_____. *Ways of Seeing*. London: Penguin, 1972.

Bibby, P. *www.smh.com.au*. 2007. http://www.smh.com.au/news/apec/call-for-inquiry-into-clash-that-felled-photographer/2007/09/10/1189276633581.html (accessed 8 22, 2011).

Bolter, Jay David. and Richard Grusin. *Remediation: Understanding New Media*. London: MIT Press, 2000.

Edwards, Betty. *Drawing on the Right Side of the Brain*. New York: Penguin Putman, 1979.

Horton, C., C. Jenkins, Colin Rhodes and J. Spalding. *Debating the Line (Minichiello's Drawings)*. Humberside: European Illustrator Gallery and Collection with Loughborough University School of Art and Design.

Keane, John, and Angela Weight. *John Keane – Gulf*. London: Imperial War museum, 1992.

McNiff, Jean, and A. Jack Whitehead. *All You Need to Know About Action Research*. London: Sage, 2011.

Wells, Paul, Jonna Quinn, and Les Mills. *Drawing for Animation*. Singapore: AVA, 2008.

NOTES

1   APEC, "Mission Statement," *www.apec.org*, 2011, http://www.apec.org/About-Us/About-APEC/Mission-Statement.aspx (accessed 8 22, 2011).

2   ABC, "Security wall to protect APEC leaders," *www.abc.net.au/news*, 2007, http://www.abc.net.au/news/2007-08-02/security-wall-to-protect-apec-leaders/2520194 (accessed 8 22, 2011).

3   P. Bibby, *www.smh.com.au*, 2007, http://www.smh.com.au/news/apec/call-for-inquiry-into-clash-that-felled-photographer/2007/09/10/1189276633581.html (accessed 8 22, 2011).

4   S. Bell, *Apes of Wrath* (London: Methuen, 2004).

5   J. McNiff and A. Whitehead, *All you need to know about action research* (London: Sage, 2011).

6   *The Sydney Morning Herald* finally published the images.

7   P. Wells, J. Quinn and L. Mills, *Drawing for Animation* (Singapore: AVA).

8   J. Keane and A. Weight, *John Keane – Gulf* (London: Imperial War museum, 1992).

9   D. Bolter and G. Grusin, *Remediation: Understanding New Media* (London: MIT Press, 2000), 155.

10 D. Bolter and G. Grusin, *Remediation: Understanding New Media* (London: MIT Press, 2000).

11 J. Berger, *Ways of Seeing* (London: Penguin, 1972), 7.

12 J. Berger, *Ways of Seeing*.

13 J. Berger, *Berger on Drawing* (Cork: Occasional Press, 2005).

14 C. Horton, C. Jenkins, C. Rhodes and J. Spalding, *Debating the Line (Minichiello's Drawings*, (Humberside: European Illustrator gallery and collection with Loughborough University School of Art and Design).

15 J. Berger, *Berger on Drawing*.

16 J. Berger, *Berger on Drawing*.

17 J. Berger, *Berger on Drawing*.

18 B. Edwards, *Drawing on the Right Side of the Brain* (New York: Penguin Putman, 1979).

19 C. Horton, et al., *Debating the Line (Minichiello's Drawings)* (Humberside: European Illustrator gallery and collection with Loughborough University School of Art and Design), 25–26.

20 C. Horton, et al., *Debating the Line (Minichiello's Drawings)*, 25–26.

14

The Sketchbook as Collection: A Phenomenology of Sketching

Raymond Lucas

THE SKETCHBOOK AS COLLECTION

Collecting is a form of conquest and collected artifacts are material signs of victory over their former owners and places of origin. From an early age non-Western artifacts brought home by soldiers, travelers, and antiquity hunters had played the role of spoils. What the modern museum particularly developed, in conjunction with this paradigm of conquest, was a model of colonization, of foreign dominion.[1]

There is an interesting parallel that is drawn between the sketchbook and the museum, both of which are understood explicitly as activities, as practices of collecting. The way in which this practice actually functions in reality is of course different, that the activity involved differs, but the intent remains similar. In a notable example, we can see from the sketchbooks of Le Corbusier that the travel journal is a persistent model, having its roots in the Grand Tour and a continued relevance through to the Modernist period. Guiliano Gresleri, introducing Corbusier's German notebooks[2] explains that the sketches, notes, and photographs had no single prescribed use, but that themes recurred in various forms throughout Corbusier's written and built works. This is maintained today in examples such as the architectural educator and theorist Simon Unwin, who contends that:

> You cannot understand architecture merely by looking at photographs. You cannot understand architecture by only reading words. Yet many books on architecture have only words and/or photographs. The only way to understand architecture is through the medium used in its creation – drawing.[3]

Unwin further argues that such drawing even has primacy over visiting buildings: that drawing a building represents a form of knowledge inherent to and essential to the discipline of architecture. The sketchbook is strongly implicated in this. 'Visiting buildings gives you the best chance to experience architecture in relation to the world of light, sound, setting, people...and to assess the performance of the abstraction when made real. But to understand the underlying architecture of buildings you need to study them through drawing.'[4] Unwin's richly illustrated works demonstrate his engagement with both literature and built architecture. The selections collected and presented in his publications are edited and curated carefully from skillfully produced sketchbooks. Collecting is of course, something of some interest to museum studies and is closely theorized by anthropologists as a form of cultural display. What is it that motivates the collector, and how can sketches be understood explicitly as collections? What is to be gained by this understanding?

SIR JOHN SOANE'S MUSEUM AS CABINET OF CURIOSITY

The Soane Museum is a curious place in several senses, representing both a prototype for later museums and as one of the most extreme examples of the type. The building sits on Lincoln's Inn Fields in London, on the Northern side of a city square. Soane established his museum in 1833, marking out his own collection for this use in what might appear now to be a rather self-aggrandising move. This is an ideal starting point of course, as it is this intention to display that we wish to interrogate within this chapter. In this sense, understanding both Soane the man and the institution is fundamental to the study.

Soane himself was an architect and educator with a strong interest in antiquity. As such, he created a vast collection of artifacts, drawings, models, and plaster casts from which to work. A classicist, his practice involved close examination of these artifacts as models or prototypes for his own work. Soane's aim was to work with direct observation wherever possible. This follows on from earlier European traditions of the Grand Tour. There was an explosion of interest in Egypt in the 19th century, fuelled by imperialist expansion from Europe. Soane's collection can be seen as being in continuity with this idea, but his intention was more direct, pragmatic and pedagogical. As indicated in item six of the *Regulations for Admission,* which remains in place today, Soane intended to learn and to teach with this collection in order to allow architecture to return to Classical universal roots. Item six states:

> *Sketching is permitted in the Museum provided that circulation is not impeded by the sketcher or his equipment. Inks, paints and charcoal are not permitted. For making measured drawings, permission must be obtained from the Director.*[5]

The archives and drawing collection remain available to scholars, and the conditions of entry remain as close as possible to Sir John Soane's original regulations as possible. This gives the museum a unique character, as there is a practice of visiting, from waiting in the street until being allowed in (there being a strict numerical limit to the numbers in the museum at any given time), the signing of a guest book, and leaving bags and other items with the attendants in the entry hall.

John Elsner, in his contribution to the edited collection *The Cultures of Collecting* explicitly explores the example of Sir John Soane's museum in the essay 'A Collector's Model of Desire: The House and Museum of Sir John Soane'.[6] This connection of collecting and desire begins to theorize the museum *as a process of accumulation*. Rather than a fixed and completed thing, the museum lives and breathes through its acquisitions and display policies. Even where the collection does not grow any more, the collection must be curated and selected, with some items remaining in storage and choices made about what to show and what to hide away.

> *Collecting is the desire of the Museum. The museum seeks to be a static hold-all, largely a finished piece (although with blurry edges caused by de-accessioning and new acquisitions), a mausoleum of previous collections; collecting is the dynamic that brought it into being. While the museum is a kind of entombment, a display of once lived activity (the activity whereby real people collected objects associated with other real people or living beings), collecting is the process of the museum's creation, the living act that the museum enbalms.*[7]

In the essay, Elsner attempts to describe the process by which museums actually happen or come in to being. This is described as a point at which a collection is transformed into a museum, the point at which these artifacts are constituted into a coherent body. A number of processes and concepts explain this, where Elsner considers the status of the collection, the ideas of nostalgia associated with the selected items, and the idea that such disparate fragments can be understood in any way as a whole. Soane's museum is the perfect case study in this regard, of course, representing as it does the collection of a single individual over a single lifetime rather than the political and colonial implications of a National collection such as the British Museum. Soane's museum represents a prototypical museum and a collection that has remained *in situ* since its institution. These implications are most pronounced in the case of the National collections, given their identification with the State. That is not to absolve the private collection from a similar critique, however, simply that the intentions are rather different: glorifying the collector as an individual rather than reinforcing the nation. Elsner questions the foundational myth of the museum:

> *In suggesting that Roman Italy was constructed as the all-plentiful provider and the Ur-collection, I wish to address a dream lying wistfully behind the collecting impulse: namely, the urge to evoke, even sometimes to fulfil, that myth of a completion, a complete ancient world, which was once itself collected in the imperial splendour of Rome.*[8]

Rome then is the Ur-source, the originating source of civilization to the 19th Century academic and architect. This is, of course, questionably Eurocentric, but was the reference point of the time, and drives many of the commonly held ideas we have of original sources, and the completion of the collection: that there is a source, an originating point like that of a river from which knowledge might flow. By limiting this to Rome, the achievement was made possible. The discovery of rich new worlds, even earlier or isolated from the Greco-Roman model complicates this substantially. Elsner is fascinated by the difference between the Museum and the Collection. What is this distinction? When did this transformation occur?

> *The exercise of translating the private into the public, the personal collection into a museum for the nation, is thus to be seen as a peculiarly textual act. It lies in the creation of the handbook, in legal formulae (such as the Act of Parliament) and in the paraphernalia of the official language with which Soane came increasingly to frame the descriptions of his collections.*[9]

This codification of the collection then marks the Museum as a quality lying in the understanding applied to the artifacts, the sense that Soane made of the works. More than a mere functional difference between the Home and the Museum, it can be understood that there is a heightened sense of intentionality behind the museum. The home has meaning, but this is always hidden and the difficulty lies in revealing, or otherwise uncovering, these unintended consequences. The museum is a deliberate construction, which often obfuscates or hides other, deeper, more politically motivated intentions.

There is an extent to which Soane's Museum helps define what may be considered collectible. Were it possible to capture entire buildings from antiquity, then this might have been Soane's ultimate aim. This illuminates some of the presuppositions of collection and the relationship with classicism's inherent universalism and the idea of original context. Soane's thinking was, to a large extent, informed by the notion of Classicism. This idea is not only out of fashion nowadays, but we must critically engage with what the very notion of the classic might mean. The critiques encompassed by Edward Said's critique of academic *Orientalism*[10] in the book of the same name are relevant to the activities of collectors such as Soane, a process of distancing and aestheticizing the Other in order to demonstrate the connoisseurship of the collector.

> *As a concept, the idea of a 'classic' indicates some sort of timeless and spaceless quality: a transcendence from that which is contextual, grounded, and mortal. The classic approaches the notion of the Platonic ideal, whereby ancient philosophers considered that there were Earthly manifestations of things, but also otherworldly ideal forms. The critique of classicism, then, is that it treats a body of antique knowledge and artifacts as originating or Ur-categories; that these represent the ultimate models from which all other responses are measured and normally found wanting.*[11]

The critique of this would be that it, firstly, ignores the original context, temporality, and use. There is undeniably a beauty and consideration for proportion in such buildings, which is sublime and worthy of investigation. Such classicism has flaws however. Politically it promotes an idea that there can be an originating (very Western) ideal from which all other things are mere shadows. More than a stylistic movement, which stripped ornamentation and displayed the interior arrangement to the outside world, Modernism is an important step away from Classicism, which began long before the 20th Century. Such Modern thought is often considered as beginning in the mid-19th Century or even earlier, certainly post-Enlightenment. Thus, architectural Modernism as a movement occurs in the mid-point of the modern period, post-war expressions are late modernism, and the 1970s onwards can be understood as post-modernist. Modernism represents a gradual movement (rather than the rupture as often understood) towards contextualism, specificity, and invention. The museum supports a continuing Classicism, intended as it was by Soane as a collection of artifacts for study. This frozen aspect of the museum is one of the keys to understanding it according to Elsner.[12]

Elsner was fascinated by the desire that drove Soane's collection, arguing that his acquisitiveness was driven by a compulsion to have, to possess. This is certainly true of early museums based on collections: that there is a material culture and economic value as well as academic interest and conservationist impulse at work. The early museum sought to save these items from ruin, but also funded expeditions to these sites of antiquity, creating a market for such things as Egyptian sarcophagi and fragments of Roman architecture. This commodification is one of the most troubling aspects, where such items are displaced from their original function of being the funeral rites of a high status individual or an essential and functional piece of architecture.

In what ways does sketching avoid some of these problems within the collecting impulse? As the foundational idea of the collection, based firmly in the Grand Tour, the Soane Museum helps us to define the very activity of collecting, marking the difficulties and importance of de-contextualization. This removal of original context is both what is: most troubling politically and ethically, but also what affords the opportunities for creative acts, of abstraction, analysis, and understanding. Notable in this regard is the work of the architect John Hejduk, whose sketchbooks exhibit the character of a Cabinet of Curiosity, and are reflective of his process as an architectural practitioner, theorist, and educator. Starting with a familiar form: The Acropolis, the work transcends the mimetic representation of objects and moves in the direction of the spiritual and poetic, structured by a linear and serial narrative.[13]

BAUDRILLARD, BACON'S STUDIO, AND THE SYSTEM OF SKETCHING

Critical theorist Jean Baudrillard's essay 'The System of Collecting' illuminates many aspects of the studio of Francis Bacon's transformation into a museum piece. He describes collecting as a systematic activity, not merely an end result, and focuses (somewhat ironically given the de-temporalization of such activities) on the practice of the museum in collecting:

> THE OBJECT DIVESTED OF ITS FUNCTION
> THE LOVED OBJECT
> THE PERFECT PET
> A SERIAL GAME
> FROM QUANTITY TO QUALITY: THE UNIQUE OBJECT
> OBJECTS AND TEMPORALITY: THE CONTROLLED CYCLE[14]

Baudrillard *is a thinker from within* the Marxist critical theory tradition. He deconstructs problems in order to understand the fundamental politics at the heart of things. He famously writes on simulations and simulacra: the mediation of life through television and other forms of communication, but he also turns to the objectivizing nature of the collection and the museum. The museum, to Baudrillard, is a process of gathering, collecting, and objectifying items. In order to be part of a collection, an object is stripped of its function, and is no longer needed for anything: it is to be placed on display and frozen. This is the aim of the gallery and museum: to *aestheticize* objects, to entomb them in this system of objects. He explicitly cites the banal example of the refrigerator in this regard:

> The fact that I make use of a refrigerator in order to freeze things, means that the refrigerator is defined in terms of a practical transaction: it is not an object so much as a freezing mechanism. In this sense, I cannot be said to possess it. Possession cannot apply to an implement, since the object I utilize always directs me back to the world. Rather it applies to that object once it is divested of its function and made relative to a subject. In this sense, all objects that are possessed submit to the same abstractive operation and participate in a mutual relationship in so far as they each refer back to the subject. They thereby constitute themselves as a system, on the basis of which the subject seeks to piece together his world, his personal microcosm.[15]

In this way, Baudrillard has something very specific in mind when he uses the word 'object'. The object is a particular way of rendering a thing, an item, as valuable and desirable that has nothing to do with its use-value. An object, then, is an object of desire. The aim of this consideration of things is to form a collection, according to Baudrillard.[16] This problem becomes all the clearer when presenting objects not originally designed for such display. A prime example being the artist's studio: the secretive machinery behind the production of Bacon's paintings. The stated aim is educational and critical, but the result is to objectify, to reify, to render precious and desirable, even valuable. As soon as the studio is placed on display, it cannot be used, and is in a way no longer a studio but an image of a studio.

Taking this on to the consideration of the loved object, Baudrillard *gives* expression *to* the passions of the collector as *being* almost sexual in nature. This is a common move in the work of theorists such as Baudrillard, and whilst at first it might seem absurd, the basis of much work in psychoanalysis suggests that there is at the very least a kernel of truth and a similar mechanism at work. Regarding architecture, the most interesting recent example of theory exploring this is by the architectural theorist Alberto Perez-Gomez in *Built Upon Love: Architectural Longing After Ethics and Aesthetics*.[17]

This psychology of the collection process is found by Baudrillard's source in this section to have the following characteristics – it is a perfect pet, a '...docile dog which receives caresses and returns them in its own way; or rather, reflects them like a mirror constructed in such a way as to throw back images not of the real but the desirable.'[18] This is one matter with objects from our own culture, but becomes much more politically undesirable once one makes the decision to attempt to show other contemporary cultures, as in an ethnographic museum. Such displays, then, are fraught with dangers and encourage us to present the 'Other' in an objectified fashion, giving value to certain items that are inducted into the gallery systems of exchange-value attribution and marketplaces. Objects enter, unwillingly, and in an unintended fashion, into the power exchanges and are accorded monetary or other economic value.

The system of collecting, for Baudrillard, only works when the objects are collected as a series. The terms for this series can be as specific as the antiquities Soane was interested in, or as narrow as everything contained in Francis Bacon's studio at the time of his death. This serial nature automatically places objects in relation, in comparison with one another. One begins to speak of that which belongs to the series and those objects excluded (such as things from Bacon's earlier studio or which he owned, but did not leave there). We also have platonic samples: the perfect object and the imperfect object. Much like the market in unlikely antiques, such as pottery or teddy bears, objects often evolve largely through its relative rarity, meaning that the work of a pottery which went out of business and existed for a brief period can be worth a great deal more than one which remained successful '…for it is invariably oneself that one collects.'[19]

The collector displays an aspect of themselves. This is certainly true of Soane, and was part of his stated intent, a kind of self-aggrandisement, culminating in his gifting of this collection to the State. The case of Bacon is of course rather different, the collectors not being a single person, but the art-historical and art-critical establishment. This leads us to consider the phenomenological implications of collecting oneself through the practice of keeping a sketchbook. A systematic approach to sketching is discussed with reference to the notebooks of Herman Hertzberger, where the editors catalogue the sketchbook entries as belonging to a class.[20] Whilst largely and pragmatically indicating the topic of the sketch, the idea of *mechanism* emerges as particularly important, as it is fundamental to the prototypes and spatial understandings developed before they become attached to the more concrete architectural schemes listed as *projects*. Hertzberger is not alone in this systematic use of sketchbooks, and examples of other architects working in this way include the rigorous analytical deconstructions of architectural history by Peter Eisenman[21] and the iterative development shown in Louis Kahn's drawings for the Dominican Motherhouse project. Whilst not a sketchbook per se, the serial quality of Louis Kahn's drawings of demonstrate the developmental quality of drawing in architecture: as noted by Michael Merrill[22] this is part of a persistent culture in architectural production, where an iterative design process is embedded in the practice of the discipline through drawing layer upon layer of transparency & tracing. These sequences of drawings are assembled after the fact into sketchbooks, the sequence playing a role as an ordering principle, which offers the reader an insight into the thinking process.

The *system* is inherent in the sketchbook, be that the underlying theoretical system described by Baudrillard or a more purposive system with regards to Hertberger's sketching practices. The sketchbook is subject to many of the issues wrapped up in collection, but avoiding the direct commodification of the object.

RESONANCE AND WONDER

This all appears very critical of the museum, the collector, and broader attempts at cultural display as well as, by extension, the sketcher. This is far from the case, however. It is important to complicate and refine our relationship with items held by museums or deliberately exhibited. Questions of who is saying what about whom should be at the forefront of our encounters with such displays. It is worth at this point returning to the potential of the museum, and therefore to end on a more positive note. This lies in the dual intentions of evoking resonance and wonder with a collection. Steven Greenblatt examines these twin concepts in his essay of the same name:

> By resonance I mean the power of the displayed object to reach out beyond its formal boundaries to a larger world, to evoke in the viewer the complex, dynamic cultural forces from which it has emerged and for which it may be taken by a viewer to stand. By wonder I mean the power of the displayed object to stop the viewer in his or her tracks, to convey an arresting sense of uniqueness, to evoke an exalted attention.[23]

This becomes for Greenblatt a discussion of the artefacts and the feelings or responses they can evoke in the museum-going public. The aim is, after all, to share and educate, to further our understanding of one another. However much we might problematize that particular activity, there is something edifying and positive in this intent – to the extent that it must remain possible and be an aim worthy of achieving. The stories of artifacts, then, are the key to this. Rather than only pointing to the perfection of the ideal or exemplar, there might be more narrative to accompany a broken item, one that shows the traces of being used, or which is everyday rather than ceremonial. This sounds subtle, but represents a huge shift in the collections' focus. Away from the best examples in a series, the one shown might be the most informative about the lives of the people who used it. We can always find traces of life and use in these artifacts, and it is this connection with others, this resonance and appeal to common humanity, that lies at the heart of the display of a culture.

> I am fascinated by the signs of alteration, tampering, and even deliberate damage that many museums simply try to efface: first and most obviously the act of displacement that is essential for the collection of virtually all older artifacts and most modern ones–pulled out of chapels, peeled off church walls, removed from decayed houses, given as gifts, seized as spoils of war, stolen, or "purchased" more or less fairly by the economically ascendant from the economically naive… even these accidents–the marks of a literal fragility – can have their resonance: the climax of an absurdly hagiographical Proust exhibition several years ago was a display case holding a small, patched, modest vase with a label that read, "This vase broken by Marcel Proust."[24]

I am drawn to a Japanese practice in this regard, however. In the display of museum quality pottery, there is an acceptance that certain hairline cracks will eventually develop into full ruptures in the fragile brittle ceramic. The solution is not efface the repair, but to celebrate it by pouring a stabilising resin into the crack and then applying gold lacquer, accentuating and highlighting the crack and showing the contrast with the remaining pottery. This shows an acceptance of use; the absurdity of museum culture is that the items most likely to be exhibited are the ones least likely to have ever been used, for these are the items that survive pristine and unbroken.

Greenblatt's account of wonder[25] takes the example of early Renaissance cabinets of curiosity, called wonder-cabinets. Like a curate's egg, the aim was not for the most valuable or most perfect, but rather for the outlandish, unusual, inexplicable, or most deeply narrative objects. Greenblatt ends with a discussion of the Musée D'Orsay in Paris, which was opened around the time of the publication, and a source of great debate. The museum was designed by Gae Aulenti, and a conversion of a large beaux-arts railway station from 1900, complete with massive barrel vault and ornamental clock. The museum gave precedence on the open ground floors to items which the art-criticism establishment felt were of minor importance compared with the masterpieces of Impressionist and Post-Impressionism displayed in less prestigious spaces deep within the museum.

The prominence instead went to furniture, crafts and other decorative arts rather than fine art. The effect, the wonder is certainly there; but Greenblatt[26] feels that this is at the expense of the resonance of the space. This is perhaps a little naively defined, for there is a great deal of drama in the display of beautifully crafted furniture placed in the context of complete room settings; set against the impressive concourse with carefully terraced display areas and balconies.

In practical terms, the museum has proven a success, albeit one with a great deal of controversy surrounding the status of the objects contained within. The viewing conditions of the acknowledged masters of painting do not afford vast numbers of visitors at once, but nor should they. The intimate setting deep within the plan is actually appropriate, ensuring a practical amount of through traffic resulting in more people spending longer with the whole collection rather than heading straight for the star painters and paintings.

There is also a question of context here, and I am reminded in particular of the galleries showing delicate pastel drawings so popular not only as studies but as alternative finished works by the artists of the time. The pastel, however, is also not as valued by the museum and art-historical establishment, partly enmeshed in the exchange value of a picture, the scale of works leaves the fragile pastel somewhere below watercolours and far below an oil painting in the pecking order of media. These are, however, important works showing the development of modernist thought in art and society more broadly. They are viewed in conditions similar to that which the artist and client might have seen them; darkened and close-up. This is not only appropriate, but evocative of the resonance and wonder that all good museums must strive to achieve; both at once, not one or the other.

Drawing is not simply a matter of memory but a medium for thought, a conceptual tool, and Gehry significantly refers to his sketches as a way of "thinking aloud."[27]

A further example of resonance and of the importance of the actual trace can be found in the well publicised work of Frank Gehry. Despite the way in which Gehry's sketching has been alternately celebrated in the popular press and somewhat derided in professional discourse, there remains a connection between the gesture collected and recorded by his sketches and the lines of his architectural works. There is resonance in the ability of the viewer to trace back the line to the gesture, and to understand the transformation of this line into the architectural form.[28]

Wonder represents our astonishment at some of the possible ways for humans to understand the world, make sense of their environment, and interact with it. Resonance is that recognition that there are a plurality and multitude of ways to live, to be human, and that we share something in common even with the most unusual of these. Confronting the material traces of these, provided the context is sufficiently appreciated, allows us some access into other peoples' worlds.

CONCLUSION: SKETCHING IN THE MUSEUM

The notions of representing difference and otherness highlighted by museum studies and anthropology also hold true for the sketchbook. This might be understood as an over-problematization of the humble sketch, but if we are to understand what it is we are doing when we sketch, then we must challenge some of the preconceived notions of what we are trying to achieve. What is the aim of the sketch, and what is the sometimes inadvertent result?

14.1 British Museum Sketchbook Pages. Selection of images from the author's sketchbook, these were drawn *in situ* at the British Museum. The multiple projections used in the sketches are particularly important in showing ways of describing and understanding objects more fully than a solely perspectival representation. Source: Image: Raymond Lucas 2011

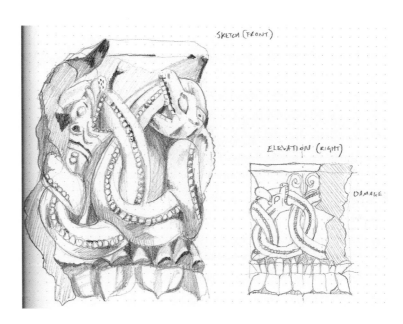

Writing on the theme of 'The Museum as a Way of Seeing,' Svetlana Alpers discusses the museum in a manner which could just as easily describe a sketchbook; in this case a large crab found at the Peabody Museum in Cambridge is described:

> I could attend to a crab in this way because it was still, exposed to view, dead. Its habitat and habits of rest, eating, and moving were absent. I had no idea how it had been caught. I am describing looking at it as an artifact and in that sense like a work of art. The museum had transformed the crab–had heightened, by isolating, these aspects, had encouraged one to look at it in this way. The museum had made it an object of visual interest.[29]

We can return to the Soane at this point, and draw a relationship with it as the prototype of the museum and also underline its facility for the sketcher. The Soane

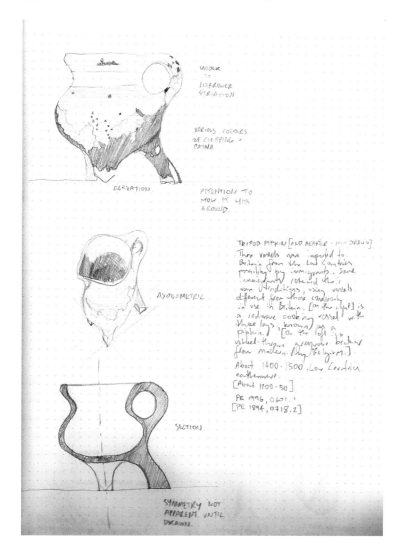

14.2   British Museum Sketchbook Pages. Selection of images from the author's sketchbook, these were drawn *in situ* at the British Museum. The multiple projections used in the sketches are particularly important in showing ways of describing and understanding objects more fully than a solely perspectival representation. Source: Image: Raymond Lucas 2011

14.3   British Museum Sketchbook Pages. Selection of images from the author's sketchbook, these were drawn *in situ* at the British Museum. The multiple projections used in the sketches are particularly important in showing ways of describing and understanding objects more fully than a solely perspectival representation. Source: Image: Raymond Lucas 2011

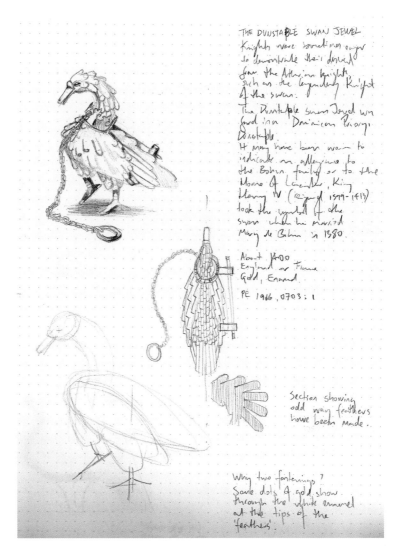

Museum itself is a potential sketchbook, the resulting drawings being a form of a personalized museum collection.

> I started with the hypothesis that everything in a museum is put under the pressure of a way of seeing. A serial display, be it of paintings or masks, stools and pitchforks, establishes certain parameters of visual interest, whether those parameters are known to have been intended by the objects' producers or not.[30]

The sketchbook is also a way of seeing, both for the sketcher and for the audience of the sketchbook, often the same individual. The imposition of order through seriality is crucial to the sketchbook. Items, scenes, and people are placed into a relationship by this simple seriality, a kind of equivalence being given to them so that a series of images are given equal weight.

BIBLIOGRAPHY

De Costa Meyer, Esther. *Frank Gehry on Line*. Princeton: Princeton University Press, 2008.

Edwards, Elizabeth, Chris Gosden and Ruth Phillips, eds. *Sensible Objects: Colonialism, Museums and Modern Culture*. Oxford: Berg, 2002.

Eisenman, Peter. *Feints*, Milan: Skira, 2006.

_____. *Ten Canonical Buildings 1950–2000*, New York: Rizzoli, 2008.

Elsner, John and Roger Cardinal, eds. *Cultures of Collecting*. London: Reaktion Books, 1994.

Forty, Adrian and Susanne Küchler, eds. *The Art of Forgetting*. Oxford: Berg, 1999.

Gunn, Wendy, ed. *Fieldnotes and Sketchbooks: Challenging the Boundaries Between Descriptions and Processes of Describing*. Frankfurt: Peter Lang, 2009.

Hallam, Elizabeth and Brian Street, eds. *Cultural Encounters: Representing Otherness*. London: Routledge, 2000.

Hejduk, John. *Architectures in Love*. New York: Rizzolli, 1995.

Karp, Ivan and Steven D. Lavine, eds. *Exhibiting Culture: The Poetics and Politics of Museum Display*. Washington: Smithsonian Institution Press, 1991.

Küchler, Susanne. *Malanggan: Art, Memory and Sacrifice*. Oxford: Berg, 2002.

Le Corbusier. *Les Voyages d'Allemagne*. Milan: Electa Architecture and Fondation Le Corbusier, 2002.

Lucas, Raymond. *"Towards a Theory of Notation as a Thinking Tool."* PhD diss., University of Aberdeen, 2006.

Merrill, Michael. *Louis Kahn Drawing to Find Out: the Dominican Motherhouse and the Patient Search for Architecture*. Baden: Lars Müller Publishers, 2010.

Perez-Gomez, Alberto. *Built Upon Love: Architectural Longing After Aesthetics and Ethics*. Cambridge Massachusetts: MIT Press, 2006.

Said, Edward. W. *Orientalism*, London: Penguin Classics, 2003.

Sherman, Daniel, J., ed. *Museums & Difference*. Indianapolis: Indiana University Press, 2008.

Sherer, D. "Critical and Palladian," in *Log* Vol. 26. New York: Anyone Corporation (2012): 135–143.

Soane, John and The Trustees of Sir John Soane's Museum. *A New Description of Sir John Soane's Museum*. London: The Trustees of Sir John Soane's Museum, 2007.

Unwin, Simon. *Twenty Buildings Every Architect Should Understand*. London: Routledge, 2010.

Van Bergeijk, Herman and Hauptmann, Deborah. eds. *Notations of Herman Hertzberger*. Rotterdam: NAI Publishers, 1998.

NOTES

1   Discusssed in "The Museum as Sensecape: Western Sensibilities and Indigenous Artifacts" by Howes and Classen in *Sensible Objects: Colonialism, Museums and Modern Culture*, eds Elizabeth Edwards, Chris Gosden and Ruth Phillips, (Oxford: Berg, 2002), 209.

2   Le Corbusier. *Les Voyages d'Allemagne*. (Milan: Electa Architecture and Fondation Le Corbusier, 2002), 13.

3   Simon Unwin, *Twenty Buildings Every Architect Should Understand* (London: Routledge, 2010), 3.

4   A discussion of this process is presented in Wendy Gunn, ed., *Fieldnotes and Sketchbooks: Challenging the Boundaries Between Descriptions and Processes of Describing* (Frankfurt: Peter Lang, 2009), 37–59.

5   Extract from the General Regulations for Admission to the Museum, 2007. Soane, John and The Trustees of Sir John Soane's Museum. *A New Description of Sir John Soane's Museum*. London: The Trustees of Sir John Soane's Museum, 2007), 167.

6   John Elsner and Roger Cardinal, eds, *Cultures of Collecting* (London: Reaktion Books, 1994), 155–176.

7   Elsner, *Cultures of Collecting*, 155.

8   Elsner, *Cultures of Collecting*, 156.

9   Elsner, *Cultures of Collecting*, 158.

10   Edward W. Said, *Orientalism* (London: Penguin Classics, 2003), 52.

11   For more on this see Raymond Lucas, "*Towards a Theory of Notation as a Thinking Tool*" (PhD diss., University of Aberdeen, 2006).

12   Elsner, *Cultures of Collecting*, 176.

13   See John Hejduk, *Architectures in Love* (New York: Rizzolli, 1995).

14   Elsner, *Cultures of Collecting*, 7–24.

15   Elsner, *Cultures of Collecting*, 7.

16   Elsner, *Cultures of Collecting*, 8.

17   Alberto Perez-Gomez, *Built Upon Love: Architectural Longing After Aesthetics and Ethics* (Cambridge Massachusetts: MIT Press, 2006).

18   Elsner, *Cultures of Collecting*, 10.

19   Elsner, *Cultures of Collecting*, 12.

20   Herman Van Bergeijk and Deborah Hauptmann, eds (*Notations of Herman Hertzberger*. Rotterdam: NAI Publishers, 1998), 39–45.

21   See Peter Eisenman, *Feints* (Milan: Skira, 2006) and Peter Eisenman, *Ten Canonical Buildings 1950–2000* (New York: Rizzoli, 2008). See also D. Sherer, "Critical and Palladian," *Log* Vol. 26. New York: Anyone Corporation (2012), 135–143.

22   Michael Merril, *Louis Kahn Drawing to Find Out: the Dominican Motherhouse and the Patient Search for Architecture* (Baden: Lars Müller Publishers, 2010), 12.

23   Ivan Karp and Steven D. Lavine, eds, *Exhibiting Culture: The Poetics and Politics of Museum Display* (Washington: Smithsonian Institution Press, 1991), 42.

24   Karp and Lavine, *Exhibiting Culture: The Poetics and Politics of Museum Display*, 44.

25   Karp and Lavine, *Exhibiting Culture: The Poetics and Politics of Museum Display*, 50–51.

26   Karp and Lavine, *Exhibiting Culture: The Poetics and Politics of Museum Display*, 54.

27   Esther De Costa Meyer, *Frank Gehry on Line* (Princeton: Princeton University Press, 2008), 22.

28   See Raymond Lucas for more on this resonance between viewer and trace in Gunn, *Fieldnotes and Sketchbooks: Challenging the Boundaries Between Descriptions and Processes of Describing*.

29   In Karp and Lavine, *Exhibiting Culture: The Poetics and Politics of Museum Display,* 25.

30   Karp and Lavine, *Exhibiting Culture: The Poetics and Politics of Museum Display,* 29.

15

Notebooks and Narratives: The Secret Laboratory of The Architect's Sketchbook

Paul Clarke

RESEARCH QUESTION

By considering architects' sketchbooks as a 'device'[1] can we discover in it a set of practices and ways of working that reveal aspects of architecture and architectural culture that have been hidden or ignored amidst other more dominant forms of architectural representation and output?

We live in an age when access to the digital is instant, unquestionable and ubiquitous. Our hands reach out to highly sophisticated digital equipment that can capture, manipulate, multiply and send images globally. Our smart-phones, iPads and laptops interface for us with a world we no longer perceive or experience in the same way we once did. In our constant rush to record and manipulate our perceptions through software and digital systems – offering seeming sophistication and complexity – we might only be flattening our sense of the individually observed world.

Over the past twenty years architectural practice and education have witnessed an accelerated shift towards digital technologies, which in turn has opened up a debate on the continuing value of traditional practices, such as hand drawing and sketching. The paradigmatic shift in the nature of the architectural design process, from that of hand produced drawings to that of CAAD (Computer Aided Architectural Design), has provoked many questions as to how this has affected the way buildings are designed, and the nature of design drawing. It is not simply about the transfer of an established process, or way of working to that of a different medium or technology, but instead the dilemma rests on a more fundamental question as to the role and significance that hand drawing and sketching play in architectural design thinking. As drawing covers such a wide area in architecture, I want to specifically focus on what I would propose to be one of the most important (but undervalued and under researched) aspects of drawing in architecture: that of the architect's sketchbook.

In examining the sketchbook I want to avoid the problematic distraction of an either/or digital/analogue divide in the consideration of the design process, which is often only a generational prejudice. Digital technologies are now fully embedded in architecture. I do not wish to re-examine the enormous potential and scope for design that this technology brings, but instead to consider the role and value of the sketchbook set amidst our digitally driven culture. I want to question if the reflective process, as facilitated by the individual sketchbook, is an important 'device' hidden amidst the current emphasis on the digital design process.

A colleague of mine who teaches in the architecture school sketches away using his soft tip pointer and Sketchbook app[2] on his iPad, capturing each idea and thought on screen. He can flash the sketches up at meetings, e-mail them to students – to get that diagram or idea just right – and then save them all as digital sketchbooks without having to find shelf space to store them. So, has the traditional process of hand drawing in the sketchbook survived in this new mechanism? However, it is not just the migration of the process of hand drawing into the digital that I am wishing to address. The Sketchbook iPad app may simply be a good example of current transfer technology from that of the analogue to the digital. Instead I want to examine what in particular takes shape in the specific nature and medium of the architect's sketchbook.

In gathering and researching architects' sketchbooks I have focused on architects engaged in different aspects of practice, teaching, writing and illustrating, and who have all continued to keep sketchbooks as fundamental to the way they think and work on a daily basis. It may now be the case that 'keeping' a sketchbook is becoming increasing rare and, as one architect described himself, '… the last of a dying species.'[3] For many contemporary architectural practices, all design work now takes place using software packages. When I asked to see their sketchbooks, many have replied that they do not have time to use them anymore, as if to historically distance the process as obsolete. However, architects' sketchbooks are not simply about design as Tordy (1983) has pointed out, but they are important documents to evidence the widest understanding of an architect's perceptions, thinking, and ideas. The suggestion is that particular ways of working are shaped by using a sketchbook in a similar fashion to that of individual creative practices. As I will describe later, several of the architects I researched were working on major international projects with complex information and production systems and yet fundamentally believed that the core of their design process and personal position in architecture was best reflected in their sketchbooks. Amidst busy travel schedules, site meetings, and the pressures of timescales and budgets, the architect's pocket notebook is always at hand, ready to capture new thoughts and ideas and to provide a 'holding space' for all the things seen and collected as inspiration. Some architects use the sketchbook to such an extent that it becomes almost unconscious, much as Peter Cook describes, '…perhaps the ideal way in which an architect can approach the act of drawing is to be unaware that he is actually doing it at all.'[4]

For the 2012 Venice Architecture Biennale, O'Donnell and Tuomey presented as part of a tableau of their 'affinities' one of their sketchbooks. Set amidst computer renderings and models the sketchbook was placed powerfully to reveal its role in the incubation and expression of an idea. The sketchbook is equally valued in this case with sophisticated computer models and physical models as a key part of their working process. For O'Donnell and Tuomey, it is as much a part of the same practice of drawing and thinking as any other aspect of their work. Their sketchbooks are presented with equal emphasis as they do with any other form of representation or drawing.

Being involved with both teaching and practice, I have noticed that in one sense the traditional pedagogic structures in architecture schools and the expectations of the professional bodies (such as the RIBA) that oversee the validation of architecture degrees, remain biased towards the paper-based studio workshop model, while in reality many younger practices and students are moving further away from this and into a wholly digitized realm of more direct modeling and CAM (Computer Aided Manufacturing). In this approach the design process has been compressed. A line can be translated immediately from CAAD into laser cut material form. Software applications seem to short circuit the need for reflective design drawing and can effectively allow a jump from an idea immediately into making it. Ever fewer students are drawing by hand, no matter what measures tutors put in place, such as setting hand drawing only projects. Students have now become feverish masters of image manipulation, morphing, prototyping, and laser cutting, without a pen or pencil in sight. Inspirational images are for scanning, not drawing.

But traditionally the practice of using a sketchbook has been firmly rooted in architectural education. The sketchbook has always been the best tool to communicate the architecture student's thinking through the different stages of the design process, and in a way that no other part of the development work could do. The pile of sketchbooks traditionally displayed at the end of year show acted like visual diaries: tracking the depth of investigation and development of the studio projects. These design 'diaries' are now fast disappearing into digital space, and to the ever larger hard drives of portable devices. In the need to produce more sophisticated digital imagery and computer animations, many students abandon or undervalue the potential of the sketchbook. Recent RIBA student awards[5] have all been for projects of incredible image complexity, which has not helped with this predicament. By contrast, the sketchbook offers a counter space to this image driven bias. I would argue also that it offers up a space more deliberately open, reflective and palpable for promoting invention and creativity, and offers a different sense of time (slower). Being less image dependant, it necessitates more focussed and personal interpretations, abstractions and readings of the things seen and imagined.

In considering the notion of what a sketchbook is: a portable blank book that absorbs all aspects of notes, sketches, lists, collages, and paste-ins, its real potential lies in its initial emptiness and scope for sequences to emerge. A void waiting to be filled, it takes shape as it evolves, and allows continual reflection over time. The architects I interviewed and who have continued the practice of keeping a sketchbook, all started the process when training as an architect, a point at which sketchbooks constitute an important thought trail of process, legitimising your ideas as a trainee designer. Laying out and demonstrating your design searches will often be the key indicator of ability. As such, sketchbooks have, with good reason, historically been a central part of any qualifying architect's portfolio.

Freed from this obligation to publicly expose your design thinking in a sketchbook, on leaving architecture school, the sketchbook becomes internalized, as it is no longer needed as evidence. It is now hidden away in the coat pocket or drawer of the qualified architect, as a private dialogue. In so doing, it takes on a very different and personal role.

The American architect Steven Holl has described his ritual of starting the day with music, coffee and his sketchbook, letting his mind wander and inducing a Zen-like meditation to start the day in preparation for the 'business' of architecture.[6] It is a very private dialogue with his sketchbook as he sits alone and independent from his large office of architects. He has published several books of these sketchbooks and highlights this as the major source of his creativity. However, architects rarely show their sketchbooks to anyone. The studio collaborators of Le Corbusier seldom caught a glimpse of his notebooks, yet they were all well aware of the importance Le Corbusier placed on them as a repository of his ideas, journeys and observations. Stored in a suitcase in his apartment (not his office), very few people had seen them until their publication in four remarkable volumes that were completed after his death.[7] Most photographs of Le Corbusier show him with the small A6 sketchbook he continually carried in his hand. These would be opened to capture an idea, note the colour of the sky, list what had to be done, whom to call, or to affirm a proposition of something he may have seen many years earlier. Only he could decipher what was a highly condensed form of encrypted notes and sketches, but we know that he continually referred to them throughout his lifetime.

This important 'secret' dimension of the content in an architect's sketchbook is central to the practice of how it works as a device. Viewable only to the architect concerned it nurtures more radical and abstract ideas than that publicly declared in the open studio. As such it holds a world of thoughts and observations that are often neglected in architectural culture and discourse as they will often remain secret. The sketchbooks can and do hold the sources of all the inspiration that drives the ideas and design of the projects and work of an architect. Used to collect all kinds of diverse observations and thoughts this 'storehouse' can trigger unexpected juxtapositions and ideas that lead to totally new insights. The publication of the 73 sketchbooks of le Corbusier testifies to this, allowing his work to be reconsidered. They reveal a lifetime of reflections and observations that are not expressed in any other medium than that of the sketchbook. Before his death, Le Corbusier arranged that his sketchbooks would be published. He carefully ordered and numbered them, essentially turning a private world of thoughts and reflections into a public one. He is one of the first architects to realize the full significance and potential of the sketchbook as an important set of documents to be published.

In researching and curating 'The Secret Laboratory' exhibition on contemporary architects' sketchbooks, I too had to find a way to make public a hidden world. Many of the architects were initially concerned that their sketchbooks were too private to be viewed. What personal information, musings and ideas would now be seen in what were previously completely private sketchbooks? Personal and private moments continually find shape in the foreground of sketchbooks. Amidst the daily life in a busy architectural practice, the notations in a sketchbook become layered in private and professional thoughts and details. Sketchbooks can, in that sense, be a highly personal space, a diary, a travel book, a confessional, a contact list, notes of books to read, food eaten, and so on. They can embody the fullness and dilemmas of our creative and private life. They reveal what we are thinking, where we have been, the shape of our imagination, and map out the priorities of our experience. As such they are highly autobiographical documents.

But are architects' sketchbooks fundamentally any different from that of artists? In a sense the sketchbook was always more fundamental to the training of the artist due to the nature of drawing and painting. For example Joseph Mallord William Turner produced over three hundred sketchbooks in his lifetime. If we were to consider the sketchbooks of the Scottish architect Charles Rennie Mackintosh,[8] it would be easy to consider him as both an artist and an architect. As Mackintosh began his architectural studies he diligently visited and drew the key buildings he was directed to study, he carefully measured details and materials, he studied construction, and all in exactly the same way as his contemporaries. His sketchbooks initially would have been no different than any other student at the time, however, it is in his continual use and development of his sketchbooks that the transformation in his work takes place. The reflective shift in the observations and abstractions of nature and the particular style and approach of his drawing dramatically evolves, as he moves to more keenly observed flowers and landscape. In essence I believe there is no difference between the architect and the artist in this regard, in that the architect's sketchbook does not implicitly carry (as many people have presumed) the obligation to direct everything towards the design of a specific building (as the direct materialization of an idea) in as much as the artist does not direct all observations onto the single work of art. But that the drawings, thoughts, and observations in a sketchbook should be considered as work in their own right. Mackintosh is a good example of this, as his sketchbooks illustrate, and I would argue also create the transformative dimension in his approach and later work.

Sketchbooks have the ability to open up a very wide field of interest. For example, Le Corbusier said several times that he was much more interested in people than he was in architecture and, in truth, a careful reading of his sketchbooks reveal this.[9] Architects have traditionally deployed the spontaneity of the sketch as a direct form of communication. One only has to consider the (often cited) lunchtime paper napkin, or the back of an envelope drawing that solves a problem in a Eureka moment. The personal sketchbook is where this is cultivated and nurtured. It is a way of 'speaking', firstly to you and then in a continual 'drawing conversation'. It collects these 'conversations' to give shape to new ideas and perceptions. Once independent of a particular project/client/site relationship, the gaze and imagination of the architect, as framed in the sketchbook, roams wide.

Historically the training of the architect has always been rooted and formed in drawing. Knowledge and skill were implicit in the architects' drawing as a direct correlation to traditional craft and knowledge. The skill of draughtsmanship, as

Edward Robbins[10] has noted, was directly related to craftsmanship. The physical skills associated with the knowledge of the master builder became translated into the physicality of large architectural renderings and drawings. Complex geometric layouts and coloured washes demanded long and physically intensive hours at drawing boards. The skilled labour associated with these large drawings came to symbolize the professional signature of the architect. When the architect moved from the role of master mason and site-based constructor, his/her knowledge base was displaced wholesale into the drawing process, thereby defining the independent professional role of architect. This transformation, from making to drawing, is key to understanding the historical emergence of the architect. Forgotten amidst this historical focus on large-scale drawings is the importance and role of the sketchbook that has inevitably led to these becoming the focus of any architecture collections and archives, and not that of sketchbooks. In the evolution of architectural training the sketchbook became embedded by much the same process as that of the artist with the emergence of the 18th century schools and academies, which opened up education beyond the individual atelier apprenticeship with that of the master. Soon the 'profession' and the newly formed architecture schools would be offering sketchbook prizes, travelling scholarships and study tours from which work was presented in definitive sketchbooks.

Often when tracing the biography of a particular architect, historians will turn to the early years and travel sketchbooks to relate the formation of the architect's imagination and influences. Most architects, as part of their education, have been on study trips and used the sketchbook as a witness to all they have seen and experienced. In this respect, if we consider Le Corbusier's famous Voyage d'Orient of 1911,[11] it typically reflects this use of a sketchbook as a travelogue. Travel shaped what he called his 'true education' and this can witnessed in his sketchbooks. For Le Corbusier the sketchbook was an important discipline that was initiated by the formative years of his Art School education at La Chaux-de-Fonds. At the height of his fame and with his emergence as an internationally known architect, Le Corbusier published the *Oeuvres Complétes,*[12] an eight-volume set of books showing all his work and ideas over almost sixty years of practice. It is no accident that the first images to appear in volume one are pages of from his travel sketchbooks. This is an important point in relation to his working method, and is often overlooked. It is a declaration as to the vital importance sketchbooks would play in his work. The final symbol of his philosophical 'Poem of the Right Angle'[13] shows a hand (his hand) drawing lines enclosed in a womb like shaped head. The head and hand combine to make a philosophers stone of transformation. The message is clear and it is the basis of his personal philosophy, for the eye that sees and the hand that draws are inseparable and together make possible the transformative nature of architecture. Drawing is the key that enables you to '…first look, and then to observe and finally perhaps to discover …'[14]

But Le Corbusier could also use his sketchbooks as a weapon. To prove his authorship of the UN building in New York[15] what more evidence was needed than to photograph his open sketchbook showing his design next to an image of the completed building, to show whom really designed it? Or to reveal the gestation and evolution of the design of his world famous chapel at Ronchamp, an outflowing of drawings in his sketchbook, miraculously conceived. Le Corbusier was careful to note that he did not run to the sketchbook to resolve something before he had thought it through, and allowed it to mull over in his mind. Instead he allowed ideas and thoughts to turn over in his mind with the sketchbook there, at hand, ready to catch his ideas as they flowed. This was not about improvization, but a careful thinking and observing process. He declared the camera was for idlers, though an architect more skilful in the use of the photograph in his work is hard to imagine. His private reflections, from the eroticism of his figure drawings, to things seen on his travels, quotes from Don Quixote and Rabelais (read while on aeroplanes), to the pain of sitting beside his dying wife, are all captured movingly in his sketchbooks. It could be argued from all this, that the best way to understand Le Corbusier the architect, is not to look at his buildings, paintings or books, but to look instead inside the world of his sketchbooks.

THE SECRET LABORATORY

Having set out something of the wider context of drawing in architecture, and the role of the architect's sketchbook, I would now like to turn to 'The Secret Laboratory' exhibition. The project started out as an idea to exhibit this hidden world of the architect's sketchbook. PLACE, an architecture centre for Northern Ireland based in Belfast, commissioned it as its first travelling exhibition. It posed the question that by looking into the sketchbooks of architects, would we gain a different understanding of how our built environment is shaped and imagined?

In all, over 250 individual sketchbooks were collated and curated from a range of many different architects and practices. They were selected on the basis of their

15.1   The secret laboratory exhibition. Source: Image: Paul Clarke

use of sketchbooks and for their differing approaches to design. Those included were also in several cases studio teachers, illustrators, and writers. Several had major international profiles, such as Grafton Architects and O'Donnell and Tuomey, and all of them were using personal sketchbooks in their daily practice and work. The sketchbooks were displayed in a long illuminated table that folded around the observer to make an enclosing space, in which the collection of sketchbooks was laid out.

Through this exhibition I wanted to explore and investigate both the content and use of contemporary sketchbooks. I wanted to ask what was really going on in these notebooks? To question their structure and their testimony as to what had been observed, collected and thought about. How were they created and used? I initially tried to form a classification system, to identify trends or themes to form a taxonomy. But as I tried to chart any particular patterns, approaches, or systems that would then allow recurrent aspects to be framed and studied, it became clear that there was a very wide variation in approaches and uses that were impossible to classify. Some of the main categorizations I developed were: the sequential field, life lessons, cross-drawing, abstraction as decoy, musings and memory, and so on. New clusters of categories continued to emerge and often multiple systems were at play in each sketchbook. Architects' sketchbooks are not usually produced to be 'read' and as such can contain almost cryptic notations as a visual shorthand. They have evolved over time and often in disparate and contrasting sections, more akin to montage techniques or a Godard film with 'jump cuts'.[16] Page after page can be worked on in one day, while months or a year may then pass without a single entry. This dimension of time is important in the way that experience and observations are sequenced and embedded in the structure of the working sketchbook. Often this can be the major dilemma when publishing a facsimile of a sketchbook, which reveals either that the sketchbook is self-consciously constructed for publication, or that it is naturally the opposite, being full of gaps, blanks and voids. Sketchbooks, I would suggest, are in a sense filmic, in that they are experienced in time. Like a flick book, once movement transforms the pages it is possible to consider them akin to walking through a building or viewing a film as a narrative with episodes and multiple paths. This was particularly the case with the sketchbooks of Tom de Paor in the aforementioned exhibition. The sequence of sketchbooks exhibited covered the period of the design of a cinema in Galway. In that sense, film as a medium was both explicit and implicit in his sketchbooks and ideas for the design of the cinema mingled with multiple interests and observations, which sometimes led back to the design, but at other times were wholly independent studies. This collection of seven sketchbooks was in turn displayed like a roll of film; running chronologically, to reinforce this analogy.

In de Paor's and many of the other architect's sketchbooks, the surprise is in how ideas can arrive at anytime and from anywhere. A cut out image may be drawn over and set next to intense notes on a poem, which in turn is placed beside a wash of thick colour, or a note concerning important personal events. The mind at work reveals itself through the pages of the sketchbook and provides intimate glimpses of private creativity. Random and simple experiences such as things cut out from newspapers can trigger drawings and multiple associations that provoke questions of research and curiosity. In this way the sketchbook is a unique creative device that 'collects' information, which can then be usefully absorbed, and transformed into new potentials.

The sketchbooks by Grafton Architects are more typical of the studio journal approach, which focuses on the development process and making of individual buildings. Moving across different scales, resolving details and plans, the drawings in them are essentially clarifications for the development of ideas and diagrams specifically related to projects. Pencil and pen studies lay out the geometric clarity of their buildings and approach. Large-scale projects that they are working on, such as Boccioni University in Milan, are condensed into definitive analytical diagrams, as visual thoughts that are all about problem solving and architectural concepts.

Seamus Lennon's biro pen sketchbooks showing his work with Sergison Bates architects, reveal a Giacometti like drawn walk through of space and detail. Though only line drawings, the sketchbooks reveal a fascination with the minimal detail of doors, windows, steps and walls. The emphasis here is on shape and contour. Abstracted and elegant human figures appear constantly across the pages to give a sense of scale and proportion to everything and serve to populate the architecture with their strange presence. While these sketchbooks, like those of Grafton Architects, demonstrate an intense focus on project work, they also provide an extraordinary glimpse of a unique and individual drawing style.

Jane Larmour and Patrick Wheeler's sketchbooks fold out like Japanese scrolls and enjoy a rich layering of images, drawings and paste-ups in different formatted notebooks. Their sketchbooks are constantly exchanged between themselves and as such individual authorship is deliberately blurred in their need to explore shared experiences and thoughts. Notes concerning places visited, food eaten, and

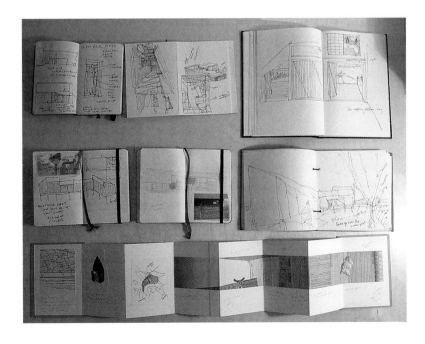

15.2   The interchanging sketchbooks of Jane Larmour and Patrick Wheeler. Source: Image: Paul Clarke

landscape studies, all combine with drawings about travel, maps and textures that provide a rich panorama of the lives and interests of these architects.

Nigel Peake's sketchbooks are in many ways the most extraordinary of those considered in the exhibition and may in part be explained by his shift from training as an architect to becoming a full time illustrator and artist. With his evident joy in drawing his sketchbooks collect a wide array of things that are carefully observed. The sketchbooks become books in themselves and he has published a number of these as such. Composed of delicate hand drawings that are more akin to fine architectural etchings of incredible intricacy, the spatial experience and composition of these notebooks is architectural in their own right. Invention and narrative merge with the meticulous observation of objects, buildings and cities. The architect's eye is at play as it zooms across many different scales. The sketchbook as an encyclopedia, a project to capture and collate drawing the whole world is manifest in Nigel's extraordinary draughtsmanship and observational eye.

Sketchbooks are almost impossible to exhibit and communicate in their entirety in any exhibition and so most visitors will only manage to see that part of the sketchbook that is open for display. However, as curator, you know the hidden life of a sketchbook is only fully revealed in the experience of holding it and looking through it. Like only viewing the stills of a film, a truer experience of the medium lies in the motion and movement of it over time. A sketchbook is by its nature inherently sequential and episodic. In order to provide this fuller experience, a series of sketchbooks from the exhibition were recorded using digital film for the web site www.secretlaboratory.co.uk. This use of digital technologies to document and investigate the analogue device has proved incredibly useful in opening up the experience of how a sketchbook can be viewed and perceived. Marshall McLuchan's notion of the 'useless'[17] is helpful in considering the current plight of the sketchbook. He suggested a thing only takes on its true value when its original purpose has been abandoned. Therefore, in this sense, the sketchbook may turn out to be even more valuable in that the new multiple forms of digital technology suggest we no longer actually need it, as there are clearly other ways to work. However, what may have radically shifted our perceptions of it, as a valued fundamental tool in design and creativity, is the very use of this digital technology to research and document it. This paradox is only just beginning to be recognized.

THE REFLECTIVE GAZE

When teaching architecture I have become increasingly more aware that students demonstrate a tendency to automatically rely on Google to validate a thought or action. Pointing to an image or film clip on screen (rather than a drawing) means that their thoughts turn to a dependency on the readymade image, rather than a drawn or abstracted interpretation of it. This seems to me to switch off the complex 'thought circuitry of creativity' and collapse the important space of reflective distance from that of the image. This 'distance' is provided by the 'filtering' process of the sketchbook, as a way of looking (I call this the 'Google Condition'), can be felt in the struggles and dilemmas of contemporary architectural design, which is over saturated in imagery. In part, it is this automatic turning to the digital onscreen image that is leading to the wholesale abandonment of the sketchbook.

By setting the sketchbook as a project brief and by awarding a yearly prize for the best sketchbook in the architecture school, I am trying to restore its position in the studio. One recipient of this prize, who used their sketchbook in an innovative way, started using it by recording their daily journey to the university. They then became interested in constructing it as a 'looking machine', before transforming it again into a digital film. Through this process their design for an Urban Film Institute evolved. Here, the sketchbook, as pedagogic device, is not only a conceptual medium through which to consider and imagine architectural ideas, but it has in a sense become architectural.

If a building implicitly contains time as memory, which is fundamental to understanding architecture, then would a similar reading of the architect's sketchbooks (as a chain of interior time processes of conceptual thinking) be possible? Between the observed and the imagined, there is a world of enormous creative potential. It seems to me that the sketchbook is best equipped to both hold and document this sense of time, to enrich our own sense of creative reflections. In the exhibition, I attempted to reveal something of this. The sketchbook cannot continue to be thought of as simply an extension of the studio into different locations and places (cafes, trains, etc.) but that it is a fundamentally different device for creativity by framing, shaping and nurturing a mechanism for our ideas and perceptions. It palpably offers a rich, time based space for ideas by 'holding' thoughts, encounters and imaginings, page after page. It is a parallel private reflective realm to that of the collective studio, and it is, I would suggest, one of the most important documents in understanding individual creativity in architecture. While in the studio, an architect's

15.3   The sketchbook as device. Source: Image: Paul Clarke

work is necessarily collaborative and participatory, whilst in the sketchbook it is the opposite, being private, reflective, abstract, personal and transitory by nature. Ideas do not assemble and evolve in a linear sequence, in contrast to how the production and design of buildings is perceived. The space afforded by the sketchbook to play out ideas and perceptions and to operate within different time frames, is much broader and richer in potential than assumed. The sketchbooks reveal who we are as architects, what we know, observe, treasure, and imagine, whether we choose to apply this to the way we build or not.

CONCLUSION

I have attempted in this text (and the exhibition) to probe and explore the creative practices and potential held within the world of the architect's sketchbook and, from this evidence, to suggest that the sketchbook lies fundamentally at the very centre of creativity in architecture. It is not in terms of digital or non digital that is important in any consideration and, as I have suggested above, this paradoxical reciprocity may be the critical factor in it being reconsidered, but instead to focus on the potential of it as a unique mechanism to collate, store, and reflect on how we see and imagine of the world in what Kirwin has called '…a history of knowing.'[18] Sketchbooks must be at the centre of both our architectural creativity and our wider culture. The Secret Laboratory exhibition aimed to change perceptions, and to open up a debate on the value of sketchbooks in architecture. For this the sketchbook as device was laid bare for all to see. Visitors to the exhibition looking down at the sketchbooks, caught their own reflected gaze on the glass, and as Edward Robbins has observed in his book *why architects draw* '…looking at drawing allows us to see, as all good drawing should, the image of itself and of its maker in all their complexity and nakedness.'[19]

BIBLIOGRAPHY

Allen, Felicity. *Your Sketchbook Yourself*. London: Tate Publishing, 2011.

Benedetti, Paul. *Forward Through the Rearview Mirror: Reflections on and by Marshall McLuhan*. Cambridge Massachusetts: MIT Press, 1997.

Bergeijk, Herman Van, and Deborah Hauptmann. *Notations of Herman Hertzberger*. Rotterdam: NAi Publishers, 1998.

Blau, Eve, and Edward Kaufman. *Architecture and its Images*. Canadian Centre for Architecture: Montreal: MIT Press, 1989.

Brawne, Michael. *Architectural Thought: The Design Process and the Expectant Eye*. London: Architectural Press, 2003.

Brereton, Richard. *Sketchbooks: The Hidden Art of Designers, Illustrators & Creatives*. London: Laurence King Publishing, 2009.

Building Material. *Paperwork. The Journal of the Architectural Association of Ireland*. Issue 15, Autumn. Dublin: AAI, 2006.

Cook, Peter. *Drawing: The Motive Force of Architecture.* Architectural Design Primer 2. London: Wiley, 2008.

Curtis, William JR. *Fragments of Invention: The Sketchbooks of Le Corbusier.* Cambridge Massachusetts: Harvard University, 1981.

Evans, Robin. *Translations from Drawing to Building and Other Essays.* AA Documents 2. London: AA Publications, 1997.

Farthing, Stephen (ed.). *The Sketchbooks of Nicholas Grimshaw.* The Royal Academy of Arts in Association with the Centre for Drawing at The University of the Arts London and Edinburgh College of Art. London: Royal Academy, 2009.

Fraser, Ian, and Rod Henmi. *Envisioning Architecture: An Analysis of Drawing.* London: Wiley, 1994.

Gresleri, Giuliano (ed). *Voyage d'Orient sketchbooks- facsimile edition.* 6 vols. New York: Rizzoli, and Milan: Electa with Foundation Le Corbusier, 2002.

Kirwin, Liza. Visual Thinking: Sketchbooks from the Archives of American Art. *Archives of American Art Journal*, Vol 27, No 1. Smithsonian Institute 1987: 21–29.

Koolhaas, Rem. *Delirious New York: A Retrospective Manifesto.* New York: Monacelli Press, 1994.

Kovats, Tania (ed.). *The Drawing Book. A Survey of Drawing the Primary Means of Expression.* London: Black Dog Publishing, 2007.

Lacy, Bill. *100 Contemporary Architects Sketches and Drawings.* London: Thames and Hudson, 1991.

Lambert, Susan. *Reading Drawings: An Introduction to Looking at Drawings.* New York: Pantheon Books, 1984.

Leach, Neil. *The Anaesthetics of Architecture.* Cambridge, Massachusetts: MIT Press, 1999.

Le Corbusier. *Creation is a Patient Search.* Praeger: New York, 1960.

_____. *Oeuvre Complète.* Originally published between 1929–70 with editor Willy Boesiger. Republished- Basel: Birkhäuser, 2006.

The Le Corbusier Sketchbooks. Vols 1–4 (1914–64) Cambridge Massachusetts and London: MIT Press, Thames and Hudson with The Architectural History Foundation. (Preface by André Wogensky and Introduction by Maurice Besset), 1981.

Maslen, Mick and Jack Southern. *Drawing Projects- An exploration of the Language of Drawing.* London: Black Dog Publishing, 2011.

O'Toole, Shane (ed.). *The Architect and the Drawing.* Dublin: Gandon with the RIAI, 1989. Pallasmaa, Juhani. *The Thinking Hand: Existential and Embodied Wisdom in Architecture.* London: Wiley, 2009.

Rappolt, Mark, and Robert Violette. *Gehry Draws.* Cambridge, Massachusetts. MIT Press with Violette Editions, 2002.

Robbins, Edward. *An Anthropology of Architecture: Some Preliminary suggestions.* In J.P. Protzen (ed.) Proceedings of the 1987 conference on Planning and Design in Architecture, American Society of Engineers. New York, 1987: 35–14.

_____. *Why Architects Draw.* Cambridge Massachusetts: MIT Press, 1994.

Robertson, Pamela (ed.). *Charles Rennie Mackintosh, Architectural Sketches.* Glasgow: University of Glasgow, 1999.

Saint, Andrew. *The Image of the Architect*. New Haven: Yale University Press, 1983.

Schank Smith, Kendra. *Architects' Sketches: Dialogue and Design*. London: Architectural Press, 2008.

Serrazanetti, Francesca and Matteo Schubert. *The Hand of the Architect*. Milan: Fondo Ambiente Italiano and Moelskine, 2009.

Tordy, William H. "Review of Le Corbusier Sketchbooks," in *Journal of the Society of Architectural Historians*, Vol. 42, No 1 (1983): 83–86.

Treib, Marc. *Thinking Through Drawing in an Electronic Age*. London: Routledge, 2008

NOTES

1   The term device takes as the starting point the idea that the sketchbook was a specific thing that was adapted for use over time. The development of available paper and binding transformed drawings on individual sheets into collections of paper, a constructed tool.

2   With the continuing development of the iPad, a series of cheaply available applications (apps) are available which transform the device into a digital sketchbook – such as Sketchbook Pro by Autodesk and Sketchbook Mobile. This software has become very popular and allows collections of drawings to be collated as sketchbooks in different formats.

3   John Tuomey and Sheila O'Donnell, interview by author, Dublin office, 2012. This interview was conducted as research for the film '*Drawing on Life*', produced and directed by the author, 2013.

4   Peter Cook, *Drawing: The Motive Force of Architecture*. (Architectural Design Primer 2. London: Wiley, 2008). The book explores the automatic nature of the unconscious act of drawing as essential to architectural thought and culture. The notion that sketches flow in a seemingly non-intellectual action is contrasted with that of complex construction drawings.

5   Every year the Royal Institute of British Architects provide awards for students of architecture for the best part I and part II students. These historically were based on the ability to draw and were started in the mid 1980s when there was a very strong interest in the value and nature of drawing. Recent winners have almost overwhelmingly been about sophisticated computer renderings and animation. One recent example was the 'Robots of Brixton', which was the 2012 part II winner. These can be viewed on www.presidentsmedals.com.

6   Steven Holl described his daily ritual of drawing and 'composing his mind' at the start of each day in his office in New York. 'For over 20 years, I have been making a morning watercolor on 5" × 7" spiral bound watercolor books. These paintings often mark the beginning concepts for a building. They can be formal studies, light studies, or anything that comes to mind at dawn with a cup of green tea. I start every day in the morning and paint for one hour. I have every drawing that I have done for the last 25 years in boxes on a shelf over my drawing board. It has become a kind of second memory bank for me. Separately I have kept journals (9.5" × 6" or 6" × 8") since my studies in Rome in 1970. I write my impressions of spaces and places, ideas, concepts, criticisms, reflections etc. The journals have allowed a continuous process, a dialogue with ideas, quotes and spontaneous captured intuitive thoughts.' From *Building Design*, 4 October, 2011.

7 Le Corbusier stored his sketchbooks in a suitcase in his apartment on the Rue Nungesser et Coli in Paris where he had his painting studio. These sketchbooks (numbering seventy three) were published in four large volumes by the Architectural History Foundation and MIT Press with the Fondation Le Corbusier in 1981–82 by Andre Wogenscky and Maurice Besset. Showing over four thousand illustrated pages from the original sketchbooks, this provided an enormous range of material for scholars for the first time. For an overview of these see William H Jordy, *Journal of the Society of Architectural Historians*, Vol 42, No 1 Mar 1983, 83–86. The introductions to each volume by Wogensky (who worked with Le Corbusier) are invaluable for his insights into how the sketchbooks were used and valued.

8 The Mackintosh sketchbooks are held in various collections. Recently a number of these have been made available online at http://www.mackintoshsketchbook.net/ and http://www.huntsearch.gla.ac.uk/Mac. Both the Glasgow School of Art and the Hunterian Gallery have extensive collections of these and have published them in a number of different formats.

9 For a useful insight into this refer to William J R Curtis, *Fragments of Invention: The Sketchbooks of le Corbusier*, (Harvard: Harvard University, 1981). This publication is a catalogue of the first exhibition of Le Corbusier's sketchbooks that was held at The Carpenter Centre For the Visual Arts, Harvard, November1981.

10 As discussed in Edward Robbins, *Why Architects Draw*, (Mass: The MIT Press, 1994). This book is critical in providing an in-depth study, through interviews, of how architects approach architectural drawing and representation. The survey of different architect's work discusses both the qualities and dilemmas of a profession so dependent on drawing.

11 Refer to Le Corbusier, *Voyage d'Orient Sketchbooks*, facsimile edition, ed. Giuliano Gresleri (New York: Rizzoli and Milan: Electa, 1988). This remarkable publication combines six whole individual sketchbooks of this period that are direct facsimiles of the original. It gives a clear indication of the way Le Corbusier used them as a form of visual note taking.

12 As discussed in *Le Corbusier's Oeuvres complètes* compiled with Will Boesigner, is one of the most comprehensive publications of an architects work ever produced. Le Corbusier exercised particular attention in all aspects of the production of these eight volumes and as such they reveal an enormous amount his ideas and working practices. Several of the sketchbooks are published in these and are strategically placed to communicate key relationships to buildings and his ideas.

13 'The Poem of the Right Angle' was composed over a period of seven years 1947–53. It encapsulates Le Corbusier's personal symbolism and philosophy as a set of cryptic drawings and paintings ordered in an iconostase. The very last section depicts a hand drawing the right angle set into a head like shape. This testifies to the power assigned to drawing by Le Corbusier.

14 This quote appears in many of le Corbusier's writings on the value of drawing. An example of this is in the 'My Work', The Architectural Press (1960), where the words are set amidst pages of pencil drawings of stones and natural forms.

15 Le Corbusier was part of a multinational team of architects from across the world that was invited to design the new United Nations building in New York in 1947. The team produced many designs but project number 23 by Le Corbusier is the one that looks like the completed building. Furious that the contract was awarded to the American architect Wallace Harrison, Le Corbusier published his sketchbook showing his designs next to an image of the completed building in the *Oeuvres complètes*. For an amusing

account of this read *Delirious New York: A Retrospective Manifesto*, Monacelli Press,1994, by Rem Koolhaas. originally published in 1978.

16   The 'jump cut' existed before Jean-Luc Godard, but he made it famous with the ability to provoke the viewer out of their aspiration for continuity by the continual disruption of action and filmic sequence. In this sense the rhythms of work in the sketchbook are continually broken and restarted each time as distinct sections and sequences.

17   McLuhan's term referred to commodities as products in the business sense but the notion can be usefully extended to the sketchbook in the context of new technologies, which could in a sense invalidate the use of this analogue device. Refer to Paul Benedetti, *Forward through the Rearview Mirror: Reflections on and by Marshall McLuchan*.

18   Liza Kirwin, *Visual Thinking: Sketchbooks from the Archives of American Art*. Archives of American Art Journal. Vol 27, No 1, (pp. 21–29) 1987, 21. This quote is in reference to the sketchbooks of David Smith.

19   Edward Robbins, *Why Architects Draw*. (Cambridge Mass: MIT Press, 1994), 49.

16

Sketchbook or Reflective Journal? Documenting the Practical PhD

Christine Turner

SKETCHBOOK OR REFLECTIVE JOURNAL?

This chapter will demonstrate the interaction between theory and practice during the process of producing a practice-based PhD. It describes the encounters between academic and creative enquiry as witnessed through the development of the sketchbook and reflective journal, and the dialogue between the respective ways of working in these documents. I will argue that, in my practice, the sketchbook is a valuable working method, generating a space for exploring ideas through drawing, rather than a means of producing artifacts. The chapter shows how the divide between theory and practice, acutely manifest in contemporary art and design higher education and contemporary debate that surrounds the practice-based PhD, is evidenced in my research. However, I also argue that this collusion is necessary to the practice.

My PhD research questions the significance of drawing and painting the human figure, both in my own artworks and within art education. The research advocates the depth of understanding that the practice of drawing produces through the intimacy of thinking and doing. Deanna Petherbridge describes this depth in that '… if drawing teaches artists how to look, then its everyday practice is an affirmation of the importance of outer as well as inner vision: the perceptual and the conceptual.'[1] The immediacy of this encounter affords drawing an unequivocal facility for astute critical practice that encompasses both practical skill and intelligent reflective understanding, a reflexive practice of the highest order. This seems logical, yet there has been a sustained division in drawing practice between practical skills and conceptual directives for centuries, arguably since the Renaissance inception of *designo*,[2] and it is acutely manifest within current debate. Six centuries have passed since Cennini's statement '…do not fail as you go on to draw something every day for no matter how little it is, it will be well worth-while, and it will do you the world of good'[3] yet drawing in contemporary art education has diminished. Simon Betts has noted '…all the foundation course teams from the University of the Arts London were increasingly seeing application portfolios that lacked confidence and competence in drawing; lacked an understanding of the wider uses and purpose of drawing, the rigor of sustained objective drawing.'[4] A general decline in drawing ability reflects a more generic trend, noted by Tom McGuirk whereby practical, situated and embodied knowledge, once so central to the study of art and design in Higher Education, has since the late 1960's become more peripheral.[5] Indeed, critic Jed Perl asks the question if artists should be drawing at all, '...whether drawing, the cultivation of the imagination through the hands manipulation of the pencil or pen or some other graphic instrument, is really an essential part of an artist's vocation any longer.'[6]

Contemporary divisions between theory and practice in art education exacerbate the existing tensions between intellectual and pragmatic learning and have affected the perception and use of the sketchbook. The impulse of fine art toward conceptualization and postmodern pluralism gains value and privilege via the increasingly academically centred ambitions of art education. The territory of art education has changed considerably during the 1990s and 2000s, as it is now developed and delivered within the relatively new sphere of university research education, requiring artists to present academic outputs. As Stephen Scrivener states '...in 1992, the binary divide was removed, polytechnics became universities and the art world found itself firmly embedded as an equal player in the academic world of the university.'[7] Furthermore, contemporary art is not necessarily produced through engagement with materials and techniques, as Rosalind Krauss suggests '...medium is not just physical object.'[8] The inception of conceptual art and the advent of experimental process as a manner of working, have led to contemporary freedom from pragmatic learning and the notion of practice in art has shifted. The 2009 revision of John Willets 1967 book *Art in the City* by Bryan Briggs and Julie Sheldon shows changes in the Liverpool Art School that point to the contemporary academic emphasis which is now evident and '...consequently education for artists who practice has demanded theoretical rather than practical and medium specific or skills training.'[9]

In recognition of the need for scholarly credibility in art school education, there are calls for more extensive use of the reflective journal, especially to record the thinking and development of a thesis in a practice-based PhD. This may not necessarily be detrimental to the process of practice-based research in the arts if the potential of the reflective journal is to clarify how practice is recognized in this capacity. As Michelle Ortlipp suggests, '...keeping and using reflective journals can make the messiness of the research process visible to the researcher who can then make it visible to those who read the research and thus avoid producing, reproducing the discourse of research as a neat and linear process.'[10] That a reflective journal may support, or even substitute for a written thesis, may be a concession toward the need for intellectual rigour and academic validation in doctoral studies that will prevent compromize in the methods of art practice. This may be a way to maintain the autonomy of art and design as it confronts the wider academic community and the perceived superiority given to a text-based thesis.

Insidious tensions between theory and practice in art higher education echo throughout contemporary debates surrounding the best method as to how to demonstrate new knowledge in practice based art and design PhD study. This portends difficulties for my project, as it is reliant upon drawing and the tradition of visual creative development that has evolved since Cennini, confronting a pragmatic process within the domain of PhD study, the apogee of art education's academic ambition. The methods I have employed typically encourage visual ideas to develop through practical experimental stages in the manner historically associated with sketchbook working. Alongside sketchbooks, a reflective journal is employed within the project and, I now shall describe how crossovers occur between the distinct documents, as drawings infuses the text of the journal and writing creeps into the drawings of the sketchbook and how the 'messiness' of this process becomes more intellectually explicit.

Whilst the reflective journal is an important tool and component of my practice-based research project, it cannot reflect the whole of the process for examination. Despite the sketchbook being the artefact that ensures the integrity of this PhD project, I demonstrate that theoretical and practical crossovers are necessary, furthermore that this relationship requires further interpretation in the form of a written thesis. The text argues that the written aspect to the project, rather than detracting from the integrity of the artwork, in fact enhances the authority of the practice to the project as a whole. Figure 16.1 shows works made at the early stage of the research, it exhibits the visual development of ideas in the traditionally understood manner of sketchbook working. The linear life drawing, made from direct observation, developed into a painting through the intuitive progression of formal ideas ('formal' here refers to pictorial construction, types of mark or medium used). Formal qualities such as fluid mark making and succinct description of the human figure identify and operate as significant progenitors to the visual process. The intention is to replicate and develop these qualities in subsequent works, in an attempt to further enhance the vitality of a life drawing. The developed oil sketch is made on a loose canvas measuring 3ft x 5ft, so that the surface could be lifted like a sheet of fabric and the liquid pooled into areas, depicting the figure within viscous swathes of colour glaze that dry in lustrous pools and signify the form. This technique produces a luminous aspect akin to stained glass, emphasizing a formal, iconic, and even theatrical quality in the painting. The confines of the physical sketchbook are breeched revealing it as primarily an exploratory and visual workspace. Likewise, my definition of drawing extends to include large works made with paint, facilitating exploration of this term and process through different formats.

At this stage, there is no apparent conceptual impulse underlying the practical enquiry, and theoretical considerations are set in a separate journal containing reading notes on artists and methodological enquiry. Complimentary to practical exploration, journal notes made from reading Juliet MacDonald's PhD thesis *Drawing Around the Body: the Manual and Visual Practice of Drawing and the Embodiment of Knowledge*[11] illustrate comments made by Deanna Petherbridge at the National Gallery which suggest the '…fluid and uncontained in drawing as a way of figuring the body.'[12] Petherbridge's notion reflects the liquid properties within my artwork and this is further explored by considering August Rodin's powerful watercolour drawings. Rodin's fluid, confident marks encouraged the evolution of a series of sketchbook watercolour drawings inspired by photographic reproductions of his work. Eventually small sketches evolved into a statuesque, life sized acrylic painting, a dramatic image that retained a state of flux by utilising the paint pooling technique described earlier. Despite the shift in format and scale, sketchbook working provides integrity to the whole process. As visual ideas evolve, a flow of sketchbook based work charts the incremental stages leading to the larger work, supporting, and revealing a developmental visual record.

A photograph taken in order to record progress shows an image of oblique divisions between the painting and the surrounding space, due to my attempt to capture all of the 'Rodin' painting in the frame. Reflection upon these distinct visual planes and gaps highlighted further properties to my way of working. The abstruseness of the photo, an intriguing pictorial quality, compliments my

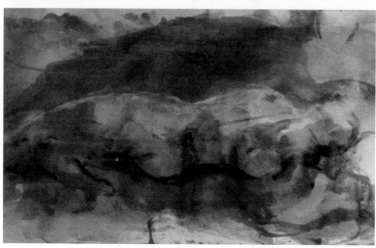

16.1   Venus Drawings. Source: Image: Christine Turner 2009

tendency toward unfinished elements and spatial ambiguity in drawings and paintings. This may be suggestive of a potential in drawing Jacques Derrida has described as 'puissance'[13] meaning a 'concealed energy.' Such thinking may demonstrate the early incursion of critical reflexive practice, coupled to the mining of intellectual research that consistently relates the process of thinking and doing, enabling further pursuit of theoretical ideas through creative practice.

Exploration of the visual intrigue within borders and gaps embodied in the artwork led to the emergence of an oil sketch made on a canvas sketchpad (Figure 16.2). This is my response to the photograph of the painting based upon a Rodin nude that considers how to re-frame the figure, both literally and metaphorically. It is possible to witness spatial ambiguity through the uncertainty of the placement of the planes of colour as for example the cobalt blue infuses all aspects on the image, even acting as a highlight on the figure. Contemplation of this potential, within the aforementioned 'gaps' in the paintings, reflects the contemporary philosophical observations of Gary Peters as he discussed Martin Heidegger's thinking in relation to knowing and unknowingness as the '...affirmation of the unknown as unknown can only take place within the known, as a gap, space or erasure.[14]

Such theoretical encounters with philosophical discourse were not necessary to my practice, but rather vitalized latent qualities within the artwork leading to the recognition of symbolic possibilities of abstract space. The thinking within the sketchbook and the journal were beginning to overlap, intellectual enquiry progressing concurrent with each visual investigation developed from previous findings. The research sketchbooks become organized more purposefully with reflections on one side of the page accompanied by visual exploration, supported

16.2   Rodin photograph and oil sketch. Source: Image: Christine Turner 2009

by practical notes, on the other. This stage reveals the inception of a subtle, mutual interchange between theory and practice, evidencing Lyn Holdridge and Katy Macleod's reasoning that '…creative practical research takes us to the edge of dialectical reason. It removes itself from the outdated insistence on a separation of theory from practice.'[15]

Segregation between the sketchbook, the reflective journal and experimental notes remain, but interestingly words begin to pervade sketches, similarly images start to creep into the journals as intellectual enquiry progresses concurrent to each visual investigation. This demonstrates clarity in engaging with theory and exposes an underlying need for examinable evidence. Scholarly references to artists are made in the journal, but the impact upon the practice shown in sketchbooks emphasizes that the driver for the research is realized through sketches, bringing visual play to the fore of the creative research impulse alongside formal spatial ideas. An important quality of sketchbook working is the enablement of serendipitous creativity, which would be inhibited if the sketchbook developed into a self-aware journal of organized documentation. If the PhD sketchbook becomes exclusively a reflective journal, the experiential nature and development of art knowledge could disappear altogether, and ideas enabled during the experience of making would be overlooked.

Whilst the importance of observing and drawing the human figure to the research can not be dismissed, a critical evaluation of the works indicates that my visual preoccupations are with formal possibilities rather than engaging with another individual. This approach privileges pictorial space, emphasizing the abstract and suppressing the authority of the subject. The relationship between the represented figure and the pictorial ground evokes a visual tension particularly relevant to drawing the nude, resulting from an incongruity that exists between human physicality and the two dimensional ground that conveys the image. An incomplete life drawing of a standing male model shows this, as the figure appears to be moving into another space. The drawing develops a more nuanced, liquid image before becoming an oil painting on canvas. Figure 16.3 offers sketches that explore the idea of mixing figure and ground with written notes that relate to the particular image. This material provides evidence of the sketchbook as an explicit, personal thinking space, a crucible for the generation of creative knowledge.

The mercurial method of oil painting seen in Figure 16.3 exacerbates my intrigue with fluidity and its significance in representing the human form. The unstable spatial context that the figure inhabits offers an ephemeral quality, encouraging a viewing that is emblematic of something other than its corporeality. Anthony Gormley, speaking during a BBC 4 Television documentary *Focus on Sculpture* in 2011 uses the phrase 'the body as a site of consciousness' to describe the function of the human figure (usually his own) in his sculptures. This echoes the significance of the human form evidenced through my research, the figure as a site of consciousness rather than a record of empirical observation or subjective expression. By drawing the life model the research is not seeking realism in a phenomenological sense, yet rather the aim is to use the figure to evoke a sense of being present in the physical world. Though this is not necessarily through a

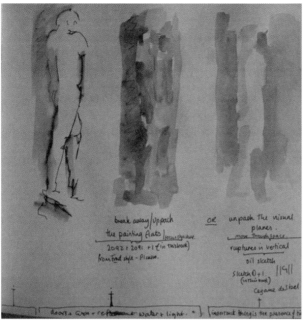

16.3   Sketchbook page and developed oil painting. Source: Image: Christine Turner 2009

depiction of an individual, for the figure may ultimately be symbolic by nature, an everyman or everywoman, a gatekeeper between the observed imperative of life drawing and the abstract domain of stillness in paint.

At this stage, a conceptual understanding of the work has occurred through the interchange between theory and practice as the developmental dialogue between theoretical reflection and reflection through drawing progresses. Sketchbook working reveals subjective responses to the practice as it related practical findings to theory and the reflective journal traced the process of theoretical thinking. The *posterior* nature of the artist's process is a facet that makes critical evaluation problematic, however, stringent records of the process offer a degree of circumspection that allows critical practice to augment art working. Gary Peters indicates this property of art practice, '…while the thinker can think outside of the aesthetic, the artist remains within it…for the artist no matter how thought-full, the work never vanishes into the task of thinking but always remains, if not as an end, then as a brute reality that is transformed by having another space (an "other beginning") opened-up within it rather than outside it.'[16]

Creative practice is difficult to align with established academic means of evaluating and discerning new knowledge. There is a vibrant debate surrounding the methodologies of practice-based PhDs and the best ways to present them for examination. On the one hand art researchers such as Katy Macleod promote the academic credibility of practical art research in that, '…we can now assert that art is a theorizing practice: it can produce the research thesis: it cannot be said to be simply illustration of it.'[17] Yet, on the other hand, this indicates the need for an appreciation of the specific properties of practical art research. Lyn Holdridge and Macleod argues that the problems with art research methodologies is that they do not take account of the *posteriori* experiential nature of art practice, that '… the teleological nature of methodologies advanced as appropriate to the artist/researcher are inappropriate as conceptual schemas because they do not take account of the posteriori nature of art knowledge.'[18]

Sally Morgan of the University of Western England (UWE) has argued that knowledge derived from practice-based PhD research is aside from general academic research validation to support this view. Morgan suggests that the PhD requirement of publication is met by exhibition, and that art is equivalent to text in that it is the same as writing a book, being '…an intelligently constructed text that embodies meaning and knowledge.'[19] However, Stephen Scrivener counters such proposals, arguing that they fail to account for the general PhD requirement of a new contribution to knowledge by suggesting that '…it is implausible to claim that the primary function of an art object is to communicate knowledge and of the art making process to create knowledge artefacts.'[20] Scrivener argues that '…artworks are essentially illustrative rather than semantic representations'[21] leading Scrivener to conclude '…the history of art cannot be understood as a process of building a body of knowledge…because the contributions were not accompanied by justification.'[22] Steven Scrivener offers a more nuanced definition of how art working contributes to the research culture, stating it '…generates novel apprehension' and that '…artworks offer perspectives or ways of seeing…ways of seeing the past, present and future rather than knowledge of the way things were or are.'[23] Negating artwork as a conveyor of knowledge and suggesting that the art making process yields knowledge, independent of the art produced, offers a contingency against an inequitable relationship between theory and practice in research. By producing knowledge gleaned explicitly through a reflective process and written thesis, by not attempting to vilify it in the research activity either as pure practice or through reflective notes, the practice is empowered because autonomy is retained.

Rob Cowdroy and Erik de Graaff's point to the need for academic contextualization, stating that '…the creativity-as-research debate suggested a present-and-defend approach as a possible alternative to conventional assessment of highly creative ability.'[24] They suggest this is preferable to letting the work speak for itself, asking '…what is there to indicate there was any creativity beyond crafting?'[25] Their argument points to the need for theoretical elucidation rather than the presentation of sketchbooks or work journals as stand alone evidence. Hypothetically, defence at viva examination should clarify and contextualize the works being presented. In considering practice-based research methods, Carole Gray made a defining statement when she declared that '…practice-based is a methodology not a type of research.'[26] Understanding practice-based research in this way focuses attention upon the doing of research and highlights the importance of recording the process through documentation within sketchbooks and reflective journals. Effective practical PhD study requires equanimity between theoretical and practical exploration, but the sketchbook, as an extraordinarily vibrant space of creative development, retains significance in this type research without conceding to theoretical precedence. By presenting this as separate to theoretical thinking, it is possible to retain the integrity of practice, as it is not required to explicate its contribution to knowledge. The sketchbook and reflective journal have been collaborative documents in the process of this discovery, for neither can claim sovereignty over the process of my art production. Nevertheless, as a practitioner, I award a special privilege to sketchbooks as my assigned working space (I recognize that this may not be so for a concept driven project), as the nature of my work maintains drawing and process as the drivers of the project. I hold that the sketchbook is a special document, one that physically and intellectually highlights art works as more than artefacts, but rather they reveal the creative and intellectual traces of process. My research has been a means of extending and refining practice, enabling and augmenting my professional practice as an artist. This is born out in the actual sketchbooks; they have developed an integrity that reveals academic rigour and the critical reflexivity necessary for this research. The pervasive nature of a fluid drawing practice, and its' ability to convene the timeless space between thinking and doing has rewarded my PhD study with equanimity and integrity. My sketchbook practice meets the two purposes traditionally assumed by sketchbook working, namely, the revelation of the artist's visual journey married to a personal creative discourse. This, like drawing, is capable of engaging with the shifting sands of thought and action and the changing environment of art practice and education.

BIBLIOGRAPHY

Biggs, Bryan, and Julie Sheldon, eds. *Art in a City Revisited*. Liverpool: Liverpool University Press, 2009.

Brew, Angela, Michelle Fava and Andrea Kantrowitz, eds. *Thinking Through Drawing: Practice Into Knowledge*. New York: Columbia University Teachers College Press, 2011.

Cowdroy, Rob, and Erik de Graaf. "Assessing Highly: Creative Ability Assessment and Evaluation," in *Higher Education*, 30:5 (2005): 507–518.

Downs, Simon Russell Marshall, Phil Sawdon, Andy Selby, and Jane Tormey, eds. *Drawing Now Between the Lines of Contemporary Art*. New York: I. B. Taurus, 2007.

Frayling, Christopher. *Research in Art and Design: Royal College of Art Research Papers* 1. London: Royal College of Art, 1993.

Garner, Steve. *Writing on Drawing, Essays on Drawing Practice and Research*. Bristol: Intellect, 2008.

Gray, Carole and Julian Malins. *Visualizing Research: a Guide to the Research Process in Art and Design*. Farnham: Ashgate Publishing, 2004.

Holdridge, Lin and Katy Macleod, Katy, eds. *The Enactment of Thinking*. Bristol: Intellect, 2002.

MacDonald, Juliet. *Drawing Around the Body: the Manual and Visual Practice of Drawing and the Embodiment of Knowledge*. PhD diss., Leeds Metropolitan University, 2009.

Krauss, Rosalind E. *The Originality of the Avant-Garde and Other Modernist Myths*. London: MIT Press, 1985.

McGuirk, Tom. *Knowing by Hand: Embodied Knowledge in Higher Education in the Discipline of Art and Design*. Proceedings of the 11th Conference of the International Society for the Study of European Ideas. July 28–August 2, 2008. Language Centre, University of Helsinki. Accessed November 25, 2010. https/:blogs.helsinki.fi:issei2008.

Morgan Sally. "A Terminal Degree: Fine Art and the PhD," in *Journal of Visual Arts Practice*, 5:15 Bristol: Intellect (2001): 5–15.

Ortlipp, Michelle. "Keeping and Using Reflective Journals in Qualitative Research Process," in *The Qualitative Report,* 13:4 (2008). Accessed March 3, 2013, http://www.nova.edu/ssss/QR/QR13-4/ortlipp.pdf.

Perl, Jed. *Eyewitness, Reports from an Art World in Crisis*, New York: Basic Books, 2000.

Peters, Gary. "Ahead of 'Yes' and 'No': Heidegger on Knowing Unknowingness." Paper presented at the *On Not Knowing* symposium, New Hall College, Cambridge, 2009. *Accesssed July 6, 2009. http://www.kettlesyard.co.uk/exhibitions/mi/papers/onn_peters.pdf.*

Scrivener, Stephen. "The Art Object Does Not Embody a Form of Knowledge," in *Working Papers in Art & Design 2* (2002): 25–32.

NOTES

1   Steve Garner, *Writing on Drawing, Essays on Drawing Practice and Research* (Bristol: Intellect, 2008), 32.

2   *'Designo'* is a slippery term that commenced in Italian Renaissance Studios to describe putting meaning (science) into action.

3   Christopher Frayling, *Research in Art and Design: Royal College of Art Research Papers* 1 (London: Royal College of Art, 1993), 55.

4   Angela Brew, Michelle Fava and Andrea Kantrowitz, eds., *Thinking Through Drawing: Practice Into Knowledge* (New York: Columbia University Teachers College Press, 2011), 28.

5   T. McGuirk, *Knowing by Hand: Embodied Knowledge in Higher Education in the Discipline of Art and Design,* accessed November 25, 2010, https/:blogs.helsinki.fi:issei2008.

6   Jed Perl, *Eyewitness, Reports from an Art World in Crisis* (New York: Basic Books, 2000), 1.

7   Stephen Scrivener, "The Art Object Does Not Embody a Form of Knowledge," in *Working Papers in Art & Design*, 2 (2002): 25–32.

8   R. E. Krauss, *The Originality of the Avant-Garde and Other Modernist Myths* (London: MIT Press, 1985), 60.

9   Bryan Biggs and Julie Sheldon, eds., *Art in a City Revisited* (Liverpool: Liverpool University Press, 2009), 177.

10   Michelle Ortlipp, "Keeping and Using Reflective Journals in Qualitative Research Process," *The Qualitative Report*, 13:4 (2008), accessed March 3, 2013. http://www.nova.edu/ssss/QR/QR13-4/ortlipp.pdf.

11   Juliet MacDonald, *Drawing Around the Body: the Manual and Visual Practice of Drawing and the Embodiment of Knowledge* (PhD diss., Leeds Metropolitan University, 2009).

12   MacDonald, *Drawing Around the Body: the Manual and Visual Practice of Drawing and the Embodiment of Knowledge,* 8.

13   Discussed in Steve Garner, *Writing on Drawing, Essays on Drawing Practice and Research* (Bristol: Intellect, 2008), 61.

14   Gary Peters, "Ahead of 'Yes' and 'No': Heidegger on Knowing Unknowingness" (paper presented at the *On Not Knowing* symposium, New Hall College, Cambridge, 2009. *Accessed July 6, 2009), http://www.kettlesyard.co.uk/exhibitions/mi/papers/onn_peters.pdf.*

15   Lin Holdridge and Katy Macleod, Katy, eds, *The Enactment of Thinking* (Bristol: Intellect, 2002), 6.

16   Peters, "Ahead of 'Yes' and 'No': Heidegger on Knowing Unknowingness."

17   Holdridge and Macleod, Katy, *The Enactment of Thinking* (Bristol: Intellect, 2002), 3.

18   Holdridge and Macleod, Katy, *The Enactment of Thinking* (Bristol: Intellect, 2002), 6.

19   Sally Morgan, "A Terminal Degree: Fine Art and the PhD," *Journal of Visual Arts Practice*, 5:15 (2001) Bristol: Intellect): 7.

20   Scrivener, "The Art Object Does Not Embody a Form of Knowledge."

21   Scrivener, "The Art Object Does Not Embody a Form of Knowledge."

22   Scrivener, "The Art Object Does Not Embody a Form of Knowledge."

23   Scrivener, "The Art Object Does Not Embody a Form of Knowledge."

24   Rob Cowdroy and Erik de Graaf, "Assessing Highly: Creative Ability Assessment and Evaluation," *Higher Education* 30:5 (2005), 517.

25   Cowdroy and de Graaf, "Assessing Highly: Creative Ability Assessment and Evaluation," 509.

26   Carole Gray and Julian Malins, *Visualizing Research: a Guide to the Research Process in Art and Design (*Farnham: Ashgate Publishing, 2004), 39.

Bibliography

Ackerman, James S. "Architectural Practice in the Italian Renaissance," in *Journal of the Society of Architectural Historians*, Vol. 13, No. 3 (October 1954): 3–11.

Alberti, Leon Battista. *On Painting*. Translated by C. Grayson. London: Penguin Books, 1991.

Allen, Felicity. *Your Sketchbook Yourself*. London: Tate Publishing, 2011.

Artaud, Antonin. *The Theater and Its Double*. Translated by M. C. Richards. New York: Grove Press, 1958.

Bachelard, Gaston. *La poétique de l'espace*. Paris: Presses universitaires de France, 2008.

Ballantyne, Andrew. *Deleuze and Guattari for Architects*. Oxon: Routledge, 2007.

Barasch, Moshe. *Theories of Art: From Plato to Winckelman*. New York: New York University Press, 1985.

Barthes, Roland. *Camera Lucida: Reflections on Photography*. London: Flamingo, 1984.

Baur, John, I.H., ed. *The Autobiography of Worthington Whittredge 1820–1910*. New York: Arno Press, 1969.

Bell, Steve. *Apes of Wrath*. London: Methuen, 2004.

Benedetti, Paul. *Forward Through the Rearview Mirror: Reflections on and by Marshall McLuhan*. Cambridge Massachusetts: MIT Press, 1997.

Benjamin, Walter. "The Work of Art in the Age of Mechanical Reproduction," trans. Harry Zohn in *Film Theory and Criticism*, eds. Gerald Mast and Marshall Cohen, Oxford: Oxford University Press (1976): 612–34.

Benthien, Claudia. *Skin: On the Cultural Border between Self and the World*. Translated by T. Dunlap. New York: Columbia University Press, 2002.

Bergeijk, Herman Van, and Deborah Hauptmann. *Notations of Herman Hertzberger*. Rotterdam: NAi Publishers, 1998.

Berger, John. *Ways of Seeing*. London: Penguin, 1972.

_____. "Drawing," in *John Berger: Selected Essays*. Ed. Geoff Dyer. London: Bloomsbury, 2001, 10–14.

_____. "Drawn to that Moment," in *John Berger: Selected Essays*, 419–423.

_____. *Berger on Drawing*. Cork: Occasional Press, 2005.

Biggs, Bryan, and Julie Sheldon (eds). *Art in a City Revisited*. Liverpool: Liverpool University Press, 2009.

Blackburn, Simon. *Oxford Dictionary of Philosophy*. Oxford: Oxford University Press, 1994.

Blau, Eve, and Edward Kaufman. *Architecture and its Images*. Canadian Centre for Architecture: Montreal: MIT Press, 1989.

Blunt, Gillian, and Gillian Rose (eds). *Writing Women and Space. Colonial and Postcolonial Geographies*. New York: The Guilford Press, 1994.

Bollas, Christopher. *The Evocative Object World*. New York: Routledge, 2009.

Bolter, Jay David, and Richard Grusin. *Remediation: Understanding New Media*. London: MIT Press, 2000.

Borges, Jorge Luis. Epilogue for "The Maker," in *Jorge Luis Borges: Selected Poems,* ed. Alexander Coleman. New York and London: Penguin, 2000.

Brawne, Michael. *Architectural Thought: The Design Process and the Expectant Eye*. London: Architectural Press, 2003.

Brereton, Richard. *Sketchbooks: The Hidden Art of Designers, Illustrators & Creatives*. London: Laurence King Publishing, 2009.

Brew, Angela, Michelle Fava and Andrea Kantrowitz (eds). *Thinking Through Drawing: Practice Into Knowledge*. New York: Columbia University Teachers College Press, 2011.

Building Material. *Paperwork. The Journal of the Architectural Association of Ireland*. Issue 15, Autumn. Dublin: AAI, 2006.

Butterfield, Jeremy, John Daintith, Andrew Holmes, Alan Isaacs, Jonathan Law, Elizabeth Martin and Elspeth Summers (eds). *Collins English Dictionary*. 6th Edition. Glasgow: Harper Collins Publishers, 2003.

Carman, Charles H. "Albert and Nicholas of Cusa: Perspective as Coincidence of Opposites," in *Explorations in Renaissance Culture*, Vol. 33 (2007): 196–219.

Carpo, Mario. *Architecture in the Age of Printing*. Cambridge Mass.: MIT Press, 2001.

Chatzichristodoulou, Maria, and Zerihan, Rachel (eds). *Intimacy Across Visceral and Digital Performance*. Basingstoke: Palgrave MacMillan, 2012.

Chwalisz, Damien. "12 Letters to the Sketch." Honours dissertation, University of South Australia, 2006.

Cixous, Hélène. "The Last Painting or the Portrait of God," in *Coming to Writing and Other Essays*, ed. Deborah Jenson. Cambridge, Mass.: Harvard University Press, 1992.

——————. "Without End, No, State Of Drawingness, No, Rather: The Executioner's Taking Off", in *Stigmata*, ed. Hélène Cixous. Oxford: Routledge, 2005, 25–40.

Clark, Justine. "Drawing out the awards", in *Architecture Australia,* Vol. 98, No. 6 (November / December, 2009): 12.

Cook, Peter. *Drawing: The Motive Force of Architecture*. Architectural Design Primer 2. London: Wiley, 2008.

Corner, James. and Alex McLean (eds). Taking Measures Across the American Landscape. New Haven: Yale University Press, 1996.

Cowan, Bainard. "Walter Benjamin's Theory of Allegory," in *New German Critique,* No. 22 (Special Issue on Modernism Winter 1981): 109–122.

Cowdroy, Rob, and Erik de Graaf. "Assessing Highly: Creative Ability Assessment and Evaluation," in *Higher Education*, Vol. 30, No. 5 (2005): 507–518.

Curtis, William JR. *Fragments of Invention: The Sketchbooks of Le Corbusier*. Cambridge Massachusetts: Harvard University, 1981.

Cusanus, Nicolaus. *Unity and Reform, Selected Writings of Nicholas de Cusa*, ed. J.P. Dolan. Notre Dame, IN: University of Notre Dame Press, 1962.

_____. "De coniecturis," in *Nicolai de Cusa Opera omnia*, Vol. 3, eds. J. Koch, C. Bormann, and I. G. Senger. Hamburg: Felix Meiner, 1972.

_____. *On Learned Ignorance*. Trans. Jasper Hopkins. Minneapolis: Banning, 1981.

Damisch, Hubert. *Théorie de la peinture*. Paris: Seuil, 1972.

_____. *Ruptures/Cultures*. Paris: Minuit, 1976.

_____. *L'origine de la perspective*. Paris: Flammarion, 1987.

Da Parma, Biagio Pelacani. *Quaestionis perspectivae*, ed. G. Federici Vescovini. Paris: Vrin, 2002.

Da Vignola, Giacomo Barozzio. *Le Due Regole della Prospettiva Pratica*. Roma: Camerale, 1611. With a comentary by Egnatio Danti.

Davies, Paul. "La Madonna delle Carceri in Prato," in *Architectural History*, Vol. 36 (1993): 1–18.

De Beistegui, Miguel. *The New Heidegger*. London: Continuum, 2005.

De Certau, Michel. *The Practice of Everyday Life*. Berkeley: University of California Press, 1984.

De Costa Meyer, Esther. *Frank Gehry on Line*. Princeton: Princeton University Press, 2008.

Deleuze, Gilles. *Bergsonism*. Translated by Hugh Tomlinson and Barbara Habberjam. New York: Zone Books, 1991.

_____. *Difference and Repetition*. Translated by Paul Patton. New York: Columbia University Press, 1994.

_____. *Francis Bacon*. Translated by Daniel W. Smith. London: Continuum, 2005.

Deleuze, Gilles, and Claire Parnet. *Dialogues II*. Translated by Hugh Tomlinson and Barbara Habberjam. London, Continuum, 1987.

Deleuze, Gilles, and Felix Guattari. *A Thousand Plateaus*. Translated by Brian Massumi. London: Continuum, 1988.

Derrida, Jacques. *De la grammatologie*. Paris: Les éditions de Minuit, 1967.

_____. *La vérité en peinture*. Paris: Flammarion, 1978.

_____. *Dissemination*. London: The Athlone Press, 1981.

_____. *Khôra*. Paris: Galilée, 1993.

_____. *Mal d'archive, une impression freudienne*. Paris: Galilée, 1995.

_____. *Foi et Savoir*. Paris: Editions du Seuil, 1996.

_____. *On Touching – Jean-Luc Nancy*. Translated by C. Irizarry. Stanford: Stanford University Press, 2005.

Desargues, Girard. *Manière universelle de Monsieur Desargues pour pratiquer la perspective par petit-pied comme le géométral*. Paris: Imprimerie de Pierre des Hayes, 1647.

Downs, Simon, Russell Marshall, Phil Sawdon, Andy Selby, and Jane Tormey (eds). *Drawing Now Between the Lines of Contemporary Art*. New York: I. B. Taurus, 2007.

Edwards, Betty. *Drawing on the Right Side of the Brain.* New York: Penguin Putman, 1979.

_____. *The New Drawing on the Right Side of the Brain.* New York: Penguin Putnam Inc., 1999.

Edwards, Elizabeth, Chris Gosden and Ruth Phillips (eds). *Sensible Objects: Colonialism, Museums and Modern Culture.* Oxford: Berg, 2002.

El-Bizri, Nader. "*Qui-êtes-vous Khôra?* Receiving Plato's *Timaeus,*" in *Existentia Meletai-Sophias,* Vol. XI, Issue 3–4 (2001): 473–90.

_____. "La perception de la profondeur: Ibn al-Haytham, Berkeley et Merleau-Ponty," in *Oriens-Occidens: sciences, mathématiques et philosophie de l'antiquité à l'âge classique (Cahiers du Centre d'Histoire des Sciences et des Philosophies Arabes et Médiévales, CNRS),* Vol. 5 (2004): 171–84.

_____. "*ON KAI KHORA*: Situating Heidegger between the *Sophist* and the *Timaeus,*" in *Studia Phaenomenologica,* Vol. IV, Issue 1–2 (2004): 73–98.

_____. "A Philosophical Perspective on Ibn al-Haytham's *Optics,*" in *Arabic Sciences and Philosophy,* Vol. 15 (2005): 189–218.

_____. "Imagination and Architectural Representations," in M. Frascari, J. Hale, and B. Starkey (eds), *From Models to Drawings: Imagination and Representation in Architecture.* London: Routledge, 2007: 34–42.

_____. "In Defence of the Sovereignty of Philosophy: al-Baghdadi's Critique of Ibn al-Haytham's Geometrisation of Place," in *Arabic Sciences and Philosophy,* Vol. 17 (2007): 57–80.

_____. "Classical Optics and the *Perspectiva* Traditions Leading to the Renaissance," in *Renaissance Theories of Vision,* eds. C. Carman and J. Hendrix. Aldershot: Ashgate, 2010: 11–30.

_____. "Creative inspirations or intellectual impasses? Reflections on relationships between architecture and the humanities," in *The Humanities in Architectural Design: A Contemporary and Historical Perspective,* eds. S. Bandyopadhyay, J. Lomholt, N. Temple, and R. Tobe. London: Routledge, 2010: 123–35.

_____. "Being at Home Among Things: Heidegger's Reflections on Dwelling," in *Environment, Space, Place,* Vol. 3 (2011): 47–71.

_____. "The Conceptual Bearings of the Intercultural Roles of Architecture," in *The Cultural Role of Architecture,* eds. Paul Emmons, John Hendrix, and Jane Lomholt. London: Routledge, 2012: 199–207.

Eisenman, Peter. *Cities of Artificial Excavation.* Montreal: Canadian Centre for Architecture / New York: Rizzoli International Publications, 1994.

_____. *Eisenman Inside Out.* New Haven and London: Yale University Press, 2004.

_____. *Feints.* Milan: Skira, 2006.

_____. *Ten Canonical Buildings 1950–2000.* New York: Rizzoli, 2008.

_____. *Barefoot on White-Hot Walls (Barfuss Auf Weiss Glühenden Mauern).* Edited by P. Noever. Ostfildern: Hatje Cantz Verlag, 2005.

Elam, Diane. *Feminism and Deconstruction: Ms en Abyme.* London: Routledge, 1994.

Elsner, John, and Roger Cardinal (eds). *Cultures of Collecting.* London: Reaktion Books, 1994.

Evans, Robin. *Translations from Drawing to Building and Other Essays.* London: Architectural Association Publications AA Documents 2, 2003.

Farthing, Stephen (ed.). *The Sketchbooks of Nicholas Grimshaw*. The Royal Academy of Arts in Association with the Centre for Drawing at The University of the Arts London and Edinburgh College of Art. London: Royal Academy, 2009.

Flam, Jack (ed.). *Robert Smithson: The Collected Writing*, Berkeley: University of Californa Press, 1996.

Forty, Adrian, and Susanne Küchler (eds). *The Art of Forgetting*. Oxford: Berg, 1999.

Foucault, Michel. *Les mots et les choses: une archéologie des sciences humaines*. Paris: Gallimard, 1966.

Franck, Frederick (ed.). *The Buddha Eye: An Anthology of the Kyoto School and its Contemporaries*. New York: World Wisdom, 2004.

Frascari, Marco. "The Drafting Knife and the Pen," in *Implementing Architecture*. Atlanta: Nexus Press, 1988.

_____. "A reflection on paper and its virtues within the material and invisible *factures* of architecture", in *From Models to Drawings: Imagination and representation in architecture,* eds. Marco Frascari, Jonathan Hale, and Bradley Starkey. London: Routledge, 2007, 23–33.

_____. "Lines as Architectural Thinking," in *Architectural Theory Review*, Vol. 14, No. 3 (2009): 200–12.

_____. *The Virtue of Architecture: A 2009 Strenna*. United Kingdom: Lulu.com, 2009.

Fraser, Ian, and Rod Henmi. *Envisioning Architecture: An Analysis of Drawing*. London: Wiley, 1994.

Frayling, Christopher. *Research in Art and Design: Royal College of Art Research Papers* 1. London: Royal College of Art, 1993.

Freud, Sigmund. *On Dreams, the Standard Edition*. Translated and edited by J. Strachey. New York: W.W. Norton, 1952.

_____. *The Interpretation of Dreams*. Translated and edited by J. Strachey. New York: Avon Books, 1965.

_____. *Civilization and Its Discontents*. Translated by J. Riviere. NewYork: Dover Publications Inc., 1994.

Frichot, Helene. "Stealing into Gilles Deleuze's Baroque House." In *Deleuze and Space,* eds. Ian Buchanan and Gregg Lambert, 61 – 79. Edinburgh: Edinburgh University Press, 2005.

Fuller, Peter. *Rock and Flesh*. Norwich: Norwich School of Art Gallery, 1985.

Garner, Steve. *Writing on Drawing, Essays on Drawing Practice and Research*. Bristol: Intellect, 2008.

Gray, Carole, and Julian Malins. *Visualizing Research: a Guide to the Research Process in Art and Design*. Farnham: Ashgate Publishing, 2004.

Gresleri, Giuliano (ed.). *Voyage d'Orient sketchbooks- facsimile edition*. 6 vols. New York: Rizzoli, and Milan: Electa with Foundation Le Corbusier, 2002.

Goffi, Federica. "Drawing Imagination and Imagination of Drawing: The Case of Tiberio Alfarano's Drawing of St. Peter's Basilica," in *Interstices: A Journal of Architecture and Related Arts: The Traction of Drawing*, Vol. 11 (2010): 20–30.

Gunn, Wendy, (ed.). *Fieldnotes and Sketchbooks: Challenging the Boundaries Between Descriptions and Processes of Describing*. Frankfurt: Peter Lang, 2009.

Haas, Robert. "Raphael's *School of Athens*: A Theorem in a Painting?" in *Journal of Humanistic Mathematics*, Vol. 2, No. 2 (July 2012): 2–26.

Hall, Marcia (ed.). *Raphael's School of Athens*. Cambridge: Cambridge University Press, 1997.

Hallam, Elizabeth, and Brian Street (eds). *Cultural Encounters: Representing Otherness*. London: Routledge, 2000.

Hankins, James. *Plato in the Italian Renaissance*, 2 vols. Leiden: E.J. Brill, 1990.

Harper, James. *Recto-Verso: The Flip Side of Master Drawings*. Cambridge: Harvard Art Museums, 2001.

Harper, Ralph. *On Presence: Variations and Reflections*. Baltimore: The John Hopkins University Press, 1991.

Harries, Karsten. *Infinity and Perspective*. Cambridge, Mass: MIT Press, 2001.

Hay, Jonathan. *Shi Tao: Painting and Modernity in Early Qing China*. Cambridge: Cambridge University Press, 2001.

Heidegger, Martin. *Holzwege*. Frankfurt am Main: Vittorio Klostermann, 1950.

——————. *Vorträge und Aufsätze*. Pfullingen: Günther Neske, 1954.

——————. *Die Technik und die Kehre*. Pfullingen: Günther Neske, 1962

——————. *Poetry, Language, Thought*. Trans. Albert Hofstadter. New York: Harper & Row, Publishers Inc., 1971.

——————. *Basic Writings*, ed. David Farrell Krell. New York: Harper Collins Publishers, 1993.

——————. *Being and Time*. Oxford: Blackwell, 1997.

Hejduk, John. *Architectures in Love*. New York: Rizzolli, 1995.

Hendrix, John. *The Relation Between Architectural Forms and Philosophical Structures in the Work of Francesco Borromini in Seventeenth-Century Rome*. Lewiston, NY: Edwin Mellen, 2002.

——————. *Architecture and Psychoanalysis: Peter Eisenman and Jacques Lacan*. New York: Peter Lang, 2006.

Holdridge, Lin, and Katy Macleod (eds). *The Enactment of Thinking*. Bristol: Intellect, 2002.

Hooks, Bell. *Yearning: Race, Gender and Cultural Politics*. New York: Turnaround Press, 1991.

Horton, C., C. Jenkins, C. Rhodes, and J. Spalding. *Debating the Line (Minichiello's Drawings)*. Humberside: European Illustrator Gallery and Collection with Loughborough University School of Art and Design.

Hubbert, Ann C. "Envisioning New St. Peter's: Perspectival Drawings and the Process of Design," in *Journal of the Society of Architectural Historians*, Vol. 68, No. 2 (2009): 158–77.

Ibn al-Haytham, al-Hasan. *Kitab al-Manazir*, 2 vols., ed. A. I. Sabra. Kuwait: National Council for Culture, Arts and Letters, 1983.

——————. *The Optics, Books I–III, On Direct Vision*, 2 vols., trans. A. I. Sabra. London: Warburg Institute, 1989.

Irigaray, Luce. *Speculum of the Other Woman*. Translated by G. C. Gill. New York: Cornell University Press, 1985.

James, Henry. *Roderick Hudson*. Boston: Houghton Mifflin, 1917.

_____. *Roderick Hudson*. Boston: James R. Osgood, 1876.

James, William. *Psychology*. New York: Macmillan, 1892.

_____. *A Pluralistic Universe*. London: Longman, Green, 1909.

_____. *The Varieties of Religious Experience*. London: Routledge, 2008.

Jones, Amelia and Andrew Stephenson. *Performing the Body / Performing the Text*. London: Routledge, 1999.

Joost-Gaugier, Christiane L. *Raphael's Stanza della Segnatura: Meaning and Invention*. Cambridge: Cambridge University Press, 2002.

Karp, Ivan, and Steven D. Lavine (eds). *Exhibiting Culture: The Poetics and Politics of Museum Display*. Washington: Smithsonian Institution Press, 1991.

Kaye, Nick. *Site-Specific Art: Performance, Place and Documentation*. London: Routledge, London, 2000.

Keane, John, and Angela Weight. *John Keane – Gulf*. London: Imperial War museum, 1992.

Kemp, Martin. *The Science of Art*: *Optical Themes in Western Art from Brunelleschi to Seurat*. New Haven: Yale University Press, *1990*.

_____. *Leonardo da Vinci: the Marvellous Works of Nature and Man*. Oxford: Oxford University Press, 2006.

Khandekar, Narayan, Gianfranco Pocobene and Kate Smith Stewart (eds). *John Singer Sargents 'Triumph of Religion' at the Boston Public Library: Creation and Restoration*. Cambridge: Harvard Art Museums, 2009.

Kimmelman, Michael. "Robert Unbound," in *Art & Auction*, 12 (1989): 24.

Kircher, Athanasius. *Prodromus Coptus Sive Aegyptiacus*. Romae: Propaganda Fide, 1636.

Kirwin, Liza. *Visual Thinking: Sketchbooks from the Archives of American Art*. Archives of American Art Journal, Vol 27, No1. Smithsonian Institute 1987, 21–29.

Koolhaas, Rem. *Delirious New York: A Retrospective Manifesto*. New York: Monacelli Press, 1994.

Kovats, Tania (ed.). *The Drawing Book. A Survey of Drawing the Primary Means of Expression*. London: Black Dog Publishing, 2007.

Krauss, Rosalind E. *The Originality of the Avant-Garde and Other Modernist Myths*. London: MIT Press, 1985.

Küchler, Susanne. *Malanggan: Art, Memory and Sacrifice*. Oxford: Berg, 2002.

Lacy, Bill. *100 Contemporary Architects Sketches and Drawings*. London: Thames and Hudson, 1991.

Lambert, Susan. *Reading Drawings: An Introduction to Looking at Drawings*. New York: Pantheon Books, 1984.

Lampugnani, Vittorio Magnago and Henry A. Millon. *The Renaissance from Brunelleschi to Michelangelo: The Representation of Architecture*. Milan: Bompiani, 1994.

Langer, Susanne. *Philosophy in a New Key*. Cambridge, Massachusetts: Harvard University Press, 1979.

Leach, Neil. *The Anaesthetics of Architecture*. Cambridge, Massachusetts: MIT Press, 1999.

Le Corbusier. *Creation is a Patient Search*. Praeger: New York, 1960.

_____. *Les Voyages d'Allemagne*. Milan: Electa Architecture and Fondation Le Corbusier, 2002.

_____. *Oeuvre Complète*, 8 vols. Originally published between 1929–70 with editor Willy Boesiger. Republished – Basel: Birkhäuser, 2006.

The Le Corbusier Sketchbooks. Vols. 1–4 (1914–64) Cambridge Massachusetts and London: MIT Press, Thames and Hudson with The Architectural History Foundation. (Preface by André Wogensky and Introduction by Maurice Besset), 1981–82.

Li, L. L. (ed.). *The Historical Records of the Development of Chinese Ancient Art Theory*. Shanghai: Shanghai People's Arts Publisher, 1997.

Licht, Meg. "I Ragionamenti – Visualising St. Peter's," in *Journal of the Society of Architectural Historians*, Vol. 44, No. 2 (May, 1985): 111–28.

Lucas, Raymond. *"Towards a Theory of Notation as a Thinking Tool."* PhD diss., University of Aberdeen, 2006.

MacDonald, Juliet. *"Drawing Around the Body the Manual and Visual Practice of Drawing and the Embodiment of Knowledge."* PhD diss., Leeds Metropolitan University, 2009.

March, Lionel. *Architectonics of Humanism: Essays on Number in Architecture*. Chichester: Academy Editions, 1998.

Maritain, Jacques. *Art and Scholasticism with Other Essays.* New York: reprinted by Kessinger Publishing (Undated), 1924.

Maslen, Mick, and Jack Southern. *Drawing Projects- An exploration of the Language of Drawing.* London: Black Dog Publishing, 2011.

Massumi, Brian. *A User's Guide to Capitalism and Schizophrenia, Deviations from Deleuze and Guattari*. Massachusetts: MIT, 1992.

_____. "Line Parable for the Virtual (On the Superiority of the Analog)," in *The Virtual Dimension: Architecture, Representation and Crash Culture*, ed. John Beckmann, 304–321. New York: Princeton Architectural Press, 1998.

May, Todd. *Gilles Deleuze, An Introduction*. Cambridge: Cambridge University Press, 2005.

Maynard, Patrick. *Drawing Distinctions: The Varieties of Graphic Expression*. Ithaca: Cornell University Press, 2005.

McGuirk, Tom. *Knowing by Hand: Embodied Knowledge in Higher Education in the Discipline of Art and Design*. Proceedings of the 11th Conference of the International Society for the Study of European Ideas. July 28–August 2, 2008. Language Centre, University of Helsinki. Accessed November 25, 2010. https/:blogs.helsinki.fi:issei2008.

McKee, Francis. *Kathy Prendergast: The End and the Beginning*. Dublin: Merrel Publishers in association with the Irish Museum of Modern Art, 1999.

McNiff, Jean, and A. Jack Whitehead. *All You Need to Know About Action Research*. London: Sage, 2011.

Mei, R. L. M. (ed.). *Shuang Xing Hui Ying*. Shijiazhuang: Hebei Education Publisher, 2006.

Merleau-Ponty, Maurice. *Phénoménologie de la perception*. Paris: Gallimard, 1945.

_____. *The Primacy of Perception*. Evanston: Northwestern University Press, 1964.

_____. *Phenomenology of Perception*. London: Routledge, 2002.

Merrill, Michael. *Louis Kahn Drawing to Find Out: the Dominican Motherhouse and the Patient Search for Architecture*. Baden: Lars Müller Publishers, 2010.

Milner, Marion. *A Life of One's Own*. London: Virago, 2000.

_____. *The Hands of the Living God*. London: Routledge, 2011.

Morgan, Sally. "A Terminal Degree: Fine Art and the PhD," in *Journal of Visual Arts Practice*,
5:15 (2001) Bristol: Intellect, 5–15.

Mulvey, Laura. *Visual and Other Pleasures*. Basingstoke: Macmillan, 1989.

Muntadas, Antoni. *On Translation: Paper BP/MVDR. Intervention in the Mies Van der Rohe
Pavilion*: Barcelona: Fundació Mies Van der Rohe, 2010.

Nancy, Jean-Luc. *Corpus*. Translated by R. A. Rand. New York: Fordham University Press, 2008.

Nesselrath, Arnold. *Raphael's School of Athens: Recent Restorations, Vatican Museums*, Vol. 1.
Vatican City State: Edizioni Musei Vaticani, 1997.

Nishida, Kitaro. *Fundamental Problems of Philosophy: The World of Action and the Dialectical
World*. Tokyo: Sophia University Press, 1970.

Olkowski, Dorothea. *Merleau-Ponty, Interiority and Exteriority, Psychic Life and the World*. New
York: State University of New York Press, 1991.

Ortlipp, Michelle. *Keeping and Using Reflective Journals in Qualitative Research Process,* The
Qualitative Report, 13:4 (2008). Accessed March 3, 2013. http://www.nova.edu/ssss/QR/
QR13-4/ortlipp.pdf.

O'Toole, Shane (ed.). *The Architect and the Drawing*. Dublin: Gandon with the RIAI, 1989.

Padovan, Richard. *Proportion: Science, Philosophy, Architecture*. London: Spon Press, 2001.

Paillet et Olivier. *Catalogue des Tableaux, Dessins, Gouaches, Estampes…Composant le
Cabinet et les Etudes de feu Hubert Robert*. Paris: Paillet et Olivier, 1809.

Pallasmaa, Juhani. *The Thinking Hand*: *Existential and Embodied Wisdom in Architecture*.
London: Wiley, 2009.

Perez-Gomez, Alberto. *Built Upon Love: Architectural Longing After Aesthetics and Ethics*.
Cambridge Massachusetts: MIT Press, 2006.

_____. "Questions of Representation: The Poetic Origin of Architecture," in
Architectural Research Quarterly, Vol. 9, Nos. 3/4 (2005): 217–25.

_____. "Architecture as Drawing," in *Journal of Architectural Education*, Vol. 36, No. 2
(Winter, 1982): 2–7.

Perl, Jed. *Eyewitness, Reports from an Art World in Crisis*, New York: Basic Books, 2000.

Peters, Gary. "Ahead of 'Yes and 'No': Heidegger on Knowing Unknowingness." Paper
presented at the *On Not Knowing* symposium, New Hall College, Cambridge, 2009.
Accesssed July 6, 2009. http://www.kettlesyard.co.uk/exhibitions/mi/papers/onn_peters.pdf.

Plato. *Timaeus, Critias, Cleitophon, Menexenus, Epistles*, ed. and trans. R. G. Bury. Cambridge
Mass.: Loeb Classical Library, 1960.

Probyn, Elspeth. "Glass Selves: Emotions, subjectivity and the research process," in *Oxford
Handbook of the Self*. Ed. Shaun Gallagher. Oxford: Oxford Handbooks Online, 2011, 29.
Accessed on 27 October 2011. http://www.oxfordhandbooks.com/oso/public/content/
oho_philosophy/9780199548019/toc.html. doi:10.1093/oxfordhb/97.

Quinlan-McGrath, Mary. "The Foundation Horoscope(s) for St. Peter's Basilica, Rome, 1506:
Choosing a Time, Changing the *Storia*," in *Isis*, Vol. 92, No. 4. (December 2001): 716–41.

Rachman, Stanley. *Anxiety*. Hove: Psychology Press Ltd, 2004.

Rappolt, Mark, and Robert Violette. *Gehry Draws*. Cambridge, Massachusetts. MIT Press with Violette Editions, 2002.

Raynaud, Dominique. "Une application méconnue des principes de la vision binoculaire: Ibn al-Haytham et les peintres du *trecento* (1295–1450)," in *Oriens-Occidens: Sciences, mathématiques et philosophie de l'Antiquité à l'Âge Classique. Cahiers du Centre d'Histoire des Sciences et des Philosophies Arabes et Médiévales*, Vol. 5 (2004): 93–131.

_____. 'Le tracé continu des sections coniques à la Renaissance: Applications optico-perspectives, héritage de la tradition mathématique arabe,' in *Arabic Sciences and Philosophy*, Vol. 17 (2007): 299–345.

Reid, Callum. "*Annibale Carracci's Holy Family at the National Gallery of Victoria.*" Honours thesis, University of Melbourne, 2010.

Rendell, Jane. *Art and Architecture A Place Between*. London: I.B. Tauris, 2008.

_____. *Site-Writing: Architecture of Art Criticism*. London: I.B. Tauris, 2011.

Robbins, Edward. *An Anthropology of Architecture: Some Preliminary suggestions*. In J. P. Protzen (ed.) Proceedings of the 1987 conference on Planning and Design in Architecture, (35–40) American Society of Engineers. New York, 1987.

_____. *Why Architects Draw*. Cambridge Massachusetts: MIT Press, 1994.

Robertson, Pamela (ed.). *Charles Rennie Mackintosh, Architectural Sketches*. Glasgow: University of Glasgow, 1999.

Rose, Paul L. "Renaissance Italian Methods of Drawing the Ellipse and related Curves," in *Physis*, Vol. 12 (1970): 371–404.

Rowland, Ingrid. *The Culture of the High Renaissance: Ancients and Moderns in Sixteenth Century Rome*. Cambridge: Cambridge University Press, 2001.

Ruskin, John. *The Elements of Drawing, in Three Letters to Beginners*. London: Smith Elder and Co, 1857.

Said, Edward. *Orientalism*, London: Penguin Classics, 2003.

Sartre, Jean-Paul. *Being and Nothingness: An Essay on Phenomenological Ontology*. Translated by H. E. Barnes. London: Methuen, 1958.

Saint, Andrew. *The Image of the Architect*. New Haven: Yale University Press, 1983.

Sbacchi, Michele. "Euclidism and Theory of Architecture," in *Nexus Network Journal,* Vol.3, Issue 2, (September 2001): 25–38.

_____. "Projective Architecture," in *Nexus Network Journal*, Vol.11, Issue 3 (December 2009): 441–54.

Scarry, Elaine. *The Body in Pain: The Making and Unmaking of the World*. Oxford: Oxford University Press, 1985.

_____. *Literature and the Body. Essays on Populations and Persons*. Baltimore: The Johns Hopkins University Press, 1988.

Schank Smith, Kendra. *Architects' Sketches: Dialogue and Design*. London: Architectural Press, 2008.

Schopenhauer, Arthur. *The World as Will and Representation*, Vol. 1. New York: Dover Publications, 1969.

Scott, David. "William James and Buddhism: American Pragmatism and the Orient," in *Religion* 30 (2000): 333–352.

Scrivener, Stephen. "The Art Object Does Not Embody a Form of Knowledge," in *Working Papers in Art & Design 2* (2002), 25–32.

Seely, Rachel Ann. "St. Peter's Basilica as *Templum Dei*: Continuation of the Ancient Near Eastern Temple Tradition in the Christian Cathedral," in *Studia Antiqua*, Vol. 4, No. 1 (Winter 2005): 63–80.

Serrazanetti, Francesca, and Matteo Schubert. *The Hand of the Architect*. Milan: Fondo Ambiente Italiano and Moelskine, 2009.

Sherer, Daniel. "Critical and Palladian," in *Log* Vol. 26. New York: Anyone Corporation (2012): 135–143.

Sherman, Daniel J. (ed.). *Museums & Difference*. Indianapolis: Indiana University Press, 2008.

Sievers, Ann H. *Master Drawings from the Smith College Museum of Art*. New York: Hudson Hills Press, 2000.

Soane, John, and The Trustees of Sir John Soane's Museum. *A New Description of Sir John Soane's Museum*. London: The Trustees of Sir John Soane's Museum, 2007.

Stam, Robert. *Subversive Pleasures: Bakhtin, Cultural Criticism, and Film*. London: The John Hopkins University Press, 1989.

Steinberg, Leo. *Borromini's San Carlo alle Quattro Fontane: A Study in Multiple Form and Architectural Symbolism*. New York: Garland Publishing, L. 1977.

Steiner, George. *Real Presences*. Chicago: Chicago University Press, 1989.

Suzuki, Daisetz T. *Zen and Japanese Culture*. Princeton: Princeton University Press, 2010.

Syed Muhammad Iyhab, Abdullah, and Ahmed Roohi. *Let's Draw the Line*. Karachi: Chawkandi Art Publications, 2008.

Symington, Joan, and Neville Symington. *The Clinical Thinking of Wilfred Bion*. London: Routledge, 1996.

Tafuri, Manfredo. "Roma Instaurata," in *Raffaello Architetto*, eds. C. L. Frommel, S. Ray, and M. Tafuri. Milan: Electa Editrice, 1984.

_____. *La ricerca del rinascimento*. Turin: Einaudi, 1992.

Taylor, Eugene. and Robert Wozniak (eds). *Pure Experience: the Response to William James*. Bristol: Thoemmes Press, 1996.

Temple, Nicholas. *Disclosing Horizons: Architecture, Perspective and Redemptive Space*. London: Routledge, 2007.

_____. *Renovatio urbis: Architecture, Urbanism and Ceremony in the Rome of Julius II*. London: Routledge, 2011.

Tordy, William H. "Review of Le Corbusier Sketchbooks," in *Journal of the Society of Architectural Historians*, Vol. 42, No. 1 (1983): 83–86.

Trachtenberg, Marvin. *Dominion of the Eye*. Cambridge: Cambridge University Press, 2008.

Treib, Marc. *Thinking Through Drawing in an Electronic Age*. London: Routledge, 2008.

Tritch, Gretta. "Questioning the Philosophical Influence of Beauty and Perception in Bramante's First Scheme for St. Peter's," in *Inquiry*, Vol. 6 (2005): 1–23.

Unwin, Simon. *Twenty Buildings Every Architect Should Understand*. London: Routledge, 2010.

Valtieri, Simonetta. "La Scuola di Atene," in *Mitteilungen des Kunsthistorischen Institutes in Florence*, XVI (1972): 63–72.

Van Bergeijk, Herman, and Deborah Hauptmann (eds). *Notations of Herman Hertzberger*. Rotterdam: NAI Publishers, 1998.

Vasari, Giorgio. *Lives of the Painters, Sculptors and Architects*. Trans. A. B. Hinds. New York: Dutton, 1963.

Vescovini, Graziella Federici. "La fortune de l'*Optique* d'Ibn al-Haytham: le livre *De aspectibus* (*Kitab al-Manazir*) dans le Moyen Age latin," in *Archives d'histoire des sciences*, Vol. 40 (1990): 220–38.

_____. 'Ibn al-Haytham vulgarisé. Le *De li aspecti* d'un manuscrit du Vatican (moitié du XIVe siècle) et le troisième commentaire sur l'optique de Lorenzo Ghiberti', in *Arabic Sciences and Philosophy*, Vol. 8 (1998): 67–96.

Wells, Paul, Joanna Quinn and Les Mills. *Drawing for Animation*. Singapore: AVA, 2008.

Wilde, Oscar. *The Decay of Lying: Pen, Pencil and Poison; the Critic as Artist; the Truth as Masks*. New York: BiblioBazaar, 2009.

Willliams, Eunice. *Drawings by Fragonard in North American Collections*. Washington DC: National Gallery of Art, 1978.

Wittgenstein, Ludwig. *Lectures and Conversations on Aesthetics, Psychology & Religious Belief*. Oxford: Blackwell, 1978.

Wittkower, Rudolf. *Architectural Principles in the Age of Humanism*, London: Academy Editions, 1977.

Wodiczko, Krzysztof. *Krzysztof Wodiczko: Instruments, Projections, Vehicles*. Barcelona: Fundacio Antoni Tapies, 1992.

Index